Practical Operating Systems: A Hands-On Approach with Python

Amir Keivan Shafiei

i

DEDICATION

Dedicated to my remarkable students, whose curiosity and enthusiasm continuously motivate me to make complex concepts accessible and tangible. It is for them that I strive to bridge theory with practice, unlocking the world of operating systems through the power of Python.

CONTENTS

ACKNOWLEDGMENTS

The journey of creating this textbook has been an immensely rewarding experience. There are several individuals without whom this book would not have come to fruition, and I am tremendously grateful for their support.

First and foremost, I would like to thank my family for their unwavering encouragement and patience at every step along this journey. Their confidence in me kept me motivated through the long hours of writing and editing.

0 INTRODUCTION

Welcome to "Practical Operating Systems: A Hands-On Approach with Python," a comprehensive guide designed to empower engineering students with a profound understanding of operating systems, blending essential theory with practical applications.

Purpose and Goals

The main goal of this book is to teach readers about operating systems in a practical, hands-on way. We want to:

1. **Practical Proficiency**: We aspire to equip engineering students with the practical skills required for adeptly navigating operating systems. By seamlessly integrating theoretical foundations with hands-on Python programming, readers will cultivate real-world expertise in OS concepts.

2. **Comprehensive Understanding**: Operating systems constitute the bedrock of contemporary computing. We are committed to presenting a holistic perspective on operating systems, encompassing core concepts and advanced topics. This ensures that readers are well-prepared to confront real-world challenges effectively.

3. **Python as a Tool**: Python serves as the cornerstone of this book for good reason. Its innate simplicity, versatility, and readability render it an ideal vehicle for conveying intricate OS concepts. We will harness Python's capabilities to elucidate and implement diverse aspects of operating systems, rendering complex ideas accessible and comprehensible.

Importance for Engineering Students

The significance of grasping operating systems is underscored for engineering students by several compelling factors:

1. **Foundation for Software Development**: Operating systems form the bedrock of software development. They oversee resource management, facilitate program

execution, and deliver indispensable services. A firm grasp of OS concepts is essential for engineers crafting software across diverse platforms.

2. **System Optimization**: Engineering solutions often necessitate optimization at the system level. Proficiency in OS knowledge empowers students to craft software that operates efficiently, harnessing hardware resources to their maximum potential.

3. **Problem-Solving Aptitude**: Operating systems pose multifaceted challenges, from process synchronization to memory management and I/O optimization. Mastery of these concepts hones students' problem-solving skills, priming them for an array of technical roles.

4. **Real-World Relevance**: In today's technology-driven landscape, operating systems are omnipresent, spanning smartphones to data centers. Engineering students equipped with insights into the inner workings of these systems are better poised to navigate the competitive job market and contribute to innovation.

Balancing Theory and Practice

This course is meticulously crafted as a harmonious fusion of theory and practice. While theory furnishes the foundational knowledge, the practical implementation in Python is the linchpin for mastering these concepts. Throughout this book, we will seamlessly guide you through hands-on exercises, provide illuminating code examples, and present engaging projects. These elements bridge the chasm between theoretical understanding and real-world application.

Why Python?

Python has been selected as the cornerstone programming language for this book owing to its distinct attributes:

- **Readability**: Python boasts a clear and concise syntax, ideally suited for learners. It fosters code that is easily comprehensible and maintainable, facilitating a seamless learning experience.

- **Versatility**: Python's versatility extends across a broad spectrum of applications, from scripting to web development, and critically, systems programming. This adaptability empowers us to delve into various OS concepts and their applications.

- **Vibrant Ecosystem**: Python is fortified by a rich ecosystem of libraries and frameworks that streamline intricate tasks. Leveraging these resources, we can effectively illustrate OS concepts.

- **Accessibility for All Levels**: Python is accessible to both novices and seasoned programmers, making it an inclusive choice for readers with diverse expertise levels.

In "Practical Operating System Concepts with Python," we harness the formidable power of Python to demystify the realm of operating systems. Our mission is not only to ensure that you comprehend these pivotal concepts but also to cultivate practical skills that will serve you astutely in your engineering odyssey. Let us embark together on this exhilarating exploration.

1 BASIC CONCEPTS AND SYSTEM ARCHITECTURES

In the opening chapter of *Practical Operating Systems: A Hands-On Approach with Python*, we embark on a journey through the fundamental terrain of operating systems. Here, we establish the bedrock of our exploration, providing readers with a solid foundation to navigate the intricate world of OS design and functionality.

We begin by demystifying essential terms and concepts, such as **processes, threads, memory management**, and **file systems**. We then delve into the fascinating realm of **computer architectures**, exploring the different ways in which hardware resources are organized and managed. We also examine various **software systems**, including the operating system itself, and the crucial interactions between them.

Finally, we introduce the concept of **interrupts** and **dual-mode operation**, which are critical aspects of ensuring system stability and security.

As we embark on this journey, our mission is to equip you with the knowledge and insights that will empower you to understand, design, and work with operating systems effectively. We will use the versatile language of Python to illustrate the concepts we discuss, and we will provide you with a variety of exercises and projects to help you solidify your understanding.

1.1 INTRODUCTION TO OPERATING SYSTEMS

In this section, we will establish the foundation for our exploration of operating systems by delving into their fundamental definition, purpose, and historical context. Operating systems are the often-overlooked heroes of modern computing, serving as the vital link between hardware and software, orchestrating the efficient utilization of computer resources.

Definition and Purpose

An operating system (OS) can be aptly compared to the conductor of an orchestra, skillfully directing the various components of a computer system to work harmoniously together. At its core, an OS is a software layer that abstracts and manages the underlying hardware. Its purpose encompasses a multitude of critical functions:

- **Resource management:** The OS allocates and oversees hardware resources, including CPU time, memory, and I/O devices, ensuring that multiple programs can run concurrently without conflicts.

- **Process and thread management:** It orchestrates the execution of processes and threads, offering users the illusion of simultaneous execution.

- **File and data management:** The OS facilitates data storage and retrieval through file systems, ensuring data persistence and organization.

- **User interface:** Often, it provides a user-friendly interface, allowing users to interact seamlessly with the computer system and execute programs.

- **Security and access control:** The OS enforces stringent security measures, safeguarding data and resources from unauthorized access.

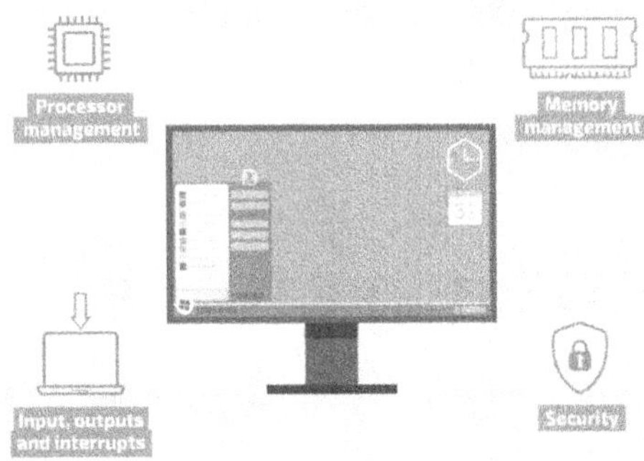

Figure 1.1: Operating System Components

In this chapter, we will delve into the world of operating systems, uncovering their essential functions and historical evolution.

Historical Perspective

To comprehend the evolutionary journey of operating systems, we must embark on a historical voyage to the inception of computing. In the early days, computers were colossal, room-filling machines operated exclusively by a select few. Complex operating systems were non-existent, and programs were manually loaded and executed one at a time.

As computing technology advanced, the necessity for efficient resource management and streamlined program execution became evident. The first-generation operating systems emerged during the 1950s and 1960s, tasked with managing hardware intricacies and simplifying the user experience.

With the advent of microprocessors and personal computers in the 1970s and 1980s, operating systems such as MS-DOS and Unix achieved household recognition. These systems introduced the groundbreaking concept of multitasking, enabling users to concurrently run multiple programs.

Today, we find ourselves immersed in a world characterized by a diverse array of operating systems. They range from Windows and macOS on personal computers to Linux on servers and Android on mobile devices. Operating systems have undergone profound evolution to become the unsung backbone of our digital lives, seamlessly managing resources, providing robust security, and serving as a platform for continuous software innovation.

In the chapters that follow, we will embark on a captivating journey to demystify the inner workings of these indispensable systems. We will explore both the theoretical underpinnings and their practical applications, leveraging the power of Python to gain deeper insights into this intricate domain.

1.3 COMPUTER ARCHITECTURES

In this section, we embark on a journey through the intriguing realm of computer architectures, gaining profound insights into the diverse architectural paradigms that have profoundly shaped the modern computing landscape. A thorough comprehension of these architectures is paramount, as they serve as the bedrock upon which the design, functionality, and performance of operating systems are built.

An Overview of Different Computer Architectures

The world of computing boasts an array of architectural flavors, each with its own unique set of principles and characteristics. Here, we introduce some of the most influential architectural paradigms:

1. **Von Neumann Architecture**

The Von Neumann architecture, named in honor of the brilliant mathematician and computer scientist John von Neumann, stands as the cornerstone of most contemporary computers. It comprises a central processing unit (CPU), memory, and input/output (I/O) devices. In this architecture, the CPU executes instructions fetched from memory, and the memory serves as the repository for both program instructions and data. Known for its simplicity and ease of implementation, the Von Neumann architecture reigns supreme in general-purpose computing systems.

2. **Harvard Architecture**

In stark contrast to the Von Neumann architecture, the Harvard architecture adopts separate memory spaces for program instructions and data. This segregation enables concurrent access to both instruction and data, potentially leading to substantial performance enhancements. The Harvard architecture finds its niche in embedded systems and microcontrollers, where efficiency and reliability are paramount.

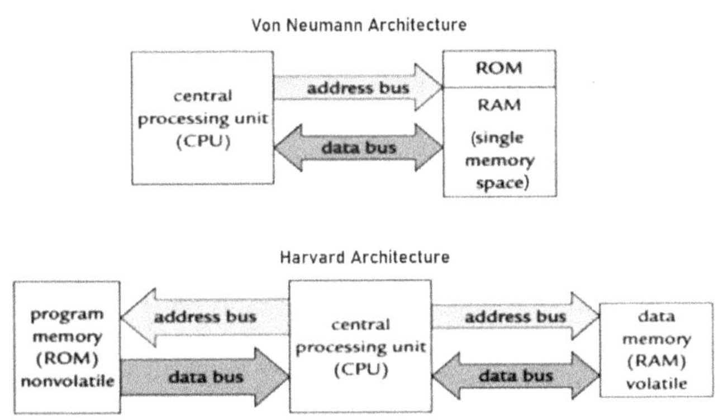

Figure 1.2: Comparison of Von Neumann and Harvard Architectures

3. **CISC (Complex Instruction Set Computer)**

CISC architecture boasts an extensive and intricate set of instructions. CISC processors can execute complex operations with a single instruction, a feature that can be advantageous for specific applications. However, this complexity may result in heightened hardware costs and potential performance trade-offs.

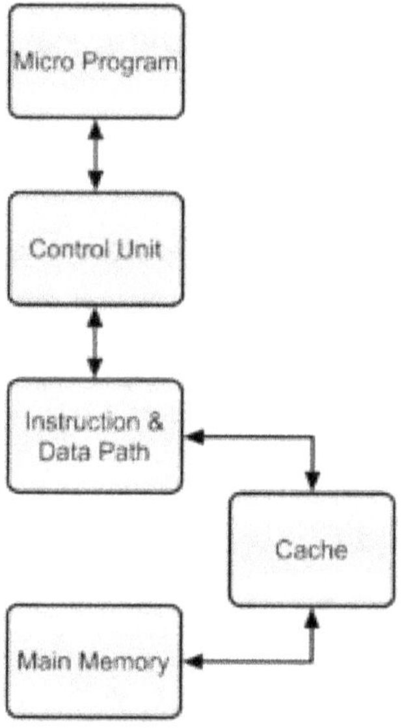

Figure 1.3: CISC Architecture

4. RISC (Reduced Instruction Set Computer)

In sharp contrast, RISC architecture follows a minimalist approach, offering a simplified and streamlined set of instructions. RISC processors excel at executing simpler instructions swiftly, often requiring multiple instructions for complex operations. This design philosophy aims to achieve superior performance and enhanced energy efficiency.

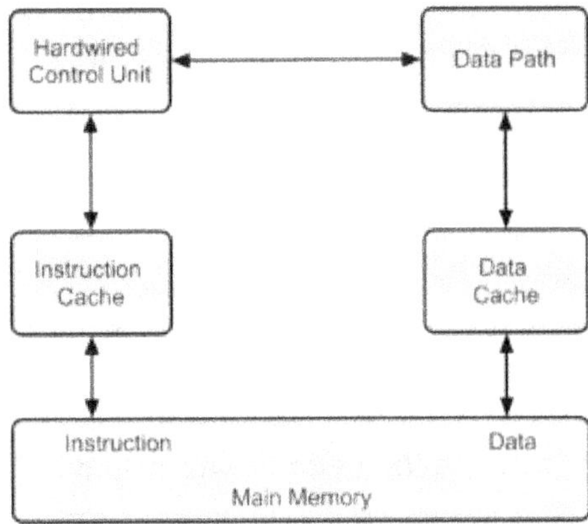

Figure 1.4: RISC Architecture

The Relevance of Architecture to Operating Systems

The choice of computer architecture exerts a profound influence on the design and performance of operating systems. Different architectures present distinct challenges and opportunities in the realm of OS development:

- **Memory Management:** The memory hierarchy and addressing schemes inherent to an architecture dictate how the operating system handles memory allocation, virtual memory management, and cache policies.

- **Instruction Set:** The architecture's instruction set profoundly influences how the OS interacts with the CPU. This interaction encompasses critical aspects such as system call handling and process scheduling.

- **I/O Handling:** Architectural features, including interrupt handling and I/O ports, shape the OS's approach to managing input and output operations.

- **Concurrency:** The architecture's support for parallelism and threading plays a pivotal role in how the OS manages concurrent processes and threads.

A comprehensive grasp of these architectural considerations is indispensable for OS developers, enabling them to optimize system performance and ensure seamless compatibility with hardware. As we advance through this book, we will delve deeper into how operating systems engage with various architectures and harness the power of Python to efficiently implement key functionalities.

1.4 SOFTWARE SYSTEMS AND THEIR ROLE

In this section, we embark on a journey to explore the intricate ecosystem of software systems and their symbiotic relationship with operating systems. Understanding the roles and interactions between these software layers is fundamental to comprehending the broader context of modern computing.

Types of Software Systems

Let us commence by categorizing software systems into three overarching types:

1. **Operating Systems**

   The operating system (OS) constitutes the bedrock of software systems within a computer. It shoulders the profound responsibility of managing the hardware resources of the computer, including the CPU, memory, and I/O devices. Beyond hardware orchestration, the OS extends its reach by providing indispensable services to other software systems, including applications and middleware.

2. **Application Software**

   Application software stands as the tangible interface through which users directly engage with computing systems. Within this realm reside a myriad of programs, ranging from word processors and web browsers to immersive games. Remarkably, application software draws heavily upon the services endowed by the OS to fulfill its myriad functions.

3. **Middleware**

   Middleware assumes a pivotal role as the bridge between the OS and application software. Positioned strategically, it bestows a realm of services designed to facilitate seamless communication between applications and, more notably, with the operating system itself. Middleware emerges as a stalwart ally, simplifying the complexities of developing and deploying distributed applications.

Interactions between Software Layers

The interactions that transpire within and between these software layers are as intricate as they are essential for the harmonious operation of a computer system. Let us delve into these pivotal interactions:

1. **OS and Application Software:**

   At the core of this interaction is the OS's role in providing indispensable services to application software. These services encompass critical functions, including memory allocation, process scheduling, and I/O management. In turn, application software draws upon these services as the very foundation upon which it executes its designated tasks.

2. **Middleware and Application Software:**

Middleware, occupying a unique vantage point, emerges as the enabler of seamless communication and data sharing among application software. Its services are harnessed by application software components to engage with one another and, significantly, with the OS. This interlayer harmony is vital for the cohesion of complex computing ecosystems.

3. **OS and Middleware:**

The OS extends its gracious hand even to middleware, providing a spectrum of services, including access to coveted hardware resources and robust security measures. Middleware, in turn, leverages these services to orchestrate its own suite of offerings, which are readily available to the eager embrace of application software.

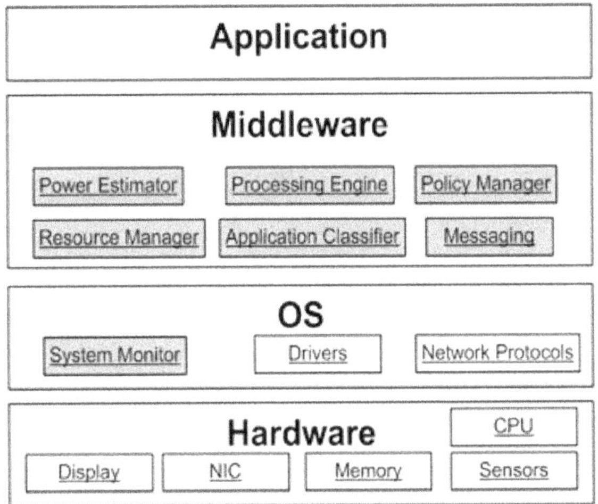

Figure 1.5: The Interplay of Software Ecosystem

This visual representation illustrates the intricate interplay of software layers in a computer system, highlighting the symbiotic relationships between operating systems, application software, and middleware.

In the forthcoming chapters, we shall embark on an even deeper exploration of these intricate relationships, unraveling the tapestry of software systems and their roles in the grand symphony of modern computing.

1.5 INTERRUPTS AND DUAL-MODE OPERATION

In this section, we discuss interrupts and dual-mode operation, two critical concepts that are essential for understanding how operating systems work.

Interrupts

An interrupt is a signal that is sent to the CPU by a hardware device or by the operating system itself. Interrupts can be used to notify the CPU of events that need its attention, such as a keystroke, a mouse movement, or the completion of an I/O operation.

There are two types of interrupts: hardware interrupts and software interrupts.

- **Hardware interrupts** are generated by hardware devices, such as the keyboard, mouse, and disk drive.
- **Software interrupts** are generated by the operating system itself. They are used to request services from the operating system, such as reading a file from disk or allocating memory.

Interrupts can be classified as maskable and non-maskable interrupts. Maskable interrupts can be disabled by the CPU, while non-maskable interrupts cannot be disabled.

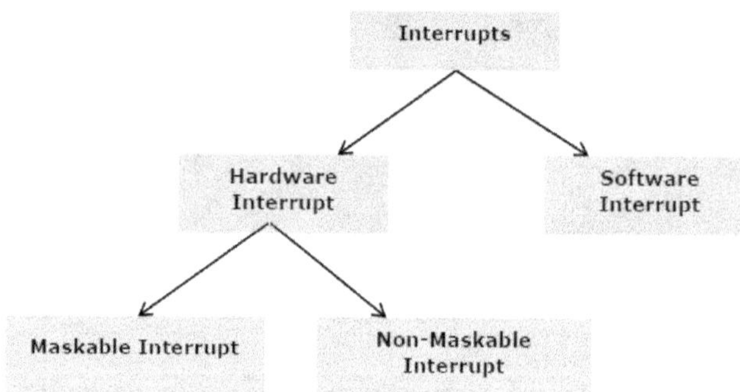

Figure 1.6: Interrupts: A way for hardware and software to notify the CPU of important events.

The operating system maintains a list of pending interrupts. When an interrupt occurs, the CPU adds the interrupt to the list of pending interrupts. The operating system will then handle the interrupts in the list one by one.

When an interrupt occurs, the CPU stops what it is doing and transfers control to a special routine called an interrupt service routine (ISR). The ISR handles the interrupt and then returns control to the CPU.

The operating system uses a variety of techniques to protect itself from unauthorized access by user programs. These techniques include dual-mode operation, privilege levels, and access control lists.

Dual-Mode Operation

Dual-mode operation is a security feature that is used to protect the operating system from user programs. In dual-mode operation, the CPU has two operating modes: kernel mode and user mode.

- **Kernel mode** is the most privileged mode. Only the operating system can run in kernel mode.
- **User mode** is less privileged than kernel mode. User programs can only run in user mode.

When a user program attempts to access a resource that is only accessible in kernel mode, the CPU will generate an exception. The operating system will then handle the exception and prevent the user program from accessing the resource.

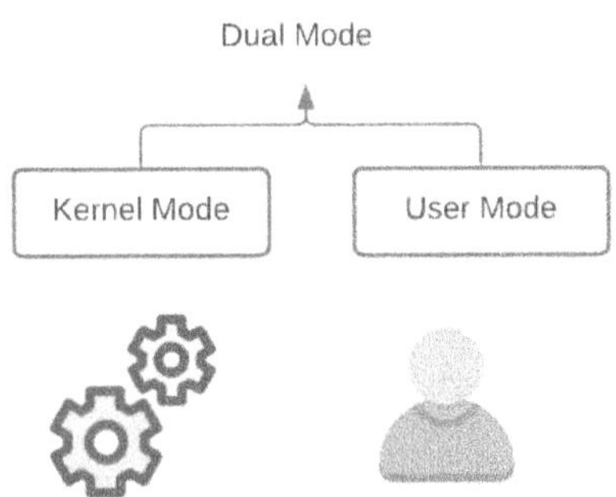

Figure 1.7: Dual mode: Kernel mode and user mode, protecting the system kernel while giving users access to resources.

Privilege Levels

In addition to kernel mode and user mode, some CPUs also have additional privilege levels. These privilege levels are used to further restrict the access of user programs to system resources.

For example, the x86 CPU has four privilege levels:

- Ring 0: The most privileged level. Only the operating system can run in Ring 0.
- Ring 1: Used by device drivers and other system software.
- Ring 2: Used by some operating systems.

- Ring 3: The least privileged level. User programs run in Ring 3.

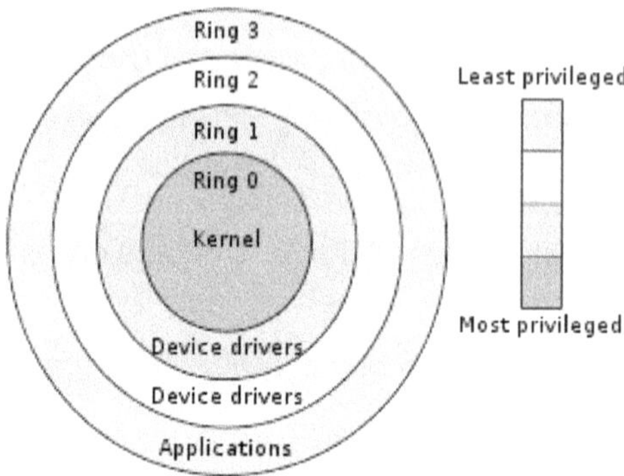

Figure 1.8: Dual mode kernel protection rings, with Ring 0 (kernel mode) at the top and Ring 3 (user mode) at the bottom.

The Importance of Interrupts and Dual-Mode Operation

Interrupts and dual-mode operation are essential for the reliable and secure operation of operating systems. Interrupts allow the operating system to respond to events quickly and efficiently, while dual-mode operation protects the operating system from unauthorized access by user programs.

In this section, we have discussed the concepts of interrupts and dual-mode operation. These concepts are essential for understanding how operating systems work. We will see how these concepts are used in operating systems in later sections.

1.6. CASE STUDY: PYTHON-BASED INTERRUPT HANDLING

In this case study, we delve into Python's capabilities for interrupt handling, a crucial aspect of operating system design. Python offers an array of modules and functions to streamline this process.

Python's Role in Interrupt Handling

Python simplifies interrupt handling through various modules and functions, including:

- **keyboard module:** Enables capturing keyboard input interrupts.
- **threading module:** Facilitates task scheduling at specified intervals.
- **signal module:** Provides tools for registering and handling interrupts.

Implementing Interrupt Handling in Python

Interrupt handling in Python involves the following steps:

1. Import the relevant modules and functions.
2. Register an interrupt handler.
3. Define the code to execute upon interrupt occurrence.

Examples of Python Interrupt Handling

Let's explore Python's interrupt handling capabilities through practical examples:

1. Handling Keyboard Input Interrupts:

This code demonstrates handling keyboard input interrupts using the 'keyboard' module:

```python
import keyboard

def handle_keyboard_input(event):
    if event.name == 'a':
        print("You pressed 'a'.")
    elif event.name == 'b':
        print("You pressed 'b'.")

keyboard.on_press(handle_keyboard_input)
```

2. Handling Timer-Based Interrupts:

The following example showcases timer interrupt handling using the 'threading' module:

```python
import threading

def periodic_task():
    print("This task runs periodically.")

# Schedule the task to run every 5 seconds
timer_interrupt = threading.Timer(5, periodic_task)
timer_interrupt.start()
```

3. Handling Hardware Interrupts:

The code below illustrates hardware interrupt handling with the 'signal' module:

```python
import signal

def handle_timer_interrupt(signum, frame):
```

```python
    print("Timer interrupt occurred.")

def main():
    # Register the timer interrupt handler
    signal.signal(signal.SIGALRM, handle_timer_interrupt)

    # Schedule a timer interrupt for 5 seconds
    signal.alarm(5)

    # Start the main loop
    while True:
        pass

if __name__ == "__main__":
    main()
```

4. Handling Multiple Interrupts:

Python's 'threading' module allows concurrent handling of multiple interrupts. Each thread can possess its interrupt handler, enabling parallel interrupt handling.

In this case study, we have explored how Python streamlines interrupt handling with its rich set of tools and libraries, presented through practical examples.

2   OPERATING SYSTEM STRUCTURES

Operating system structures are the foundation of how operating systems work. They define how the operating system interacts with hardware and software, and they determine the performance and scalability of the system.

In this chapter, we will explore the different types of operating system structures, including monolithic kernels, microkernels, and hybrid kernels. We will also discuss the role of APIs (Application Programming Interfaces) in enabling software applications to communicate with the operating system.

We will then take a closer look at system calls, which are the mechanisms through which processes request services from the operating system. System calls are essential for performing tasks such as file I/O, memory management, and process scheduling.

Finally, we will discuss how operating system structures are evolving to meet the demands of modern computing. Cloud computing and virtualization are two key trends that are changing the way operating systems are designed and implemented.

2.1. UNDERSTANDING OPERATING SYSTEM ARCHITECTURES

In this section, we embark on an exploration of various operating system architectures. Architectural decisions in OS design profoundly impact performance, security, and flexibility. Familiarity with these choices and their trade-offs is vital for those delving into the world of operating systems.

Overview of OS Architectures

Operating systems exhibit distinct architectural paradigms, each with its advantages and drawbacks. Let's delve into these architectures:

- **Monolithic Kernel:** This architecture boasts a single, extensive kernel housing essential OS functions like device drivers and file systems. It excels in inter-component communication efficiency. However, its size can lead to error vulnerability and maintenance complexities.

  Linux is a well-known OS that employs the monolithic kernel architecture. It centralizes core functionalities, offering efficient communication between components.

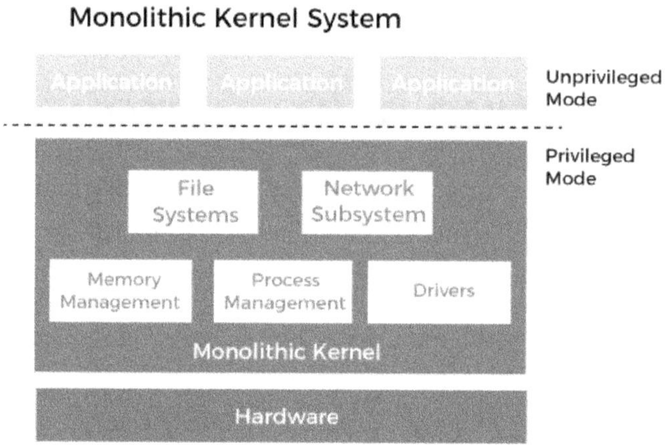

Monolithic Kernel System

Figure 2.1: Monolithic kernel system: A single unified kernel that manages all resources and applications.

- **Microkernel:** In contrast, the microkernel houses only core functions like process scheduling and IPC within the kernel space. Other services, such as device drivers, reside as user-level processes. This minimizes the kernel's size but introduces inter-process communication overhead.

  QNX, an OS often used in embedded systems, follows the microkernel architecture. It prioritizes a small kernel for enhanced reliability.

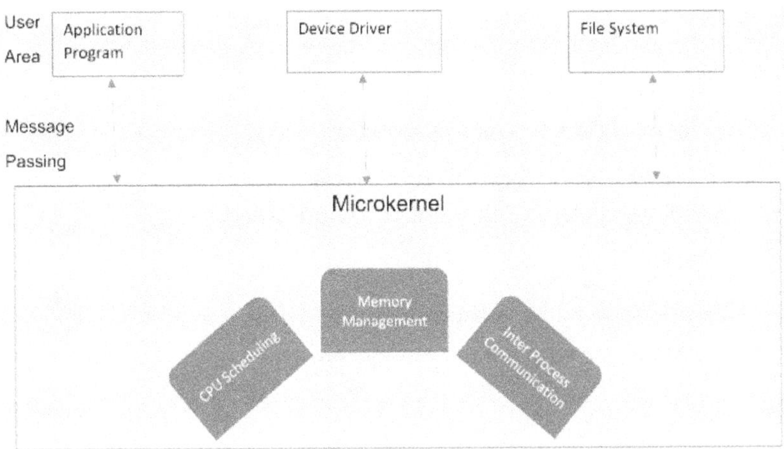

Figure 2.2: Microkernel architecture: The kernel provides only the essential services to applications, which run in user space.

- **Hybrid Kernel:** The hybrid kernel combines aspects of monolithic and microkernel designs, retaining a compact kernel while integrating additional functionality from user-level processes. This aims to balance efficiency and modularity, offering better performance with security benefits.

  Windows operating systems, like Windows NT and later versions, employ a hybrid kernel. They strike a balance between performance and reliability by incorporating some components as user-level processes.

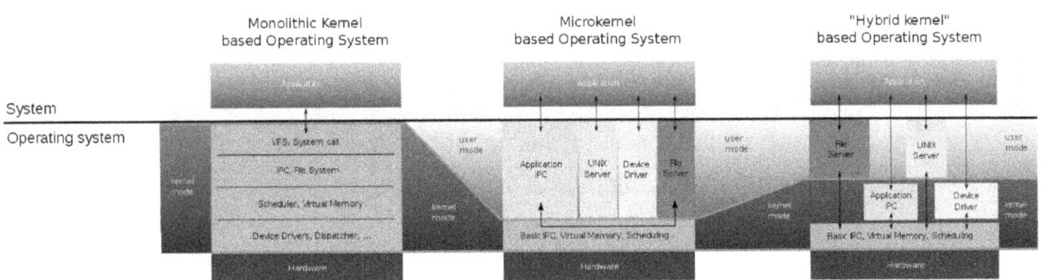

Figure 2.3: Hybrid kernel architecture: Combines the best features of monolithic and microkernel architectures.

Understanding Architectural Choices and Trade-offs

Architectural selection in operating systems reflects specific goals and priorities. Each architecture presents trade-offs:

Monolithic Kernel:

- *Advantages:*

    - Efficient direct access to hardware.
    - Minimal context switching overhead.
    - Simplified inter-component communication.

- *Disadvantages:*

    - Error-prone and crash-prone due to size.
    - Modularity and scalability hindered.

Microkernel:

- *Advantages:*

    - Enhanced modularity and component isolation.
    - Easy maintenance and extensibility.
    - Improved fault tolerance via isolation.

- *Disadvantages:*

    - Increased overhead due to inter-process communication.
    - Potential user-level component performance bottlenecks.

Hybrid Kernel:

- *Advantages:*

    - Balance between efficiency and modularity.
    - Improved fault tolerance.
    - Flexibility for diverse use cases.

- *Disadvantages:*

    - May not reach monolithic kernel performance levels.
    - Complexity managing hybrid architectures.

Throughout this chapter and the book, we will delve deeper into these architectural choices, offering insights into their effects on OS design, performance, and functionality.

2.2. THE SIGNIFICANCE OF APIS IN OPERATING SYSTEMS

This section delves into the central role of APIs (Application Programming Interfaces) in the realm of operating systems. APIs function as intermediaries, enabling software applications to communicate and interact with the underlying OS. Understanding API definition, significance, and design principles is fundamental for harnessing modern OS capabilities.

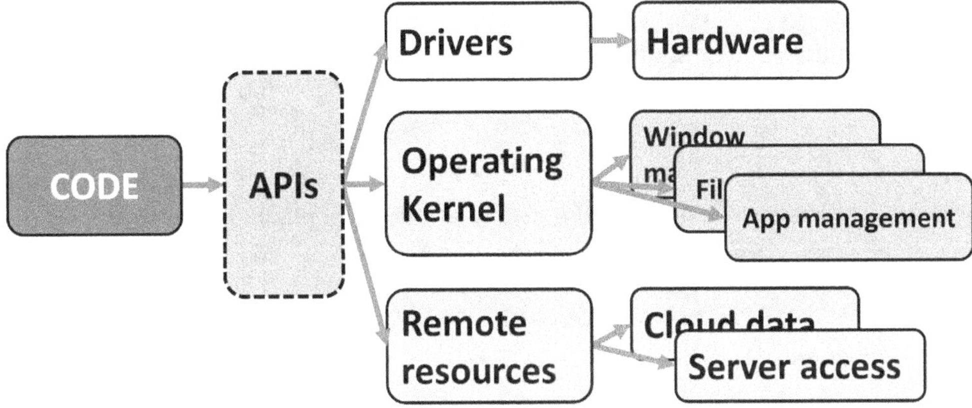

Figure 2.4: APIs: Enabling developers to build powerful and innovative applications on top of operating systems.

Defining APIs and Their Significance

APIs, or Application Programming Interfaces, are defined sets of rules, protocols, and tools facilitating communication between software applications. In the context of operating systems, APIs serve as gateways through which user-level programs request services and resources from the OS kernel.

APIs hold immense importance in operating systems, serving multiple key purposes:

- **Abstraction:** APIs abstract the complexities of low-level hardware interactions and kernel functionality. They shield developers from hardware intricacies, allowing them to focus on specific tasks.

- **Interoperability:** APIs standardize interactions with the OS, ensuring seamless compatibility among applications from different sources. This fosters interoperability and ecosystem growth.

- **Security:** APIs enforce access controls and permissions. Only resources and actions exposed through the API can be accessed, preventing unauthorized access to critical system functions.

How APIs Enable Interactions with the OS

APIs act as bridges between user-level code and the OS kernel. When a user-level application needs to perform an action requiring kernel-level privileges or hardware access, it requests it through the relevant API. The API communicates with the kernel, which executes the request and returns the result to the application.

This interaction is crucial for various operations, including file I/O, process management, memory allocation, and hardware access. APIs define the syntax and semantics of these interactions, ensuring effective communication with the OS.

Examples of Key OS APIs

Operating systems expose numerous APIs for various functionalities. Key examples of OS APIs include:

- **File System API:** Enables file creation, reading, writing, deletion, and directory navigation.

- **Process Management API:** Facilitates process and thread creation, execution, termination, and inter-process communication.

- **Memory Management API:** Provides memory allocation, deallocation, virtual memory management, and memory protection functions.

- **Networking API:** Defines network communication protocols, socket operations, and data transfer methods.

API Design Principles

Effective API design is essential for seamless application-OS interaction. Key API design principles encompass:

- **Consistency:** APIs should maintain uniform naming conventions, parameter orders, and return values to reduce confusion.

- **Clarity:** Comprehensive API documentation should provide developers with clear instructions on usage.

- **Simplicity:** APIs should offer necessary functionality with minimal complexity, reducing the learning curve.

- **Flexibility:** APIs should accommodate diverse use cases, allowing developers to adapt them as needed.

In subsequent chapters, we will delve into specific APIs and provide practical examples of their use in interacting with the OS. These hands-on experiences will deepen your understanding of how APIs empower software applications to leverage modern OS capabilities.

2.3. THE ESSENCE OF SYSTEM CALLS

In this section, we delve into system calls, the core interfaces connecting user-level programs to the operating system's heart. System calls act as conduits through which applications request essential services and resources from the OS kernel. By grasping the nature, categories, and error handling intricacies of system calls, you'll gain profound insights into how software interacts with the OS's inner workings.

Understanding System Calls and Their Purpose

System calls, often known as syscalls, are functions or routines provided by the OS kernel. They grant user-level applications privileged access to hardware resources and critical system services. The purposes of syscalls are diverse:

- **Resource Access:** Syscalls enable applications to interact with hardware resources, encompassing file systems, network interfaces, and peripheral devices.

- **Process Control:** They facilitate process management, including creation, termination, and execution control, empowering applications to manage concurrency.

- **Memory Management:** Syscalls manage memory, including allocation, deallocation, and protection, optimizing memory usage.

- **I/O Operations:** They support input and output operations, allowing applications to read from and write to files, devices, and communication channels.

Categories of System Calls

Syscalls fall into distinct categories, each tailored for specific tasks. Let's explore three primary categories:

- **File and I/O System Calls**

    - Open: Opens files or devices for reading, writing, or both.
    - Read: Reads data from open files or devices into buffers.
    - Write: Writes data from buffers to open files or devices.
    - Close: Closes open files or devices, freeing resources.
    - Seek: Moves the file pointer within files.
    - Dup/Dup2: Duplicates file descriptors for input/output redirection.
    - Pipe: Creates inter-process communication channels (pipes).
- **Process Control System Calls**

- Fork: Creates new processes by duplicating the caller.
- Exec: Replaces the current process, often for running different programs.
- Exit: Terminates the caller and returns an exit status.
- Wait/Waitpid: Suspends the caller until a child process exits.
- Kill: Sends signals to processes for inter-process communication.
- **Memory Management System Calls**

  - Brk/Sbrk: Adjusts the data segment's size for dynamic memory allocation.
  - Mmap/Munmap: Maps and unmaps memory regions, including file mapping.
  - Mprotect: Modifies memory protection attributes, e.g., read, write, execute permissions.

Handling System Call Errors

System calls may encounter errors due to various reasons like invalid arguments or resource shortages. Proper error handling ensures application robustness and reliability. Error handling methods include checking system call return values for error codes and using error-specific functions like perror or strerror to obtain human-readable error messages.

In upcoming chapters, we'll delve into practical Python examples that employ system calls for crucial operations such as file I/O, process management, and memory allocation. Mastering system calls is essential for crafting efficient and resilient software that seamlessly interacts with the operating system.

APIs vs. System Calls: What's the Difference?

APIs (Application Programming Interfaces):

APIs serve as intermediaries between software applications and the operating system (OS). They define a set of rules, protocols, and tools that facilitate communication between applications and the OS. APIs abstract the complexities of low-level hardware interactions and kernel functionality, shielding developers from these intricacies. They provide a standardized way for applications to request services and resources from the OS.

System Calls:

System calls are a subset of APIs. They are low-level interfaces that allow user-level programs to interact with the OS kernel. System calls provide direct access to the kernel's core functionalities, such as process management, memory allocation, and hardware access. When an application needs to perform an action that requires kernel-level privileges or hardware access, it makes a system call. The OS kernel executes the requested action and returns the result to the application.

Examples:

API Example - File System API:

```python
# Python's os module provides an API for file system operations
import os

# Create a new directory using the os API
directory_name = "new_directory"
os.mkdir(directory_name)

# List files in the current directory using the os API
files = os.listdir(".")
print(files)
```

In this example, we use Python's os module, which offers an API for file system operations. We create a new directory and list files in the current directory using the API functions.

System Call Example - File Opening (Unix-like systems):

```c
// C code for opening a file using a system call
#include <fcntl.h>

int main() {
    int fd;

    // Open a file using the system call open()
    fd = open("example.txt", O_RDONLY);

    if (fd == -1) {
        perror("Error opening file");
        return 1;
    }

    // File opened successfully, perform operations...

    // Close the file using the system call close()
    close(fd);

    return 0;
}
```

In this C code example, we use system calls to open and close a file. The `open()` and `close()` functions are system calls that directly interact with the OS kernel to perform file operations.

Python itself doesn't have a direct system call interface like lower-level programming languages such as C or assembly. In Python, system calls are typically abstracted away and provided through higher-level interfaces like the Python standard library and various third-party libraries.

For example, Python's `os` module provides functions for interacting with the operating system, such as file operations (`open()`, `read()`, `write()`, etc.), directory manipulation (`mkdir()`, `rmdir()`, etc.), and process control (`fork()`, `exec()`, etc.). These functions are implemented using system calls under the hood, but Python developers typically use the `os` module to interact with the OS, which abstracts the low-level system calls.

So, while Python doesn't expose raw system calls in the same way languages like C do, you can achieve similar functionality by using Python's built-in modules or by creating Python extensions in C that directly interact with system calls. These extensions can then be imported and used in Python scripts.

In essence, Python provides a higher-level and more user-friendly interface for working with system-related functionality, making it easier for developers to write cross-platform code without needing to deal directly with system calls.

2.4. THE POWER OF VIRTUALIZATION AND CLOUD COMPUTING

In this section, we dive into virtualization and cloud computing, technologies that have reshaped modern operating systems. These innovations bring unprecedented flexibility, scalability, and efficiency to both personal and enterprise computing.

Virtualization Fundamentals

Virtualization, the bedrock of cloud computing, abstracts and isolates computing resources like CPU, memory, and storage from the underlying hardware. It comes in two main flavors:

- **Hardware Virtualization**

    - **Overview:** It employs specialized software, known as hypervisors, to create and manage virtual machines (VMs). Each VM operates as an independent instance of an OS on the same physical hardware.
    - **Advantages:** Strong isolation between VMs for security and

compatibility. Running multiple OSes on a single machine.

- **Examples:** VMware, VirtualBox, Hyper-V, KVM.

- **Software Virtualization**

  - **Overview:** Also called containerization, it uses the host OS's kernel to create lightweight, isolated environments called containers. Containers share the OS kernel but run separate user spaces.
  - **Advantages:** Swift deployment and efficient resource usage. Ideal for microservices and lightweight apps.
  - **Examples:** Docker, Kubernetes, Podman.

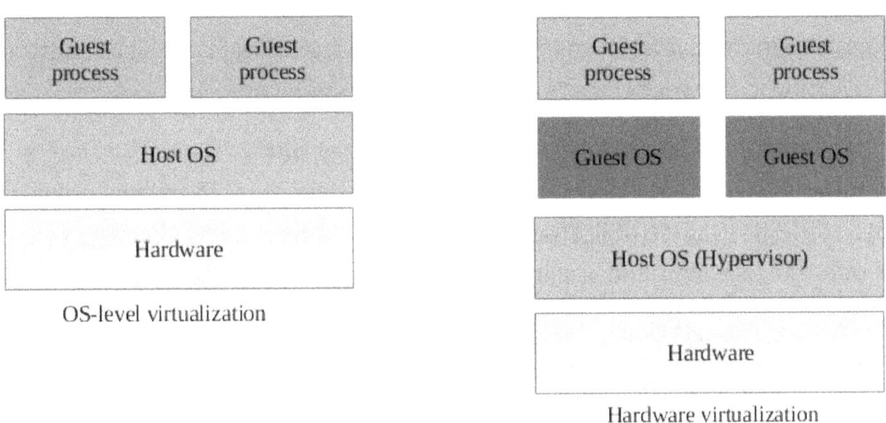

Figure 2.5: Virtualization: Running multiple operating systems on a single physical machine.

Cloud Computing in a Nutshell

Before delving into virtualization's role in cloud computing, let's briefly demystify cloud computing itself. At its core, cloud computing is a paradigm that delivers computing services, such as servers, storage, databases, networking, software, over the internet. These services are hosted on remote servers (often referred to as "the cloud") instead of on local servers or personal devices.

Now, let's explore how virtualization fits into this ecosystem:

Virtualization's Role in Cloud Computing

Virtualization serves as the cornerstone of cloud computing, enabling efficient resource allocation and management. Its key roles include:

- **Resource Pooling:** Virtualization allows cloud providers to dynamically allocate resources based on demand. This dynamic resource pooling ensures efficient utilization of computing power and scalability. When you need more resources, they're just a click away.

- **Isolation:** In a cloud environment, it's crucial to ensure that resources are isolated between different users and applications. Virtualization provides this isolation, enhancing security and preventing resource conflicts. Each virtual machine or container operates independently, unaware of others running on the same physical hardware.

- **Flexibility:** The cloud offers a vast array of virtual machine configurations and containerized services. This flexibility accommodates diverse workloads and use cases. Whether you're running a small website, a big data analytics platform, or anything in between, the cloud's flexibility has you covered.

With this foundation in cloud computing and its synergy with virtualization, we're prepared to explore practical aspects in the upcoming chapters. These technologies empower efficient resource utilization, scalability, and the seamless operation of modern operating systems and applications.

Cloud Processing Models (IaaS, PaaS, SaaS)

Cloud computing provides different service models tailored to user needs:

- **Infrastructure as a Service (IaaS)**

    - **Overview:** Virtualized computing resources (VMs, storage, networking) with user control over OS and apps. Cloud provider manages infrastructure.
    - **Use Cases:** Ideal for users needing full OS and software stack control, suitable for hosting applications.
- **Platform as a Service (PaaS)**

    - **Overview:** Abstracts infrastructure to focus on app development, deployment, and management. Cloud provider handles infrastructure.
    - **Use Cases:** Developers deploy apps without worrying about infrastructure. Streamlines app development.
- **Software as a Service (SaaS)**

    - **Overview:** Fully hosted and managed software applications delivered over the internet. Accessed via web browsers, no installation or maintenance.
    - **Use Cases:** Designed for end-users and organizations seeking easy

access to applications like email and productivity suites.

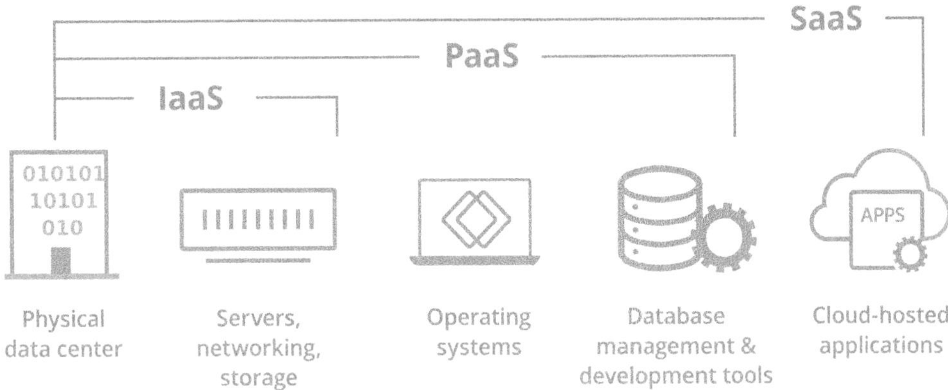

Figure 2.6: Cloud computing: Delivering computing resources on demand over the internet.

Understanding virtualization and cloud computing is paramount In today's landscape. These technologies empower efficient resource utilization and seamless scalability. In upcoming chapters, we'll explore practical aspects, showcasing their role in modern operating systems and applications.

2.5. PRACTICAL PYTHON FOR SYSTEM CALLS AND APIS

In this section, we'll delve into the hands-on side of using Python to work with system calls and interact with operating system APIs. Python's popularity, readability, and extensive library support make it an excellent choice for tackling system-level tasks. We'll introduce key Python modules, namely os and subprocess, and demonstrate how they simplify essential system operations, including file manipulations and process control.

Python's Handy os and subprocess Modules

Python equips developers with two crucial modules, os and subprocess, for seamless interaction with the operating system and effortless execution of system calls.

os Module:

- **Overview:** The os module is a Swiss Army knife for OS-related tasks, offering functions to access the file system, manipulate directories, and manage processes.

- **Use Cases:** Employ the os module for file and directory manipulations, environment variable management, and process-related operations.

- **Example:**

```python
import os

# Check if a file exists
if os.path.exists("myfile.txt"):
    print("File exists.")
else:
    print("File does not exist.")
```

subprocess Module:

- **Overview:** The subprocess module empowers Python programs to create and interact with additional processes, making it invaluable for running external commands, executing shell scripts, and managing subprocess input and output.

- **Use Cases:** Rely on the subprocess module for launching external programs, automating system tasks, and capturing their output.

- **Example:**

```python
import subprocess

# Run an external command and capture its output
result = subprocess.run(["ls", "-l"],
stdout=subprocess.PIPE, text=True)
print(result.stdout)
```

Mastering File Operations with Python

Python's os module provides an array of functions for file and directory operations, enabling developers to create, read, write, move, and delete files and directories. We'll explore these common file operations through illustrative Python code examples.

File Creation and Writing:

```python
import os

# Create a new file and write content to it
with open("myfile.txt", "w") as file:
    file.write("Hello, world!\n")
```

File Reading:

```python
# Read the contents of a file
with open("myfile.txt", "r") as file:
    content = file.read()
print(content)
```

File Deletion:

```python
import os

# Delete a file
if os.path.exists("myfile.txt"):
    os.remove("myfile.txt")
```

Efficient Process Control with Python

Python's os and subprocess modules empower developers to control and manage processes effectively. Whether you need to initiate, halt, or interact with processes, Python equips you with the tools for streamlined process control.

Process Execution with subprocess:

```python
import subprocess

# Run an external command
subprocess.run(["ls", "-l"])
```

Process Termination with os:

```python
import os
import signal  # Import the signal module

# Terminate a process by its process ID (PID)
pid_to_terminate = 12345
os.kill(pid_to_terminate, signal.SIGTERM)
```

In the upcoming chapters, we'll delve deeper into these Python modules, showcasing their applications for interacting with system calls and APIs. This knowledge will empower you to perform a broad spectrum of system-related tasks efficiently and with confidence.

2.6. USING PYTHON TO INTERACT WITH OS APIS

In this section, we'll explore the world of operating system APIs and demonstrate how Python can act as a powerful intermediary between your applications and these APIs.

Specifically, we'll introduce Python's ctypes library, which facilitates seamless interaction with OS-specific APIs. Through practical examples, we'll illustrate how to access and utilize these APIs while considering important factors for cross-platform compatibility.

Python's ctypes Library for API Interaction

Python's ctypes library enables the direct invocation of functions within shared libraries (DLLs on Windows, shared libraries on Unix systems) from Python code. It serves as a bridge between Python and lower-level languages like C, facilitating the utilization of OS-specific APIs and external libraries. Here's an overview of how ctypes works:

1. Loading Shared Libraries:

To access OS-specific APIs, the corresponding shared library must be loaded using ctypes. This step establishes a connection between Python and the API functions offered by the library.

```python
import ctypes

# Load a shared library (DLL on Windows)
my_library = ctypes.CDLL('my_library.dll')  # Replace with the
library name
```

2. Accessing Functions:

Once the library is loaded, functions within it can be accessed using dot notation. These functions correspond to the API calls provided by the library.

```python
# Call a function from the loaded library
result = my_library.my_function(arg1, arg2)
```

3. Data Types and Function Signatures:

ctypes necessitates the definition of data types for function arguments and return values to ensure proper interaction with the API. These details must be specified for accurate API function calls.

Examples of Accessing OS-Specific APIs

Let's dive into practical examples of using ctypes to interact with OS-specific APIs. We'll explore two common scenarios: calling a Windows API function to retrieve system information and invoking a Unix API function to manipulate files.

Example 1: Accessing Windows API

In this example, we'll utilize ctypes to call the Windows API function GetSystemInfo, which retrieves information about the system's hardware and operating system.

```python
import ctypes

# Load the Windows kernel32 library
kernel32 = ctypes.WinDLL('kernel32.dll')

# Define the SYSTEM_INFO structure
# (Omitted for brevity; it's a complex structure)

system_info = SYSTEM_INFO()

# Call the GetSystemInfo function
kernel32.GetSystemInfo(ctypes.byref(system_info))

# Access system information
print(f"Number of processors: {system_info.dwNumberOfProcessors}")
```

Example 2: Accessing Unix API

In this example, we'll use ctypes to call the Unix API function mkdir, which creates a new directory.

```python
import ctypes

libc = ctypes.CDLL('libc.so.6')   # You can specify the exact
library name for the C library

# Define the required arguments and return type
libc.mkdir.argtypes = [ctypes.c_char_p]
libc.mkdir.restype = ctypes.c_int

# Call the mkdir function
directory_name = "new_directory"
result = libc.mkdir(directory_name.encode('utf-8'))

if result == 0:
    print(f"Directory '{directory_name}' created successfully.")
else:
    print(f"Error creating directory '{directory_name}'")
```

Cross-Platform Considerations and Compatibility

While ctypes offers a powerful means of accessing OS-specific APIs, cross-platform compatibility is essential. Here are some key points to keep in mind:

- **Library Names:** Shared library names and paths may vary across operating systems. Use platform-specific library names or utilize tools like `ctypes.util.find_library` to locate the appropriate library.

- **Function Availability:** Not all functions are available on all platforms. Ensure that the functions you intend to call exist on the target operating system.

- **Data Types:** Be mindful of differences in data types, especially when dealing with data structures passed to and returned from API functions.

By understanding and addressing these considerations, you can fully leverage OS-specific APIs in your Python applications while maintaining cross-platform compatibility.

In the upcoming chapters, we'll explore more advanced use cases of interacting with OS APIs using Python, demonstrating how to leverage these capabilities for a wide range of system-related tasks.

3 UNDERSTANDING PROCESSES IN OPERATING SYSTEMS

Processes are the core units of execution in modern computing, governing how our computers perform tasks and allocate resources. This chapter delves into the world of processes, exploring their essential characteristics and their central role in operating systems. From grasping the importance of processes to unraveling the intricacies of Process Control Blocks (PCBs) and multitasking through context-switching, this chapter provides a comprehensive understanding of processes. It also examines the functions of different schedulers in optimizing process management and explores the mechanisms involved in process creation and communication. Furthermore, we'll demonstrate the practical applications of Python in process management, offering code examples that bridge theory with real-world usage. By the end of this chapter, you'll have a solid grasp of processes, both in theory and practice, laying the foundation for a deeper exploration of operating systems.

3.1 INTRODUCTION TO PROCESSES

Processes are the fundamental units of modern computing, serving as self-contained entities responsible for specific tasks. In this section, we'll dive into what processes are and why they are critical in the world of computing.

3.1.1 Definition and Importance

A process can be defined as an independent unit of work within a computer program. It includes program code, data, and the resources needed to execute a particular task. Processes are the tools through which an operating system manages and executes multiple tasks concurrently.

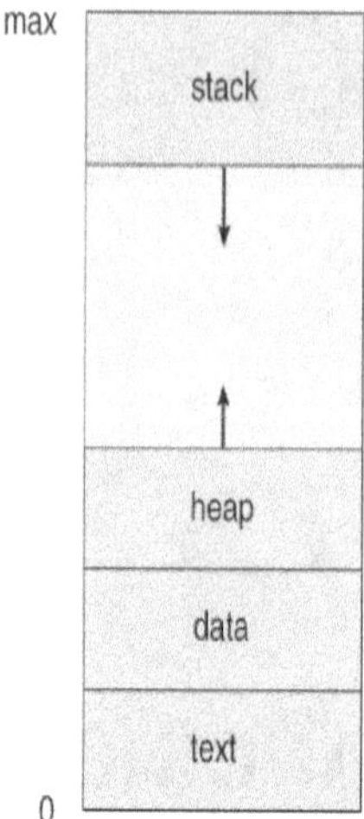

Figure 3.1: Process: Memory layout of a running program

Processes are crucial for several reasons:

- **Concurrency**: They enable a computer to perform multiple tasks at the same time, appearing as if they run in parallel. This is vital for efficient application execution, system services, and background task management.

- **Isolation**: Each process operates in isolation with its memory space. This isolation prevents one process from interfering with another's memory or resources, enhancing system stability and security.

- **Resource Management**: Processes efficiently allocate and manage system resources like CPU time, memory, and input/output devices. The operating system ensures fair resource sharing among processes.

- **Fault Tolerance**: Isolated processes are resilient. If one process encounters an error or crashes, it typically does not affect other processes, ensuring system reliability.

Process States:

Processes can exist in various states as they execute within the operating system. These states include:

- **New**: This is the initial state when a process is created, but it has not yet started execution.

- **Ready**: In this state, a process is prepared to execute but is waiting for the CPU to be assigned to it by the scheduler.

- **Running**: When a process is actively using the CPU, it is in the running state. At any given time, only one process can be in this state on a single CPU core.

- **Wait**: Processes in the wait state are temporarily halted, often waiting for some event or resource, such as user input or data from a file.

- **Terminated**: This is the final state when a process has completed its execution or has been terminated by the system.

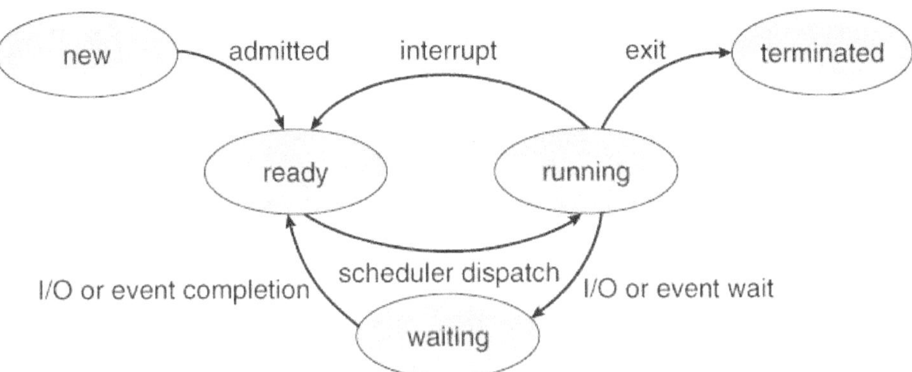

Figure 3.2: Process states: New, ready, running, waiting, terminated

3.1.2 The Role of Processes in Computing

Processes are the linchpin of multitasking operating systems, enabling them to execute multiple programs simultaneously. Here are key roles processes play in computing:

- **Program Execution**: Processes allow programs to run on a computer. Each program becomes a process, loaded into memory for execution.

- **Resource Management**: They handle system resources like CPU time and memory, requesting and releasing them as needed for efficient resource utilization.

- **Concurrency**: Computers achieve concurrency by running multiple processes concurrently, vital for multitasking and user responsiveness.

- **Isolation and Security**: Processes provide isolation between applications. One misbehaving process or a crash does not impact others, enhancing system security and stability.

- **Inter-Process Communication (IPC)**: Processes often need to communicate and share data. IPC mechanisms facilitate this, enabling processes to collaborate when necessary.

Understanding processes is fundamental to grasping how modern operating systems manage the myriad tasks and applications running on your computer. In the following sections, we'll delve deeper into process functionality, exploring concepts like Process Control Blocks (PCBs) and context-switching that underpin their operation.

Now, let's delve into the inner workings of processes.

3.2 PROCESS CONTROL BLOCKS (PCBS)

Processes in the realm of operating systems are tangible entities managed by the system itself. The backstage players that enable this management are Process Control Blocks (PCBs). In this section, we'll dive into the nuances of PCBs, understanding their definition and their pivotal role in achieving efficient process management.

3.2.1 Understanding PCBs

A Process Control Block (PCB) is, at its core, a data structure used by the operating system to handle and oversee processes. Think of it as a virtual file containing all crucial information about a process, enabling the system to monitor, control, and manipulate the process efficiently.

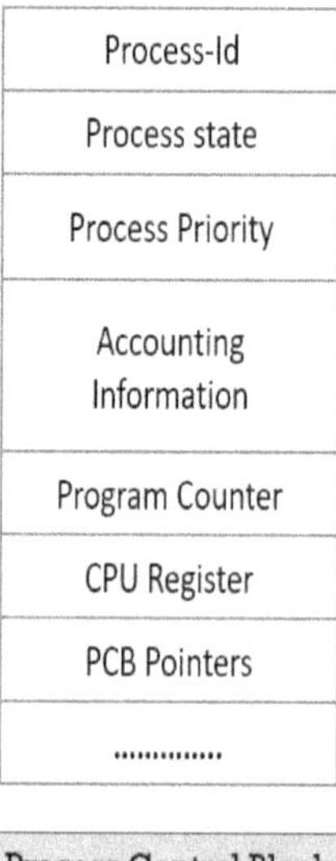

Figure 3.3: PCB: Data structure tracking process state and information

PCBs are indispensable for several reasons:

- **Process Management**: PCBs store vital process information, such as its current state, program counter, registers, and memory allocation. This data facilitates efficient process switching, a fundamental aspect of multitasking.

- **Resource Management**: PCBs house data regarding the process's resource usage, including open files, allocated memory, and CPU utilization. This data guides intelligent resource allocation and deallocation.

- **Context-Switching**: PCBs play a pivotal role in context-switching, the mechanism by which the system saves the state of one process and loads another. This enables seamless process transitions, creating the illusion of concurrent execution.

3.2.2 PCB Components and Their Significance

A typical PCB comprises various components, each serving a specific role in process management. Let's explore these components and their significance:

- **Process ID (PID)**: Each process is assigned a unique identifier called the Process ID (PID). PIDs are critical for tracking and managing processes effectively.

- **Program Counter (PC)**: The PC holds the memory address of the next instruction to be executed by the process. It plays a pivotal role in context-switching and allows the process to resume from where it left off.

- **CPU Registers**: PCBs store the values of CPU registers, including general-purpose registers, stack pointers, and program status flags. These values are vital for preserving the process's state during context-switching.

- **Process State**: This component indicates the process's current state, such as "Running," "Waiting," or "Ready." The state provides insights into the process's activity and aids in its management.

- **Priority**: Processes are assigned priority levels, allowing the system to determine the execution order based on factors like importance and time sensitivity.

- **Memory Management Information**: PCBs contain details about the process's memory allocation, including the base and limit registers. This information ensures processes cannot access each other's memory, enhancing system security.

- **Open Files**: A list of open files associated with the process, along with file pointers indicating the current position in each file, is recorded. This data enables processes to read and write files without conflicts.

- **Accounting Information**: Information regarding resource usage, such as CPU time consumed and I/O operations performed by the process, is documented in the PCB. This data assists in resource allocation and tracking.

Understanding PCBs is pivotal for grasping how the operating system efficiently manages and controls processes. PCBs serve as the linchpin in orchestrating processes, allowing the system to juggle multiple tasks concurrently while maintaining stability and optimal resource utilization. In the upcoming sections, we'll delve further into process management, including context-switching and the role of schedulers in optimizing process execution.

3.3 CONTEXT-SWITCHING AND MULTITASKING

In the world of operating systems, multitasking is the art of efficiently managing processes, creating the illusion of executing multiple tasks simultaneously. This illusion is achieved through a remarkable process known as context-switching. In this section, we'll dive deep into the mechanics of context-switching, uncovering its significance, and understanding the associated overhead.

Introduction

Visualize your computer as a juggler, skillfully handling a set of balls in the air, with each ball representing a running process. To maintain this juggling act seamlessly, your computer accomplishes a remarkable feat: it rapidly switches between these processes, ensuring that each receives its fair share of CPU time. This swift transition is what we call context-switching, and it serves as the core of multitasking in modern operating systems.

3.3.1 Context-Switching Explained

Context-switching is the process of preserving the state of one process while loading the state of another, enabling the operating system to transition between processes effortlessly. Think of it as momentarily setting one juggling ball aside to catch and juggle another.

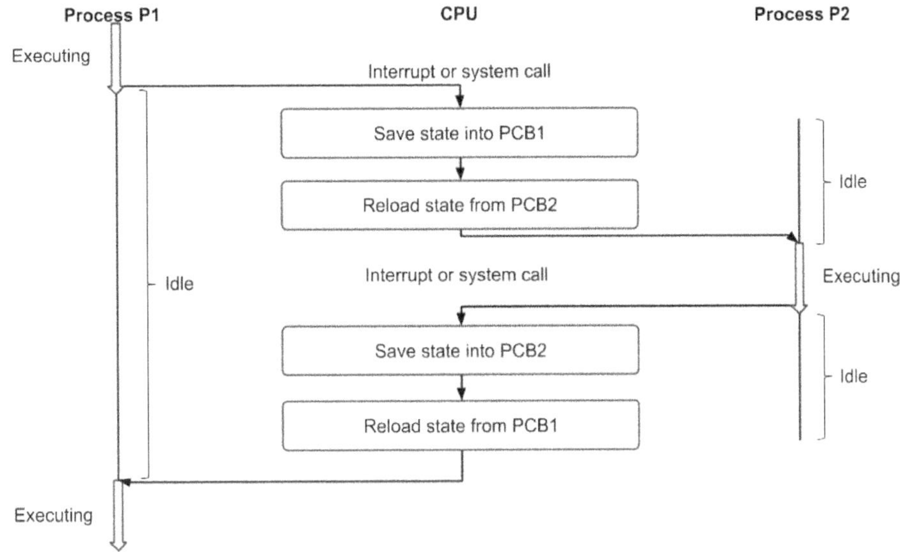

Figure 3.4: Context switching: Saving and restoring process state

Let's dissect the steps involved in context switching:

- **Save Current State**: When the operating system decides to switch to another process, it diligently saves the current process's state. This includes preserving the program counter, CPU registers, and other vital information.

- **Load New Process State**: The system then loads the state of the next process scheduled for execution. This entails setting the program counter to the correct memory address, injecting CPU registers with the new process's values, and preparing it for execution.

- **Resuming Execution**: With the new process's state seamlessly loaded, the operating system resumes its execution. This appears to users as if the processes are running in parallel, even though the CPU is rapidly toggling between them.

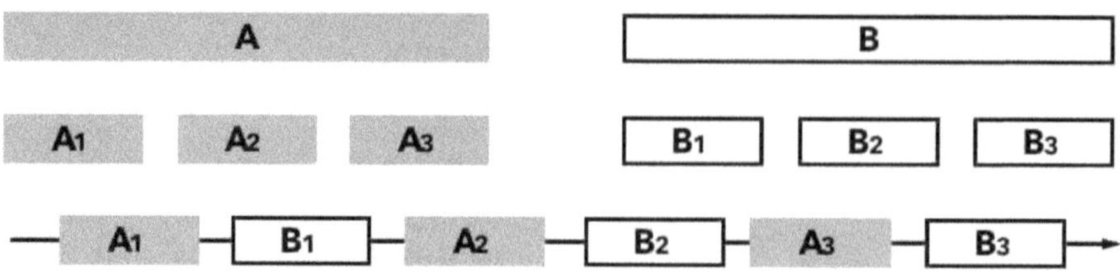

Figure 3.5: Concurrent processes: Interleaving execution of two processes.

3.3.2 The Role of Context-Switching in Multitasking

Context-switching is the magic wand that empowers multitasking in operating systems. It ensures processes efficiently share the CPU's finite resources, providing responsiveness and creating the illusion of concurrent execution for users.

Let's consider a real-world example: a user running a word processor, a web browser, and a music player concurrently. Each of these applications represents a distinct process. Context-switching empowers the operating system to allocate CPU time to each process in a round-robin fashion, giving the user the perception that all three tasks are happening simultaneously.

Example: Multitasking in Action

Imagine listening to music on your computer while composing a document in a word processor. At any given moment, the operating system is rapidly toggling between these two processes, ensuring that you enjoy uninterrupted music while simultaneously typing in your document. This seamless transition between processes is the result of efficient context-switching.

3.3.3 Context-Switch Overhead

Although context-switching is vital for multitasking, it's not devoid of costs. Each context-switch incurs overhead, which encompasses the time and resources needed to save and load process states. This overhead can impact system performance, particularly in scenarios with numerous processes vying for CPU time.

Efficient context-switching is a delicate balance. Too frequent context-switches can lead to excessive overhead, diminishing overall system throughput. Conversely, infrequent context-switches can result in poor responsiveness.

In the upcoming sections, we'll delve into the strategies and techniques employed by operating systems to optimize context-switching and strike the right equilibrium between multitasking and system performance.

3.4 SCHEDULERS IN OPERATING SYSTEMS

Schedulers are the essential decision-makers behind the efficient allocation of CPU time to processes in an operating system. In this section, we'll explore the distinct types of schedulers that operating systems employ to guarantee smooth process execution. We'll delve into the functions of short-term, medium-term, and long-term schedulers, unveiling the algorithms and policies guiding their actions.

Imagine a bustling traffic control center efficiently managing the flow of vehicles on a busy road. In a similar vein, schedulers in an operating system undertake the responsibility of managing the flow of processes competing for CPU time. Each scheduler has a specific function, ensuring equitable, prompt, and priority-based execution of processes.

3.4.1 Short-Term Scheduler (CPU Scheduler)

The short-term scheduler, often referred to as the CPU scheduler, can be likened to a traffic cop at a bustling intersection, determining which process gains the next slot for execution. Its primary objective is to distribute CPU time among processes in a manner that maximizes system throughput and ensures responsiveness.

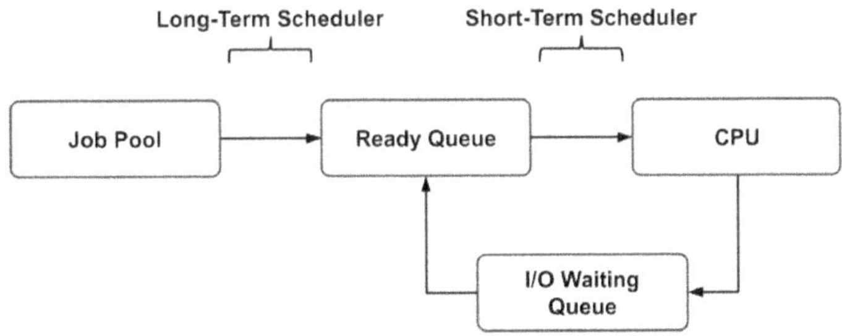

Figure 3.6: Job scheduling: Short-term and long-term

Example: Short-Term Scheduling

Consider a scenario where you're running a compute-intensive program on your computer. The CPU scheduler guarantees that this program receives its fair share of CPU time while also accommodating other processes, such as your web browser, to run seamlessly in the background.

3.4.2 Medium-Term Scheduler

The medium-term scheduler acts as a traffic director, overseeing processes as they transition between main memory (RAM) and secondary storage (e.g., a hard drive). When a process is moved from RAM to disk (swapped out) or vice versa (swapped in), the medium-term scheduler plays a pivotal role in managing this process.

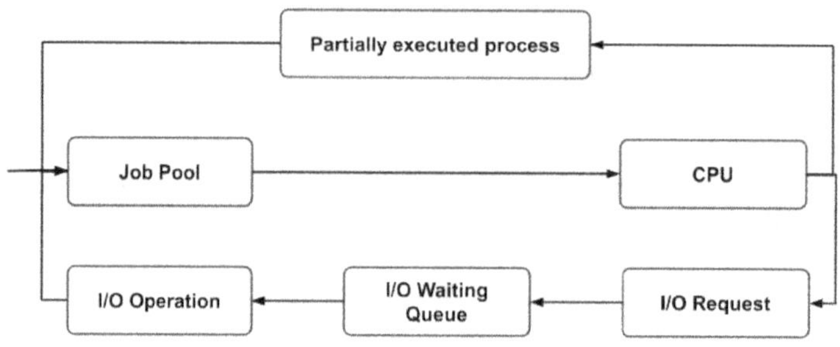

Figure 3.7: Medium-Term Scheduler: Swapping processes to/from memory

Example: Medium-Term Scheduling

Imagine a computer equipped with limited RAM. As you open more applications, some processes may need to be temporarily moved to disk to free up memory for others. The medium-term scheduler orchestrates these movements to optimize memory utilization and overall system performance.

3.4.3 Long-Term Scheduler

The long-term scheduler, occasionally referred to as the admission scheduler, determines which processes are permitted to enter the system from a pool of waiting processes. It evaluates factors like process priority, available resources, and system load to make informed decisions.

Example: Long-Term Scheduling

Visualize a server responsible for handling incoming network requests. The long-term scheduler assesses which requests can be accepted based on the server's capacity and the priority of the incoming requests. It ensures that the server maintains efficient service without becoming overwhelmed.

3.4.4 Scheduling Algorithms and Policies

Scheduling algorithms are used to determine the order in which processes are executed by the operating system. The choice of scheduling algorithm depends on a number of factors, such as the type of system, the number of processes, and the priorities of the processes.

Some of the most common scheduling algorithms include:

- **First-Come, First-Served (FCFS)**: FCFS is the simplest scheduling algorithm. It schedules processes in the order they arrive in the queue. For example, if processes P1, P2, and P3 arrive in that order, then P1 will be executed first, followed by P2, and then P3.

FCFS (Example)

Process	Duration	Oder	Arrival Time
P1	24	1	0
P2	3	2	0
P3	4	3	0

Gantt Chart :

P1 waiting time : 0
P2 waiting time : 24
P3 waiting time : 27

The Average waiting time :

(0+24+27)/3 = 17

- **Round Robin (RR)**: RR is a preemptive scheduling algorithm. It schedules each process for a fixed time quantum, and then preempts it and schedules the next process. The time quantum is the amount of time that a process is allowed to run before it is preempted. For example, if the time quantum is 2 milliseconds, then process P1 will run for 2 milliseconds, then process P2 will run for 2 milliseconds, and so on.

TIME SLICE = 4

PROCESS	ARRIVAL TIME	BURST TIME	
		TOTAL	REMAINING
P1	0	8	8
P2	1	6	6
P3	3	3	3
P4	5	2	2
P5	6	4	4

READY QUEUE:

P1	P2	P3	P1	P4	P5	P2

GANTT CHART:

P1	P2	P3	P1	P4	P5	P2

0   4   8   11   15   17   21   23

- **Priority Scheduling:** Priority Scheduling assigns a priority to each process. The process with the highest priority executes first. For example, if process P1 has a priority of 10, process P2 has a priority of 5, and process P3 has a priority of 1, then P1 will be executed first, followed by P2, and then P3.

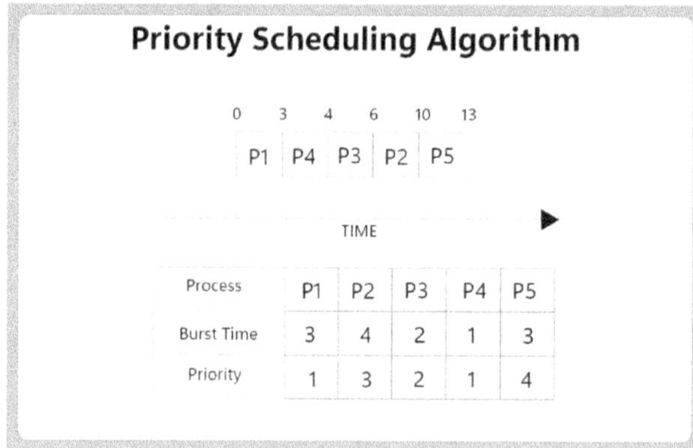

- **Shortest Job First (SJF):** SJF schedules the process with the shortest estimated execution time next. For example, if processes P1, P2, and P3 have estimated execution times of 10 milliseconds, 20 milliseconds, and 30 milliseconds, respectively, then P1 will be scheduled first, followed by P2, and then P3.

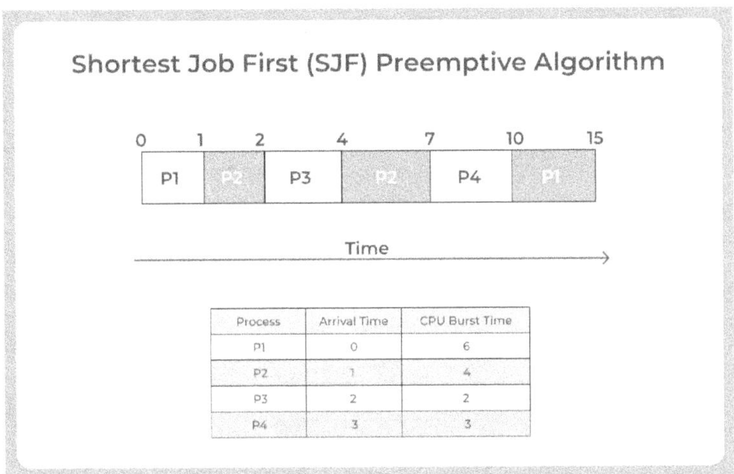

- **Shortest Remaining Time First (SRTF)**: SRTF is similar to SJF, but it schedules the process with the shortest remaining execution time next. For example, if the current time is 10 milliseconds, and processes P1, P2, and P3 have estimated execution times of 10 milliseconds, 20 milliseconds, and 30 milliseconds, respectively, then P3 will be scheduled first, followed by P2, and then P1.

Process	Burst Time	Arrival Time
P1	7	0
P2	3	1
P3	4	3

The Gantt Chart for SRTF will be:

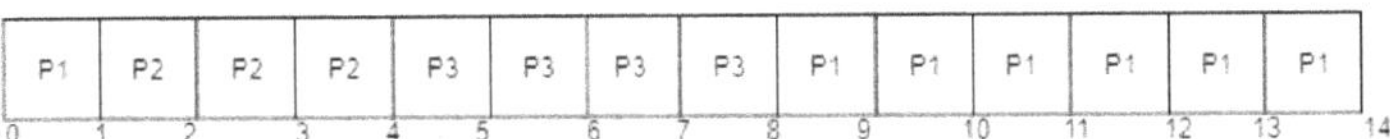

- **Multilevel Feedback Queue (MLFQ)**: MLFQ divides the processes into a number of queues, each with its own scheduling algorithm. The queues are typically arranged in order of priority, with the highest priority queue having the shortest time quantum. For example, if there are two queues, the high-priority queue has a time quantum of 1 millisecond and the low-priority queue has a time quantum of 10 milliseconds, then a process with a high priority will be scheduled for 1 millisecond, preempted, and then a process with a low priority will be scheduled for 10 milliseconds.

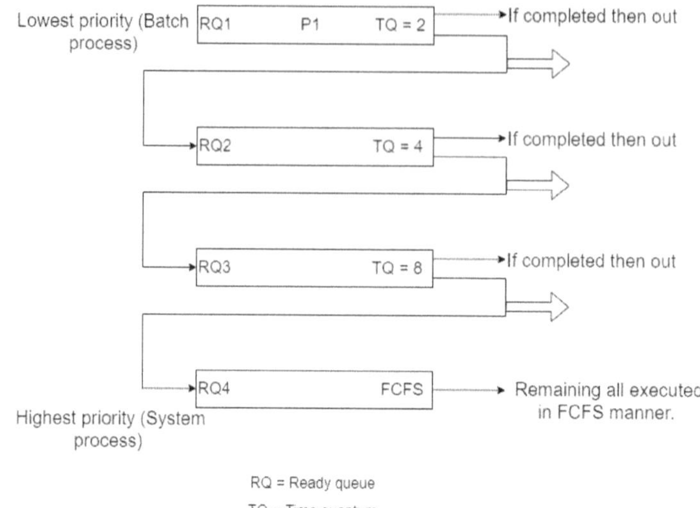

- **Weighted Round Robin (WRR)**: WRR is a preemptive scheduling algorithm that is similar to Round Robin, but it assigns each process a weight that determines how much CPU time it gets. The weight is a number that represents the relative importance of the process. For example, if process P1 has a weight of 2 and process P2 has a weight of 1, then process P1 will get twice as much CPU time as process P2.

- **Deadline Scheduling**: Deadline scheduling is a scheduling algorithm that prioritizes processes based on their deadlines. The deadline is the time by which the process must complete execution. For example, if process P1 has a deadline of 10 milliseconds and process P2 has a deadline of 20 milliseconds, then P1 will be scheduled first.

The choice of scheduling algorithm is a trade-off between **fairness, efficiency**, and **responsiveness**. FCFS is the fairest algorithm, but it may not be the most efficient or responsive. RR is more efficient than FCFS, but it may not be as fair. Priority Scheduling can be more efficient than FCFS and RR, but it may not be as fair if the priorities are not assigned carefully. SJF and SRTF are the most efficient scheduling algorithms, but they may not be as responsive if the processes have different execution times. MLFQ is a compromise between fairness, efficiency, and responsiveness. WRR can be more fair than RR, but it may not be as efficient. Deadline scheduling is used in real-time systems where it is important to ensure that critical processes meet their deadlines.

In addition to the scheduling algorithm, the scheduling policy also plays an important role in determining how processes are scheduled. The scheduling policy determines how the scheduler reacts to events such as the arrival of new processes, the completion of processes, and the preemption of processes.

Some of the most common scheduling policies include:

- **Preemptive:** The scheduler preempts a running process and schedules another process if the new process has a higher priority.
- **Non-preemptive:** The scheduler does not preempt a running process, even if the new process has a higher priority.
- **Cooperative:** The scheduler relies on the processes to voluntarily relinquish the CPU when they are done using it.

The choice of scheduling policy depends on the specific needs of the system. Preemptive scheduling is more efficient than non-preemptive scheduling, but it may not be as fair. Cooperative scheduling is the most fair scheduling policy, but it may not be as efficient.

The choice of scheduling algorithm and policy is a complex decision that depends on a number of factors. There is no single "best" scheduling algorithm or policy, and the best choice will vary depending on the specific system.

3.5 PROCESS CREATION AND COMMUNICATION

Processes don't operate in isolation; they often need to collaborate and communicate to accomplish more complex tasks. In this section, we'll explore how processes are created, both by duplicating existing ones and by spawning new ones. Additionally, we'll delve into inter-process communication (IPC), which allows processes to exchange data and collaborate efficiently.

Think of processes as individual workers in a vast factory. While they can perform tasks independently, their ability to collaborate and share information enhances productivity. Process creation and communication mechanisms act as the tools and channels that enable these workers to work together effectively.

3.5.1 Process Creation

Process creation is fundamental in shaping how tasks are managed and executed in an operating system. It can be compared to hiring new employees in an organization, each with unique roles and responsibilities. In this section, we explore two common methods of process creation: forking processes and spawning new ones.

3.5.1.1 Forking Processes

Forking is akin to cloning an existing worker. When you fork a process, you create an exact copy, known as the child process, of the original process, referred to as the parent process. Initially, both the parent and child processes run the same code, but they can diverge and perform different tasks as needed.

Example: Forking a Process

Imagine a text editor application. When you open a new file, the editor may fork a process for each open file. These child processes start with the same code as the parent process, including the text editor's functionalities. However, each child process handles specific file operations, such as reading, writing, and saving, while sharing the editor's core codebase. This approach allows multiple files to be edited simultaneously, with each file operation occurring independently within its respective child process.

3.5.1.2 Spawning New Processes

Spawning a new process is akin to hiring a specialized worker with a specific skill set tailored for a particular task. Unlike forking, where processes start identical, spawning allows you to create processes with different program code and roles.

Example: Spawning a Process

Consider a web server that needs to handle multiple client requests concurrently. Each incoming client request requires its process to manage the communication and response. In this scenario, the web server employs the method of spawning new processes. When a new client connection is established, the server creates a new process with code dedicated to handling that client's requests. Each spawned process is specialized in serving client requests, ensuring efficient and responsive web service. This approach enables the server to serve multiple clients simultaneously, with each spawned process executing unique code tailored to the client's needs.

Process creation methods offer flexibility in managing tasks within an operating system. Whether through forking or spawning, processes can be tailored to perform specific functions, allowing for efficient multitasking and resource utilization. In the subsequent sections, we'll delve into inter-process communication (IPC) mechanisms, which enable these processes to collaborate and share information effectively.

3.5.2 Inter-Process Communication (IPC)

Processes in an operating system often need to collaborate, exchange data, or coordinate their activities to achieve more complex tasks. Inter-Process Communication (IPC) provides the essential means for processes to share information and work together effectively. There are several IPC mechanisms, each tailored to specific use cases, facilitating various forms of communication and coordination.

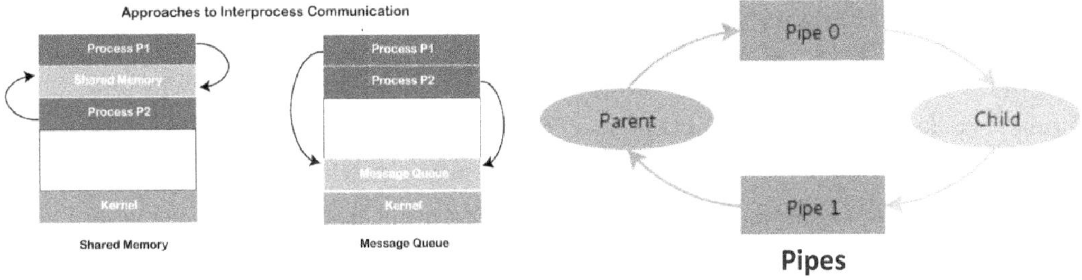

Figure 3.8: IPC: Processes communicating with each other

3.5.2.1 Pipes

Pipes are a simple yet powerful unidirectional communication mechanism. They allow processes to send data in one direction, typically used for straightforward, sequential data transfer between processes.

Example: Using Pipes

In a command-line environment, pipes enable the output of one process to serve as the input to another. For instance, the output of a file listing command (ls) can be piped (sent) as input to a text search command (grep). This allows you to filter specific files from the list seamlessly.

3.5.2.2 Message Queues

Message queues provide a versatile way for processes to communicate asynchronously, allowing processes to send and receive messages. They are ideal for scenarios where processes need to exchange information without waiting for each other.

Example: Message Queue Usage

In a distributed system, components often need to communicate without causing delays. Message queues offer a solution in such cases. For instance, consider an e-commerce platform that handles order processing. As new orders arrive, they can be placed in a message queue. Separate processes can then retrieve and process these orders at their own pace, ensuring efficient and responsive order management.

3.5.2.3 Shared Memory

Shared memory is a highly efficient IPC mechanism that allows processes to share a portion of their memory space. This shared region of memory enables processes to read and write data quickly and effectively, making it well-suited for scenarios requiring high-speed data exchange.

Example: Shared Memory Usage

In a multimedia application, one process might be responsible for decoding video frames, while another process is tasked with rendering and displaying these frames in real-time. Shared memory can be used to transfer video frames efficiently from the decoding process to the rendering process, ensuring smooth and responsive video playback.

3.5.2.4 Synchronization Mechanisms

When multiple processes concurrently access shared resources or communicate through IPC mechanisms, synchronization becomes crucial to maintain order and consistency. Various synchronization mechanisms, such as locks, semaphores, and mutexes, ensure that interactions occur in an orderly and predictable manner.

Example: Synchronization

In a multi-threaded application, where multiple threads may need to access a shared data structure, synchronization mechanisms come into play. Mutexes can be employed to ensure that only one thread accesses the shared data structure at any given time, preventing data corruption and ensuring data integrity.

Understanding and effectively utilizing IPC mechanisms is pivotal in developing robust, collaborative, and efficient systems. These mechanisms enable processes to work together harmoniously, sharing data and resources while maintaining the integrity and reliability of the overall system. In the subsequent sections, we'll delve deeper into process management in Python, exploring how these concepts can be applied in practice.

3.6 PROCESS MANAGEMENT IN PYTHON

Process management is crucial for controlling and overseeing the execution of processes, ensuring system stability and efficiency. Python, a versatile programming language, provides robust support for process management. In this section, we'll explore how Python can be utilized for creating, managing, and interacting with processes, covering essential aspects such as process creation, control, termination, and real-world applications.

3.6.1 Leveraging Python for Process Management

Python offers a comprehensive set of modules and libraries for managing processes, making it an invaluable tool for system administrators, developers, and engineers. Its simplicity and cross-platform compatibility make it an ideal choice for various process management tasks.

3.6.2 Creating Processes in Python

Creating processes in Python is straightforward, thanks to the multiprocessing module. This module enables us to spawn new processes and execute functions concurrently, facilitating efficient parallel processing.

Example: Creating Processes in Python

Let's consider a scenario where you need to download multiple files concurrently. We can leverage Python's multiprocessing module to create a separate process for each file download, significantly speeding up the process.

```python
import multiprocessing
import urllib.request

def download_file(url, save_path):
    try:
        urllib.request.urlretrieve(url, save_path)
        print(f"Downloaded: {url}")
    except Exception as e:
        print(f"Error downloading {url}: {e}")

if __name__ == "__main__":
    urls = ["https://example.com/file1.pdf",
"https://example.com/file2.pdf", "https://example.com/file3.pdf"]
    save_paths = ["file1.pdf", "file2.pdf", "file3.pdf"]

    # Create a process for each download
    processes = []
    for url, path in zip(urls, save_paths):
        process = multiprocessing.Process(target=download_file,
args=(url, path))
        processes.append(process)
        process.start()

    # Wait for all processes to complete
    for process in processes:
        process.join()

    print("All downloads completed.")
```

This creates a separate process for each file download, significantly speeding things up compared to a sequential approach.

Performing Calculations in Parallel

We can also use multiprocessing to perform CPU-bound tasks in parallel:

```python
import multiprocessing

def perform_calculation(operation, a, b):
    if operation == 'add':
        result = a + b
    elif operation == 'subtract':
        result = a - b
    elif operation == 'multiply':
        result = a * b
    elif operation == 'divide':
        if b != 0:
            result = a / b
        else:
            result = "Cannot divide by zero"
    else:
        result = "Invalid operation"

    print(f"{operation}({a}, {b}) = {result}")

if __name__ == "__main__":
    operations = ['add', 'subtract', 'multiply', 'divide']
    values = [(10, 5), (15, 7), (8, 4), (12, 0)]  # Some example
values

    # Create a process for each calculation
    processes = []
    for operation, (a, b) in zip(operations, values):
        process =
multiprocessing.Process(target=perform_calculation,
args=(operation, a, b))
        processes.append(process)
        process.start()

    # Wait for all processes to complete
    for process in processes:
        process.join()

    print("All calculations completed.")
```

Here we perform simple math operations in parallel processes.

The `multiprocessing` module makes it easy to leverage multiple CPUs for concurrent execution. This allows us to speed up all kinds of parallel workloads in Python.

3.6.3 Managing Processes in Python

The `psutil` library provides ways to monitor and control processes in Python.

Checking Process Status

For example, we can launch a process and then check if it is still running:

import psutil

```python
import time

process = psutil.Popen(["notepad.exe"])

while True:
    if not psutil.pid_exists(process.pid):
        print("Process has exited.")
        break
    time.sleep(1)
```

This loops and checks the process ID to see if the process is still alive.

TERMINATING PROCESSES

We can also forcibly terminate processes:

```python
import psutil

process = psutil.Popen(["notepad.exe"])

# Some time later...

process.terminate()
process.wait()
```

Here we use `terminate()` to send a SIGTERM signal, then wait for the process to exit.

LISTING ALL PROCESSES

To view all running processes, we can use:

```python
import psutil

for proc in psutil.process_iter():
    try:
        pinfo = proc.as_dict(attrs=['pid', 'name'])
    except psutil.NoSuchProcess:
```

```
        pass
    else:
        print(pinfo)
```

This provides a snapshot of all processes running on the system.

The `psutil` library makes managing and monitoring external processes easy in Python. This helps ensure robust process control in complex scripts and applications.

3.6.4 Process Termination and Cleanup

It's important to properly terminate Python processes to avoid resource leaks or data corruption.

Handling Termination Signals

We can handle termination signals like CTRL+C to terminate gracefully:

```python
import time

running = True

def main_loop():
    global running
    while running:
        print("Processing...")
        time.sleep(1)

if __name__ == "__main__":
    try:
        main_loop()
    except KeyboardInterrupt:
        print("Terminating...")
        running = False
```

This allows the process to finish up any critical operations before exiting when it receives a termination signal.

Using Context Managers

We can also use context managers to ensure cleanup code executes:

```python
import time
from contextlib import contextmanager

@contextmanager
def managed_loop():
```

```python
    print("Starting ... ")
    try:
        yield
    finally:
        print("Cleaning up ... ")

with managed_loop():
    while True:
        print("Processing ... ")
        time.sleep(1)
```

The cleanup code in the `finally` block will execute even if the loop terminates early.

Terminating Child Processes

If a parent process spawns children, it should terminate them before exiting:

```python
import subprocess

child = subprocess.Popen(["python3", "child.py"])

# Terminate child before exiting
child.terminate()
child.wait()
```

This ensures no orphaned processes are left behind.

Properly handling termination makes Python programs more robust and stable. This is especially important for long-running processes like daemons and servers.

3.6.5 Real-World Use Cases and Examples

Python's process management capabilities extend far beyond the previously discussed use cases. In fact, Python proves invaluable for a wide array of process management tasks, including:

- **Managing concurrent processes**: Python excels at handling multiple processes concurrently, enabling parallel execution of tasks.

- **Terminating processes gracefully**: Python provides mechanisms to gracefully terminate processes, ensuring that resources are released efficiently.

- **Monitoring process performance**: Python can be used for real-time monitoring of process performance, allowing for proactive management.

- **Scheduling processes**: Python facilitates process scheduling, ensuring tasks are executed in a timely and organized manner.

- **Logging process activity**: Python enables the logging of process activities, aiding in debugging and analysis.

- **Interacting with processes**: Python offers versatile tools for interacting with processes, including data exchange and control.

Python's process management capabilities continually evolve, with new features and enhancements added regularly. This makes Python an adaptable and powerful tool for process management across various environments.

These practical examples illustrate how Python's process management capabilities can be applied to address real-world challenges effectively:

Use Case 1: Parallelizing Data Processing

In scenarios involving the efficient processing of large datasets, Python's process management capabilities shine. By parallelizing data processing tasks, Python significantly reduces computation time.

Example: Parallelizing Data Processing

Suppose you have a dataset of customer reviews and need to perform sentiment analysis on each review. Python's multiprocessing module can distribute the sentiment analysis task across multiple processes, speeding up the analysis.

```python
import multiprocessing

def analyze_sentiment(review):
    # Perform sentiment analysis here
    pass

if __name__ == "__main__":
    reviews = [...]  # List of customer reviews
    num_processes = 4

    # Create a process pool
    pool = multiprocessing.Pool(processes=num_processes)

    # Parallelize sentiment analysis
    results = pool.map(analyze_sentiment, reviews)

    pool.close()
    pool.join()
```

Use Case 2: System Monitoring and Resource Management

Python is a valuable asset for system monitoring and resource management tasks. Whether you're a system administrator overseeing server networks or an application developer optimizing resource usage, Python can efficiently manage processes and system resources.

Example: System Monitoring and Resource Management

Imagine the responsibility of monitoring a server's CPU usage and taking actions if it exceeds a certain threshold. Python, in combination with libraries like psutil, can handle this task seamlessly.

```python
import psutil
import time

def monitor_cpu_threshold(threshold):
    while True:
        cpu_percent = psutil.cpu_percent(interval=1)
        if cpu_percent > threshold:
            # Take necessary actions, e.g., send alerts or scale resources
            print(f"CPU Usage exceeds {threshold}%")
        time.sleep(60)  # Check every minute

if __name__ == "__main__":
    threshold = 90  # Define the CPU usage threshold
    monitor_cpu_threshold(threshold)
```

Use Case 3: Task Automation

Python's process management capabilities simplify task automation. Whether automating routine system maintenance or orchestrating complex workflows, Python can create scripts that reliably and efficiently execute tasks.

Example: Task Automation

Consider automating the daily backup of important files. Python can create a script that identifies files to be backed up and manages the backup process.

```python
import shutil
import os
import datetime

def backup_files(source_dir, backup_dir):
    today = datetime.date.today()
```

```python
    backup_folder = os.path.join(backup_dir, str(today))

    os.makedirs(backup_folder, exist_ok=True)

    for root, _, files in os.walk(source_dir):
        for file in files:
            source_path = os.path.join(root, file)
            backup_path = os.path.join(backup_folder, file)
            shutil.copy2(source_path, backup_path)
            print(f"Backed up: {source_path} to {backup_path}")

if __name__ == "__main__":
    source_directory = "/path/to/source/files"
    backup_directory = "/path/to/backup/location"

    backup_files(source_directory, backup_directory)
```

These real-world use cases demonstrate the versatility and power of Python in process management. Whether parallelizing data processing, monitoring system resources, or automating tasks, Python's process management capabilities make it a valuable tool for a wide range of applications.

4   THREADS

In the digital world, multitasking and efficient resource utilization are paramount. Threads play a pivotal role in enabling concurrent execution of tasks within a single process. They are lightweight processes that share the same memory space and resources.

This chapter explores the fascinating realm of threads, shedding light on their definition, significance, and the models they operate within. We'll delve into how operating systems handle threads, focusing on key concepts such as thread scheduling and synchronization.

Advantages of multi-threading are numerous. For instance, it can significantly improve the responsiveness of a program by allowing multiple tasks to be executed simultaneously. It also enhances resource utilization and simplifies program structures.

In the context of Python, a versatile programming language, we will introduce the threading module and demonstrate how to harness its power for creating, managing, and orchestrating threads. Expect to find plenty of code examples to help you grasp the practical aspects of multi-threaded programming in Python. By the end of this chapter, you'll have a comprehensive understanding of threads and be ready to embark on the journey of multi-threaded programming in Python.

4.1 UNDERSTANDING MULTI-THREADING

Multi-threading is a fundamental concept in modern computing, revolutionizing the way processes execute tasks concurrently. In this section, we will delve into the essence of multi-threading, defining it and unraveling its significance in the world of software development and system efficiency.

4.1.1 Definition and Concept

At its core, multi-threading refers to the concurrent execution of multiple threads within a single process. A thread can be thought of as a lightweight, independent unit of a process, capable of executing code concurrently with other threads in the same process. Threads share the same memory space, which means they can access and modify the same data without having to copy it, making them highly efficient for tasks that require coordination and communication.

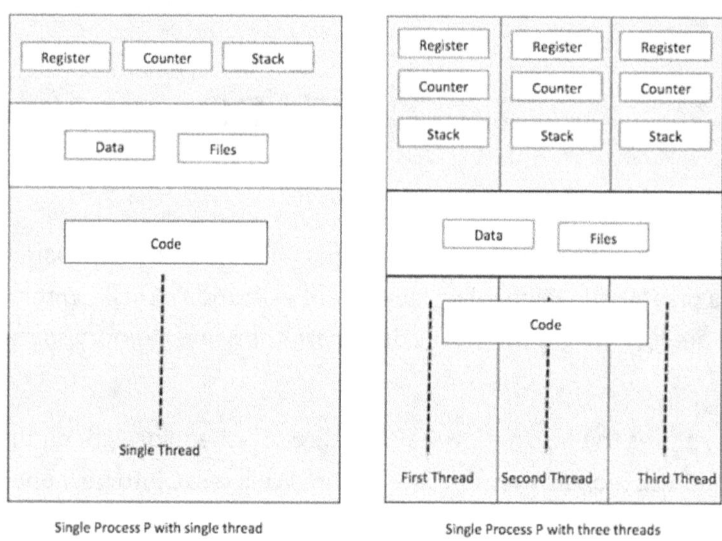

Figure 4.1: Threads: Lightweight processes sharing the same address space

The significance of multi-threading lies in its ability to harness the full potential of modern computing hardware, particularly multi-core processors. By breaking down a program into smaller threads, each handling a specific task or subtask, multi-threading allows for parallel execution. This, in turn, leads to improved program responsiveness, enhanced resource utilization, and the ability to tackle complex tasks more efficiently.

For example, consider a web server responsible for serving multiple client requests simultaneously. Without multi-threading, the server might process requests sequentially, leading to slow response times. However, by employing multi-threading, each incoming request can be assigned to a separate thread. These threads work concurrently to handle client requests, significantly improving the server's responsiveness and overall performance.

In essence, multi-threading empowers software developers to write programs that can juggle multiple tasks concurrently, delivering faster execution times and better resource utilization. In the chapters that follow, we'll explore the intricacies of thread management, synchronization, and multi-threading in the context of Python, demonstrating how this powerful concept can be put into practice.

4.1.2 Multi-Threading Models

Multi-threading models in operating systems encompass various approaches to managing threads. These models differ in how threads are created, scheduled, and synchronized. In this section, we will explore different multi-threading models, specifically focusing on user-level and kernel-level thread approaches, to provide a comprehensive understanding of how threads are managed.

User-Level Threads (ULTs)

User-level threads are threads managed entirely by user-level libraries and the application itself, without direct involvement from the operating system kernel. These threads are lightweight and are created, scheduled, and synchronized by the application code. User-level threads are highly portable, suitable for any operating system supporting multi-threading. However, their limitation lies in efficiently utilizing multiple processor cores, as the operating system kernel remains unaware of their existence.

Advantages of User-Level Threads:

- **Portability**: User-level threads can run on any operating system with a multi-threading library, ensuring high portability.

- **Custom Scheduling**: Application developers have full control over thread scheduling, allowing them to design custom algorithms tailored to specific needs.

Disadvantages of User-Level Threads:

- **Limited Concurrency**: User-level threads may not fully leverage multi-core processors since they depend on the operating system for actual execution.

- **Blocking Threads**: If one user-level thread in an application blocks (e.g., due to I/O), it can potentially block all other threads in the application.

Kernel-Level Threads (KLTs)

Kernel-level threads, on the other hand, are directly managed by the operating system kernel. Each thread is considered a separate process by the kernel, enabling independent scheduling across multiple processor cores. Kernel-level threads offer better parallelism and suit applications requiring intensive multi-core utilization. However, they may involve more overhead in thread creation and management due to kernel involvement.

Advantages of Kernel-Level Threads:

- **Parallel Execution**: Kernel-level threads can execute concurrently on multiple processor cores, maximizing resource utilization.

- **Fault Tolerance**: Blocking one kernel-level thread does not affect the execution of other threads in the same process.

Disadvantages of Kernel-Level Threads:

- **Overhead**: Creating and managing kernel-level threads typically involves more overhead compared to user-level threads, impacting performance for applications with many threads.

- **Less Portability**: Kernel-level thread implementations can vary between operating systems, reducing portability compared to user-level threads.

In practice, the choice between user-level and kernel-level thread approaches depends on specific application requirements. Some systems employ a hybrid model, combining both approaches to leverage their respective advantages. Understanding these models is crucial for designing multi-threaded applications that efficiently utilize system resources while meeting performance goals.

Mapping User Threads to Kernel Threads

There are three main models for mapping user threads to kernel threads:

- **One-to-one:** In this model, each user thread is mapped to a kernel thread. This is the simplest and most straightforward model, but it can also be the most inefficient, as it can lead to a lot of context switching between kernel and user threads.
- **Many-to-one:** In this model, multiple user threads can be mapped to a single kernel thread. This can improve performance by reducing the amount of context switching, but it can also make it more difficult to synchronize threads.
- **Many-to-many:** In this model, any number of user threads can be mapped to any number of kernel threads. This is the most flexible model, but it can also be the most complex to manage.

The choice of mapping model depends on the specific application requirements. For example, an application that requires a high degree of synchronization between threads may choose a one-to-one mapping, while an application that is CPU-intensive may choose a many-to-one mapping.

Here is a table summarizing the key characteristics of each mapping model:

Mapping Model	Advantages	Disadvantages
One-to-one	Simplest and most straightforward	Least efficient
Many-to-one	Improves performance by reducing context switching	Can make it more difficult to synchronize threads
Many-to-many	Most flexible	Most complex to manage

The support for mapping user threads to kernel threads varies depending on the operating system.

- **Linux:** Linux supports all three mapping models. The default mapping model is one-to-one, but it can be changed to many-to-one or many-to-many using the `ulimit` command.
- **Windows:** Windows supports only the one-to-one mapping model.
- **macOS:** macOS supports both the one-to-one and many-to-one mapping models. The default mapping model is one-to-one, but it can be changed to many-to-one using the `sysctl` command.

The choice of mapping model is also affected by the operating system's thread scheduler. The thread scheduler is responsible for determining which thread to run next. The scheduler can be preemptive or non-preemptive.

- **Preemptive scheduler:** In a preemptive scheduler, the operating system can interrupt a running thread and switch to another thread at any time. This can improve performance by ensuring that all threads are given a fair chance to run.
- **Non-preemptive scheduler:** In a non-preemptive scheduler, a thread will continue to run until it blocks or voluntarily yields. This can improve performance for threads that are performing long-running operations.

The choice of mapping model and thread scheduler depends on the specific application requirements. For example, an application that requires a high degree of responsiveness may choose a preemptive scheduler with a one-to-one mapping, while an application that is CPU-intensive may choose a non-preemptive scheduler with a many-to-one mapping.

4.2 THREAD MANAGEMENT IN OPERATING SYSTEMS

Thread management encompasses critical aspects of modern operating systems, enabling the efficient and concurrent execution of tasks. In this section, we will delve into the intricacies of thread management, focusing on how operating systems handle threads, with a specific emphasis on the role of the kernel in creating, scheduling, and synchronizing threads.

4.2.1 Kernel Support for Threads

Operating systems play a pivotal role in managing threads, providing a framework for their creation, scheduling, and coordination. The kernel, which is the core component of the operating system, is central to this process. Let's explore how the kernel provides support for threads:

Thread Creation:

- **Thread Creation API**: Typically, the operating system offers an API (Application Programming Interface) for creating threads. Applications can utilize this API to request the creation of new threads.

- **Resource Allocation**: Upon thread creation, the kernel allocates essential resources such as a thread control block (TCB), stack space, and program counter to facilitate the management of the thread's execution.

Thread Scheduling:

- **Thread Scheduler**: Housed within the kernel, the thread scheduler assumes responsibility for determining which threads should run and for how long. It employs scheduling algorithms to make these decisions.

- **Context Switching**: During a context switch, the kernel performs a crucial task. It saves the current thread's state, including registers and the program counter, in memory and restores the state of the thread that will run next.

Thread Synchronization:

- **Synchronization Primitives**: The kernel furnishes synchronization mechanisms such as locks, semaphores, and mutexes. These mechanisms ensure orderly and secure access to shared resources among threads, preventing data races and maintaining data consistency.

- **Blocking and Wake-Up**: The kernel efficiently manages thread blocking and wake-up operations. When one thread attempts to access a resource held by another, it may be temporarily blocked. The kernel ensures that blocked threads are awakened efficiently when the resource becomes available.

Kernel-Level vs. User-Level Threads:

- **Kernel Involvement**: In the case of kernel-level threads, the kernel independently manages each thread, making scheduling decisions and context switches directly. User-level threads, on the other hand, are managed by user-level libraries, with the kernel remaining unaware of their existence.

- **Resource Allocation**: Kernel-level threads typically enjoy dedicated kernel resources for each thread, rendering them well-suited for multi-core utilization. In contrast, user-level threads share the same kernel-level resources.

A comprehensive understanding of the kernel's central role in thread management is vital for developers seeking to create efficient and scalable multi-threaded applications. In the forthcoming sections, we will explore various thread states, transitions between these states, and the critical importance of synchronization mechanisms in greater detail.

4.2.2 Thread States and Transitions

Thread states represent the different stages of a thread's execution within an operating system. Grasping these states and the transitions that occur between them is fundamental for effective thread management. In this section, we will delve into the common thread states, elucidating how threads move between these states, and explore the events that trigger these transitions.

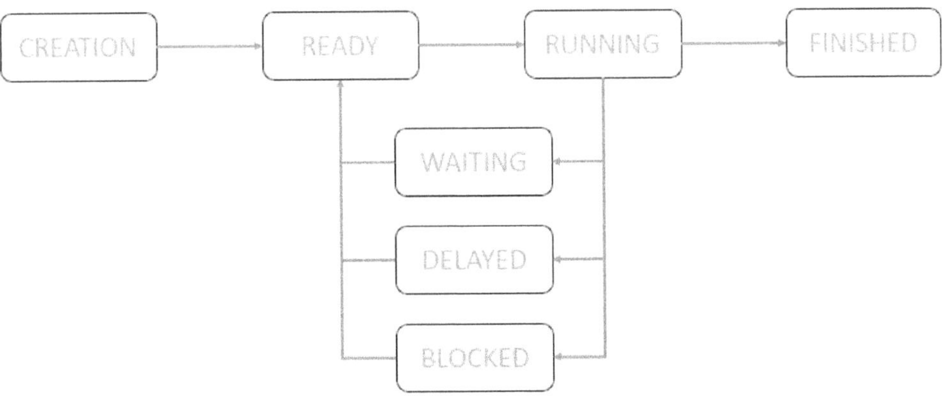

Figure 4.2: Thread states: The lifecycle of a thread

Thread States:

- **Running**: A thread in the running state is actively executing its code on a processor core. At any given moment, only one thread from a process can be in the running state.

- **Ready**: Threads in the ready state are prepared to run but await the scheduler's allocation of CPU time. Multiple threads in the ready state can coexist within a process.

- **Blocked** (or **Waiting**): Threads in the blocked state are temporarily unable to run due to specific conditions, such as waiting for a particular resource or the completion of an I/O operation. These threads remain ineligible for execution until they return to the ready state.

Thread State Transitions:

Threads transition between these states in response to specific events or operations. Here are the key state transitions:

- **Running** to **Ready**: A running thread may shift to the ready state when its allocated time quantum expires, prompting the scheduler to allocate CPU time to another thread.

- **Running** to **Blocked**: A running thread may transition to the blocked state when it initiates a blocking operation, such as waiting for user input or file I/O. This transition occurs voluntarily by the thread itself.

- **Blocked** to **Ready**: A blocked thread returns to the ready state when the event or condition it was waiting for (e.g., data availability) is satisfied.

- **Ready** to **Running**: When the scheduler selects a thread from the ready queue for execution, the chosen thread transitions from the ready state to the running state.

- **Ready** to **Blocked**: A thread in the ready state may voluntarily shift to the blocked state, such as when it relinquishes the CPU to wait for a specific event or resource.

- **Blocked** to **Running** (or **Ready**): When a blocked thread returns to the ready state, it becomes eligible for execution by the scheduler. If selected, it moves to the running state.

Events Triggering Transitions:

- **Timer Interrupt**: A timer interrupt can initiate a transition from running to ready when a thread's allocated time quantum expires.

- **I/O Completion**: Threads blocked on I/O operations transition to the ready state when the I/O operation reaches completion.

- **Resource Availability**: Threads awaiting resources (e.g., locks or semaphores) transition from the blocked state to the ready state when the resources become accessible.

A profound comprehension of these thread states and transitions is pivotal for efficient thread management and the responsiveness of the overall system. Operating system kernels employ sophisticated algorithms to effectively manage these transitions, ensuring the efficient scheduling and synchronization of threads.

4.2.3 The Significance of Thread Synchronization

In the intricate realm of multi-threaded programming, thread synchronization emerges as a pivotal concept, wielding a profound influence on the prevention of data races and the maintenance of data consistency. In this section, we will embark on a journey to unearth the profound importance of thread synchronization. We shall also introduce the cornerstone synchronization primitives—locks, semaphores, and mutexes—revealing them to be indispensable instruments for orchestrating the intricate dance of thread interactions.

The Crucial Role of Thread Synchronization

In the multi-threaded arena, a multitude of threads can concurrently access shared resources. In the absence of meticulous synchronization, this simultaneous foray into shared territories can lead to an undesirable and chaotic phenomenon known as a "data race." Data races, aptly named, can yield catastrophic outcomes: data corruption, program crashes, and cryptic and elusive bugs that confound even the most seasoned developers.

Here's an example to illustrate a "data race" in a multi-threaded program:

Imagine a simple program with two threads that are trying to increment a shared counter variable. The threads perform the following steps:

Thread 1:

1. Reads the current value of the shared counter (e.g., it reads 5).
2. Increments the counter by 1 (5 + 1 = 6).
3. Writes the new value back to the shared counter (sets it to 6).

Thread 2:

1. Reads the current value of the shared counter (still the old value, i.e., 5).
2. Increments the counter by 1 (5 + 1 = 6).
3. Writes the new value back to the shared counter (also sets it to 6).

Now, let's consider the sequence of events in a multi-threaded environment:

1. Thread 1 reads the counter's value as 5.

2. Thread 2 reads the counter's value as 5 (before Thread 1 has a chance to update it).
3. Thread 1 increments its local copy of the counter to 6.
4. Thread 2 also increments its local copy of the counter to 6 (since it read 5).
5. Both Thread 1 and Thread 2 write their local copies (6) back to the shared counter.

In this scenario, two threads were simultaneously trying to modify the shared counter without proper synchronization. As a result, both threads incremented the counter from 5 to 6, even though the expected outcome should have been 7 (5 + 1 + 1). This inconsistent behavior is what we refer to as a "data race."

Data races can lead to incorrect program behavior, unpredictable outcomes, and even program crashes in more complex scenarios. To prevent data races and ensure proper synchronization, synchronization mechanisms like locks, mutexes, and semaphores are used to coordinate access to shared resources among threads.

Thread synchronization assumes a multitude of vital roles, each contributing to the order and harmony of the multi-threaded symphony:

1. Ensuring Data Consistency: Above all, synchronization stands as a vigilant guardian of data consistency. It possesses the power to ensure that shared data retains its integrity, shielding it from the disarray that concurrent access may unleash. It acts as the sentinel, ensuring that no thread reads data currently under the surgeon's scalpel of modification by another.

2. Enforcing Orderly Access: Thread synchronization mechanisms don the mantle of order keepers, orchestrating a structured procession for thread access to shared resources. They deftly avert conflicts and safeguard the pristine essence of data, preventing disorderly clashes.

3. Fostering Cooperation: Threads, like members of a finely tuned orchestra, often need to synchronize their efforts. They must harmonize, waiting for specific conditions to align or coordinating their actions to create a harmonious symphony. Synchronization primitives serve as the conductor's baton, enabling threads to communicate and collaborate effectively.

Embarking on the Synchronization Odyssey

Synchronization in the realm of multi-threaded programming is a multifaceted endeavor, achieved through a pantheon of primitives and mechanisms. Let us venture forth and unravel some of the most revered and frequently employed:

Locks:

- **Mutex (Mutual Exclusion):** Mutex, a sentinel of solitude, is a synchronization primitive that extends the privilege of access to a single thread at a time. When a thread secures a mutex, it ascends to the pinnacle of exclusivity, gaining sovereign rights over the protected resource. Other threads, yearning for the same privilege, must stand in line, patiently waiting their turn for the throne.

- **Semaphore:** A semaphore, a more flexible sentinel, orchestrates the entry of a specified number of threads into a realm of shared resources. Semaphores, akin to discerning gatekeepers, ensure that a predetermined count of threads may access the domain concurrently. This versatility finds expression in scenarios such as resource pooling and the imposition of concurrency constraints.

- **Condition Variables:** Condition variables, the heralds of condition-based enlightenment, provide a platform for threads to convey their yearnings and anxieties. Threads may opt to pause, awaiting specific conditions to ripen before they venture forth into the unknown. Condition variables often find their purpose intertwined with the dance of locks, signaling and orchestrating transitions between states.

- **Read-Write Locks:** Distinguished patrons of the literary world, read-write locks wield the quill of differentiation. They discern between those seeking to peruse the pages and those endeavoring to pen new chapters. The fraternity of readers enjoys the privilege of concurrent perusal, while the lone author, aiming to inscribe the masterpiece, must seize the quill exclusively. This dichotomy finds resonance in scenarios where reading prevails frequently, and writing occurs sporadically.

A Synchronization Odyssey: The Mutex as the Protagonist

Synchronization is a critical concept in multi-threaded programming. It ensures that multiple threads can safely access shared resources without interfering with each other.

In this section, we will explore the concept of synchronization using the mutex as an example. A mutex is a synchronization primitive that allows only one thread to access a shared resource at a time.

To illustrate the use of a mutex, let's consider the following code:

```python
import threading

# Shared resource
shared_counter = 0

# Mutex for synchronization
```

```python
mutex = threading.Lock()

def increment_counter():
    global shared_counter
    with mutex:   # Acquire the mutex
        shared_counter += 1   # Perform a synchronized operation
        print(f"Counter: {shared_counter}")

# Create multiple threads
threads = []
for _ in range(5):
    thread = threading.Thread(target=increment_counter)
    threads.append(thread)

# Start the threads
for thread in threads:
    thread.start()

# Wait for all threads to finish
for thread in threads:
    thread.join()
```

This code creates five threads that all increment the shared_counter variable. Without a mutex, it is possible for the threads to interleave their operations, resulting in an incorrect value for the counter.

The `with mutex` statement acquires the mutex before the `shared_counter` variable is incremented. This ensures that only one thread can access the variable at a time.

The `print()` statement releases the mutex after the variable has been incremented. This allows other threads to acquire the mutex and access the variable.

The output of this code is always 5, because each thread is only able to increment the counter once.

The mutex is a simple but powerful synchronization primitive that can be used to prevent race conditions in multi-threaded programs.

A Symphony of Synchronization Awaits

Thread synchronization is a complex and challenging topic, but it is essential for writing correct and reliable multi-threaded programs.

In addition to mutexes, there are many other synchronization primitives available, such as semaphores, condition variables, and barriers. Each primitive has its own strengths and weaknesses, and the best choice for a particular application will depend on the specific requirements.

The mastery of synchronization primitives is an essential skill for any multi-threaded programmer. By understanding the different synchronization primitives and how to use them effectively, you can write programs that are safe, efficient, and reliable.

The Future of Synchronization

The field of synchronization is constantly evolving as new technologies emerge. For example, the rise of cloud computing has led to the development of new synchronization primitives that are designed to work in a distributed environment.

As the world becomes increasingly interconnected, the need for efficient and reliable synchronization primitives will only grow. The future of synchronization is bright, and it is an exciting time to be a multi-threaded programmer.

4.3 UNLOCKING THE BENEFITS OF MULTI-THREADING

Multi-threading is a potent programming technique that bestows several remarkable advantages, making it an indispensable tool for developers. In this section, we will delve into these advantages, commencing with an exploration of how multi-threading elevates a program's responsiveness by facilitating concurrent task execution.

4.3.1 Improved Responsiveness

One of the primary merits of multi-threading lies in its ability to enhance a program's responsiveness. In conventional single-threaded applications, tasks follow a sequential path. When a task involves substantial computation or awaits external resources, it can lead to unresponsive user interfaces and lackluster performance.

Improved Responsiveness: Multi-threading bolsters a program's capacity to swiftly respond to user input or events, eliminating delays. In single-threaded setups, time-consuming tasks can cause the user interface to freeze or become unresponsive. Multi-threading tackles this issue by enabling concurrent task execution.

How Multi-Threading Improves Responsiveness:

- **Concurrent Execution:** In multi-threaded programs, different tasks can run concurrently in separate threads. This means that while one thread is immersed in a time-consuming operation, other threads continue their work in the background.
- **User Interface Responsiveness:** In applications equipped with graphical user

interfaces (GUIs), multi-threading safeguards the UI from freezing during resource-intensive operations. For instance, a file download can progress in the background while users interact with the interface.

- **Faster Task Completion:** By efficiently harnessing available CPU cores, multi-threading accelerates task completion. Operations amenable to parallelization, like data processing, reap substantial benefits from multi-threading.

Example: Improving Responsiveness with Multi-Threading

Imagine a web browser that leverages multi-threading to enhance responsiveness. When you open a web page, the browser assigns one thread to render the page's content, another to download images, and yet another to handle user input. While rendering the content may take time, the browser remains responsive because user input processing occurs in a separate thread. This allows seamless scrolling, clicking links, or interacting with the page as it loads.

```python
import threading

def render_web_page():
    # Simulate rendering a web page
    print("Rendering web page...")

def download_images():
    # Simulate downloading images
    print("Downloading images...")

# Create threads for rendering and downloading
render_thread = threading.Thread(target=render_web_page)
download_thread = threading.Thread(target=download_images)

# Start both threads
render_thread.start()
download_thread.start()

# Wait for both threads to finish
render_thread.join()
download_thread.join()

print("Web page fully loaded and responsive.")
```

Enhancing responsiveness is but one facet of multi-threading's advantages. In the following sections, we will explore additional benefits, such as heightened efficiency and resource optimization, which amplify the allure of multi-threading as a formidable programming technique.

4.3.2 Enhanced Resource Utilization

Multi-threading brings forth another compelling advantage: enhanced resource utilization, especially in the realm of multi-core systems. In this section, we will delve into how multi-threading harnesses CPU resources effectively, culminating in improved system efficiency.

Utilizing Multi-Core Systems

Contemporary computers often house multi-core processors, comprising multiple independent processing units (cores) on a single chip. These cores can execute instructions in parallel, unlocking hardware-level parallelism. However, for software to fully tap into these multi-core systems, it must be adept at parceling out tasks across multiple threads.

Enhanced Resource Utilization: Multi-threading augments resource utilization by apportioning tasks among multiple threads, permitting concurrent task execution. This parallelism translates into markedly improved performance and throughput, optimizing CPU cores and other system resources efficiently.

Benefits of Multi-Threading in Multi-Core Systems

In multi-core systems, multi-threading proves to be a game-changer, enhancing performance and throughput by enabling multiple tasks to run concurrently on different cores. This boon extends to various applications, including those encompassing extensive computational tasks, data processing endeavors, and scientific simulations.

Example: Utilizing Multi-Core Systems

Let's contemplate a multi-threaded image processing application. In its single-threaded counterpart, image processing tasks would unfold sequentially, underutilizing available CPU cores. Yet, through the implementation of multi-threading, each image can undergo processing concurrently in distinct threads, making efficient use of the multi-core processor.

```python
import threading

# List of images to process
images = ["image1.jpg", "image2.jpg", "image3.jpg", "image4.jpg"]

def process_image(image):
    # Simulate image processing
    print(f"Processing {image} on thread
{threading.current_thread().name}")
```

```python
# Create a thread for each image
threads = []
for image in images:
    thread = threading.Thread(target=process_image, args=(image,))
    threads.append(thread)

# Start all threads
for thread in threads:
    thread.start()

# Wait for all threads to finish
for thread in threads:
    thread.join()

print("Image processing complete.")
```

Resource Optimization

Multi-threading not only enhances CPU utilization but also optimizes other system resources. For instance, in a multi-threaded web server, threads can concurrently handle incoming client requests, reducing idle time and making efficient use of network and memory resources.

Conclusion

Enhanced resource utilization stands as a formidable advantage of multi-threading, especially within the realm of multi-core systems. By distributing tasks across threads and cores, multi-threaded programs unlock the full potential of available hardware resources. The result is improved system efficiency and performance, a boon of immense value in performance-critical applications like scientific simulations, video rendering, and data processing.

4.3.3 Simplified Program Structure

Multi-threading offers a significant advantage when it comes to simplifying program structure. This advantage stems from the ability to divide complex tasks into smaller threads, each handling a specific aspect of the overall task. In this section, we will delve into how multi-threading simplifies program design and enhances code readability.

Dividing Complex Tasks

Many real-world applications involve intricate and multifaceted tasks that can be challenging to manage in a single-threaded environment. Multi-threading allows developers to break down these complex tasks into smaller, more manageable threads, each responsible for a specific subtask. This approach leads to several benefits:

- **Modularity**: By dividing tasks into threads, developers create a modular program structure. Each thread focuses on a well-defined portion of the task, making the code easier to understand and maintain.

- **Concurrent Execution**: The use of multiple threads enables concurrent execution of subtasks. This means that while one thread is busy with its part of the task, other threads can execute their portions in parallel, reducing overall execution time.

- **Improved Readability**: Code that employs multi-threading tends to be more readable and comprehensible. Each thread can be written as a self-contained unit, with a clear purpose and responsibility.

Example: Simplified Program Structure

Imagine a scenario where we need to develop a web scraper, a tool designed to extract data from websites. In a single-threaded implementation of this program, handling tasks such as fetching web pages, parsing HTML content, and storing data can become a convoluted and intertwined endeavor. This often leads to complex and hard-to-maintain code.

However, when we employ multi-threading, we can segment each facet of the scraping process into distinct threads. For instance, one thread can be responsible for fetching web pages, another for parsing HTML content, and yet another for storing the extracted data. This modular approach results in a more structured and comprehensible program, easing both development and maintenance efforts.

```python
import threading
import requests
from bs4 import BeautifulSoup

# List of URLs to scrape
urls = ["https://example.com", "https://another-example.com",
"https://yet-another-example.com"]

# Function to fetch and parse a web page
def scrape_page(url):
    response = requests.get(url)
    if response.status_code == 200:
        soup = BeautifulSoup(response.text, 'html.parser')
        # Parse and store data here

# Create a thread for each URL
threads = []
for url in urls:
```

```python
    thread = threading.Thread(target=scrape_page, args=(url,))
    threads.append(thread)

# Start all threads
for thread in threads:
    thread.start()

# Wait for all threads to finish
for thread in threads:
    thread.join()

print("Web scraping complete.")
```

In this example, each URL is processed by a separate thread, simplifying the overall program structure. The `scrape_page` function is responsible for fetching and parsing a single web page, making the code more modular and easier to comprehend.

Conclusion

Multi-threading simplifies program structure by breaking down complex tasks into smaller threads, each with a well-defined role. This approach enhances modularity, promotes concurrent execution, and results in more readable code. It is particularly advantageous in applications where tasks involve multiple components or require parallelism, such as web scraping, data processing, and simulations.

4.4 MULTI-THREADING IN PYTHON

Python, a versatile and powerful programming language, provides built-in support for multi-threading through its threading module. In this section, we'll introduce Python's threading module and explore how it simplifies thread management.

4.4.1 Python's Threading Module

Python's threading module is a robust library for working with threads. It offers a high-level, object-oriented interface for creating, managing, and synchronizing threads. This module simplifies multi-threading, making it accessible to both beginners and experienced Python programmers.

Key Features of Python's Threading Module

- **Thread Creation:** Python's threading module simplifies creating and managing threads. Threads are represented as objects of the Thread class.
- **Thread Synchronization:** The module provides synchronization primitives like locks, semaphores, and condition variables to manage thread interactions and

prevent data races.

- **Thread Safety:** Python's threading module is designed with thread safety in mind, offering mechanisms to protect shared resources and ensure data integrity in multi-threaded programs.
- **Concurrency Control:** Developers can use this module to implement concurrent execution of tasks, effectively utilizing multi-core processors and enhancing program performance.

Example: Using Python's Threading Module

Let's see a simple example to illustrate Python's threading module. In this example, two threads perform tasks concurrently.

```python
import threading
import time

# Function to simulate a time-consuming task
def task(name):
    print(f"Thread {name} is starting...")
    time.sleep(2)  # Simulate work
    print(f"Thread {name} is done.")

# Create two threads
thread1 = threading.Thread(target=task, args=("A",))
thread2 = threading.Thread(target=task, args=("B",))

# Start both threads
thread1.start()
thread2.start()

# Wait for both threads to finish
thread1.join()
thread2.join()

print("All threads have completed.")
```

In this example, we define a task function that simulates a time-consuming operation. We create two threads, thread1 and thread2, and assign the task function to them. These threads run concurrently, executing the task function and simulating parallelism.

Conclusion

Python's threading module is a valuable tool for implementing multi-threading in Python applications. It simplifies thread creation, synchronization, and management, making it easier to leverage the benefits of multi-threading in your Python programs. Whether you're developing a web server, data processing application, or any other concurrent system, Python's threading module can help you achieve efficient multi-threaded execution.

4.4.2 Creating and Managing Threads in Python

In this section, we'll provide step-by-step instructions on how to create and manage threads using Python's threading module, covering essential topics such as thread creation, starting, and joining. Let's dive into the details.

Creating Threads

To create a thread in Python, follow these steps:

1. Import the threading module.
2. Define a function that represents the task you want the thread to perform.
3. Create a Thread object, passing the task function as the target argument.

Here's a practical example:

```python
import threading

# Define a function that represents the task
def print_numbers():
    for i in range(1, 60):
        print(f"Number: {i}")

# Create a Thread object
number_thread = threading.Thread(target=print_numbers)
```

Starting Threads

Once you have created a thread, start it using the start() method. Starting a thread initiates its execution, and it runs concurrently with other threads.

```python
# Start the thread
number_thread.start()
```

Joining Threads

To ensure that a thread completes its execution before the main program exits, use the join() method. Calling join() on a thread blocks the main program's execution until the thread finishes.

```python
# Wait for the thread to finish
number_thread.join()
```

Complete Example

Here's a complete example that creates and manages two threads to print numbers concurrently:

```python
import threading

# Define a function that represents the task
def print_numbers():
    for i in range(1, 60):
        print(f"Number: {i}")

# Create two Thread objects
thread1 = threading.Thread(target=print_numbers)
thread2 = threading.Thread(target=print_numbers)

# Start both threads
thread1.start()
thread2.start()

# Wait for both threads to finish
thread1.join()
thread2.join()

print("All threads have completed.")
```

In this example, we define a print_numbers function representing the task. We create two threads, thread1 and thread2, and start them concurrently. We use join() to wait for both threads to complete before printing the final message.

By following these steps, you can easily create and manage threads in Python using the threading module, enabling concurrent execution of tasks in your Python applications, enhancing performance and responsiveness.

4.4.3 Examples of Multi-Threaded Python Programs

In this section, we'll explore real-world examples of multi-threaded Python programs to highlight the advantages and use cases of multi-threading.

Example 1: Web Scraping

Web scraping involves extracting data from websites, often requiring fetching multiple web pages concurrently. Multi-threading can significantly boost efficiency. Let's create a simple web scraping program using Python's requests library and threading module.

```python
import requests
```

```python
import threading

# Function to fetch a web page
def fetch_url(url):
    response = requests.get(url)
    print(f"Fetched content from {url}, length:
{len(response.text)}")

# List of URLs to scrape
urls = [
    "https://msn.com",
    "https://google.com",
    "https://yahoo.com",
]

# Create threads for each URL
threads = [threading.Thread(target=fetch_url, args=(url,)) for url
in urls]

# Start the threads
for thread in threads:
    thread.start()

# Wait for all threads to finish
for thread in threads:
    thread.join()

print("Web scraping tasks completed.")
```

In this example, we define a function, `fetch_url`, to retrieve web pages. Multiple threads are created, each responsible for fetching a different URL concurrently. This approach significantly speeds up web scraping tasks, especially when dealing with numerous URLs.

Example 2: Image Processing

Tasks like resizing, filtering, or enhancing images benefit from multi-threading, especially when processing a batch of images. Here's an example of resizing multiple images using threads:

```python
from PIL import Image
import os
import threading

# Function to resize an image
```

```python
def resize_image(input_path, output_path, size):
    image = Image.open(input_path)
    image = image.resize(size)
    image.save(output_path)

# List of image files to process
image_files = ["image1.jpg", "image2.jpg", "image3.jpg"]

# Create threads for resizing images
threads = []
for input_file in image_files:
    output_file = os.path.splitext(input_file)[0] + "_resized.jpg"
    thread = threading.Thread(target=resize_image,
args=(input_file, output_file, (300, 300)))
    threads.append(thread)

# Start the threads
for thread in threads:
    thread.start()

# Wait for all threads to finish
for thread in threads:
    thread.join()

print("Image resizing tasks completed.")
```

In this example, multiple threads are created to resize images concurrently. This approach enhances the efficiency of image processing tasks.

These examples showcase how Python's multi-threading can parallelize tasks, significantly improving program performance in various applications, from web scraping to image processing.

5   PROCESS SYNCHRONIZATION

In the world of computer systems, smooth teamwork among processes is crucial. This chapter explores process synchronization, a core aspect of operating systems. Here, we learn how processes can collaborate seamlessly, preventing conflicts and data issues. We uncover the importance of synchronization tools like monitors, semaphores, and critical sections, which ensure tasks run smoothly together. Furthermore, we address classic synchronization challenges, offering elegant solutions applicable across computing domains. This chapter also highlights CPU scheduling algorithms, essential for multi-core systems and real-time tasks. Finally, we demonstrate how Python's versatile threading module can put these synchronization ideas into practice with real code examples. Join us on this journey where order emerges from chaos, and parallelism finds its harmony.

5.1 UNDERSTANDING PROCESS SYNCHRONIZATION

In the world of computer systems, where multiple processes run concurrently, the need for coordination and synchronization is clear. Process synchronization ensures that multiple processes cooperate and communicate effectively, preventing conflicts and ensuring orderly execution. This concept is fundamental to modern operating systems, and in this section, we'll define it, explore its importance, and address the inherent challenges it tackles.

5.1.1 Definition and Importance

Process synchronization involves techniques and mechanisms to control the execution order of processes, preventing interference. Its importance lies in:

- **Data Consistency**: Concurrent access to shared resources or data can lead to data corruption. Synchronization maintains coordinated access, preserving data integrity.

- **Resource Management**: In multi-process environments, efficient allocation of resources like CPU time and memory is crucial. Synchronization optimizes resource utilization.

- **Preventing Deadlocks**: Deadlocks, where processes wait for each other's resources, can disrupt operations. Process synchronization techniques help prevent and recover from deadlocks.

- **Real-Time Systems**: Timing is critical in real-time systems. Process synchronization ensures tasks meet deadlines and ensures system reliability.

5.1.2 The Need for Synchronization

Consider two processes updating a shared bank account balance simultaneously. Without synchronization, chaos can result. One process may read the balance before the other updates it, leading to incorrect results and financial discrepancies. This example emphasizes the critical role of synchronization in data consistency.

Another common challenge arises when multiple processes try to print data to a shared printer. Without synchronization, simultaneous print jobs may overlap or mix up output. Such scenarios underscore the importance of synchronized resource access for maintaining order and reliability.

In essence, process synchronization is key to achieving harmony in multi-process environments. It ensures processes work cohesively, preventing conflicts and data races, resulting in a more efficient and reliable computing system. In the following sections, we'll explore synchronization mechanisms and solutions that enable this harmony.

5.2 SYNCHRONIZATION MECHANISMS

In the world of computer processes, synchronization mechanisms play a pivotal role as choreographers, ensuring processes collaborate seamlessly to prevent conflicts, maintain data integrity, and ensure smooth operation. This section explores three key synchronization mechanisms: Mutexes, Monitors, and Semaphores.

5.2.1 Critical Sections

Critical sections involve code segments demanding uninterrupted, atomic execution. These sections often deal with shared resources, and their execution by only one process at a time is crucial to prevent conflicts.

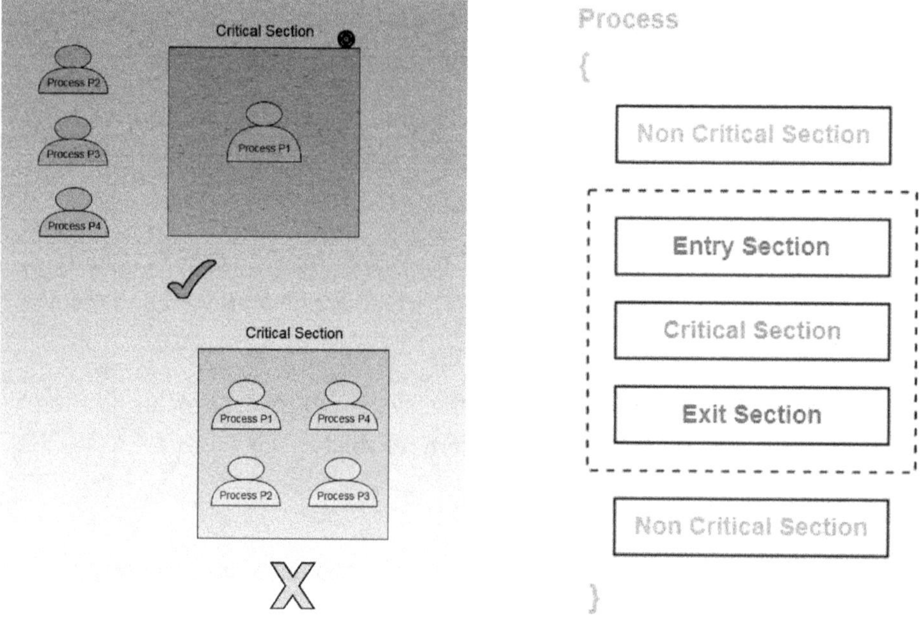

Figure 5.1: Critical sections: Code that must be executed atomically

Example: Safeguarding a Critical Section

Imagine two processes updating a shared bank account balance. The code responsible for balance updates constitutes a critical section. Without synchronization, simultaneous execution can lead to erroneous results. Critical sections ensure only one process enters at a time, averting conflicts.

5.2.2 Mutexes: Ensuring Exclusive Access

In the world of concurrent programming, mutexes (short for mutual exclusion) play a vital role in ensuring that only one process or thread can access a shared resource at a given time. Mutexes are synchronization primitives used to prevent data corruption and race conditions in multithreaded or multiprocess applications.

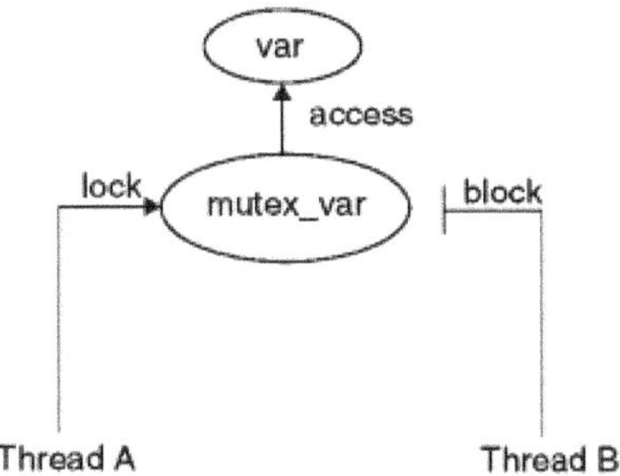

Figure 5.2: Mutex lock:
Ensuring exclusive access to
shared resources

Here's how mutexes work:

1. **Mutex Initialization:** To use a mutex, you first initialize it. In Python, you can create a mutex using the `threading` module.

```python
import threading

# Create a Mutex
mutex = threading.Lock()
```

2. **Acquiring the Mutex:** When a process or thread wants to access a shared resource within a critical section, it must acquire the mutex. If the mutex is available (i.e., no other process holds it), the requesting process gains exclusive access.

```python
mutex.acquire()
```

3. **Executing the Critical Section:** Once the mutex is acquired, the process can safely execute the critical section of code. This ensures that no other process can enter the same critical section concurrently.

4. **Releasing the Mutex:** When the process finishes its work within the critical section, it releases the mutex to allow other processes to acquire it and access the shared resource.

```python
mutex.release()
```

Mutexes are particularly useful in scenarios where multiple threads or processes need to access shared data structures, files, or resources without interfering with each other.

They help prevent race conditions, where the outcome of a computation depends on the order of access.

Here's a simple Python example of using a mutex to protect a shared counter:

```python
import threading

# Create a Mutex
mutex = threading.Lock()

# Shared counter
counter = 0

def increment_counter():
    global counter
    # Acquire the Mutex
    mutex.acquire()
    try:
        for _ in range(100000):
            counter += 1
    finally:
        # Release the Mutex, even if an exception occurs
        mutex.release()

# Create and start multiple threads
threads = []
for _ in range(4):
    thread = threading.Thread(target=increment_counter)
    threads.append(thread)
    thread.start()

# Wait for all threads to finish
for thread in threads:
    thread.join()

# Print the final counter value
print(f"Final counter value: {counter}")
```

In this example, the mutex ensures that only one thread can increment the `counter` at a time, preventing conflicts and ensuring data consistency.

5.2.3 Monitors: Safeguarding Shared Resources

In the realm of operating systems, a monitor stands as a synchronization construct, ensuring the secure access of shared resources by multiple processes. Monitors are adept data structures, encapsulating both data and the procedures associated with it.

Within these constructs, entry sections are guarded pathways, permitting the passage of only one process at any given moment.

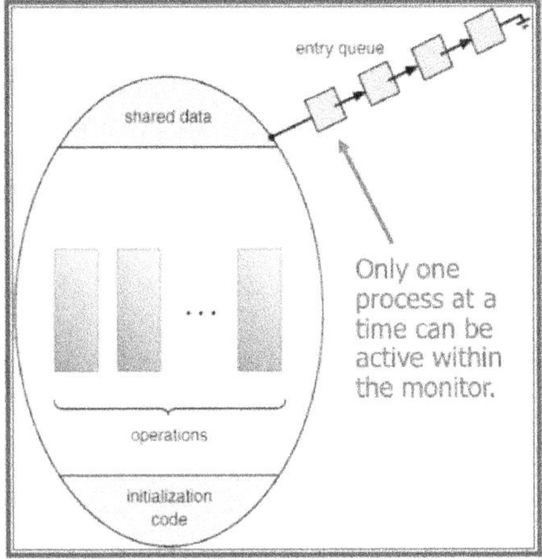

Figure 5.3: Monitors: High-level synchronization primitives for concurrent programming

Monitors function by employing mutual exclusion locks, granting exclusive access to a single process within an entry section. When a process seeks entry, it must first secure the lock, relinquishing it upon exit.

Monitors offer distinct advantages over alternative synchronization mechanisms like semaphores and mutexes:

- **Safety:** Monitors are guardians of order, ensuring solitary access to shared resources, effectively deterring race conditions and deadlock scenarios.
- **Expressiveness:** Monitors provide a richer vocabulary for processes to harmonize their shared resource access, simplifying coordination.
- **Efficiency:** Monitors can outperform semaphores and mutexes, as they sidestep the overhead of acquiring and releasing locks with each resource access.

Nonetheless, monitors do have their limitations:

- **Complexity:** Utilizing monitors can be more intricate compared to semaphores and mutexes.
- **Heterogeneity:** Monitors may not seamlessly integrate with heterogeneous systems, comprising processes of diverse languages and programming models.

Consider a scenario where numerous processes vie for access to a shared printer, with the monitor as the vigilant overseer. It manages the print queue, granting exclusive access to one process at a time. This meticulous orchestration averts conflicts, preserves a harmonious print order, and optimizes resource utilization. In this setup, the shared printer serves as the resource, and the processes act as users. The monitor encompasses two entry sections: one for submitting print jobs and another for retrieving them. When a process intends to submit a print job, it seizes the lock for the submission entry section, sends the print job, and then releases the lock. Conversely, when a process aims to receive a print job, it acquires the lock for the retrieval entry section, awaits an available print job, retrieves it, and then releases the lock.

5.2.3.1 Monitors in Action: Safeguarding Shared Resources

Let's delve deeper and see how monitors work in practice, using a Python implementation:

```python
import threading

# Define a monitor to manage printer access
class PrinterMonitor:
    def __init__(self):
        self.lock = threading.Lock()

    # Entry section for sending a print job
    def send_print_job(self, process_id):
        with self.lock:
            print(f"Process {process_id} is sending a print job.")
            # Simulate printing
            threading.Event().wait()
            print(f"Process {process_id} completed printing.")

    # Entry section for receiving a print job
    def receive_print_job(self, process_id):
        with self.lock:
            print(f"Process {process_id} is receiving a print
job.")
            # Simulate job retrieval
            threading.Event().wait()
            print(f"Process {process_id} received the print job.")

# Create a shared printer monitor
printer_monitor = PrinterMonitor()

# Simulate processes sending and receiving print jobs
def process_send(printer_monitor, process_id):
    printer_monitor.send_print_job(process_id)
```

```python
def process_receive(printer_monitor, process_id):
    printer_monitor.receive_print_job(process_id)

# Create and start multiple threads (simulating processes)
threads = []
for i in range(5):
    send_thread = threading.Thread(target=process_send,
args=(printer_monitor, i))
    receive_thread = threading.Thread(target=process_receive,
args=(printer_monitor, i))
    threads.extend([send_thread, receive_thread])
    send_thread.start()
    receive_thread.start()

# Wait for all threads to finish
for thread in threads:
    thread.join()
```

In this Python implementation, we define a `PrinterMonitor` class to manage access
to a shared printer. The monitor uses a lock to ensure exclusive access to its entry
sections: `send_print_job` for submitting print jobs and `receive_print_job` for
retrieving them.

Multiple threads (simulating processes) send and receive print jobs concurrently, with
the monitor orchestrating access, preventing conflicts, and ensuring orderly printing.

This meticulous orchestration averts conflicts, preserves a harmonious print order, and
optimizes resource utilization. In this setup, the shared printer serves as the resource,
and the processes act as users. The monitor encompasses two entry sections: one for
submitting print jobs and another for retrieving them. When a process intends to submit
a print job, it seizes the lock for the submission entry section, sends the print job, and
then releases the lock. Conversely, when a process aims to receive a print job, it
acquires the lock for the retrieval entry section, awaits an available print job, retrieves
it, and then releases the lock.

5.2.4 Semaphores: Safeguarding Shared Resources

In the realm of operating systems, semaphores play a pivotal role as synchronization
constructs that enable multiple processes to access shared resources securely. These
semaphores, akin to versatile variables, hold integer values that signify the availability of
resources.

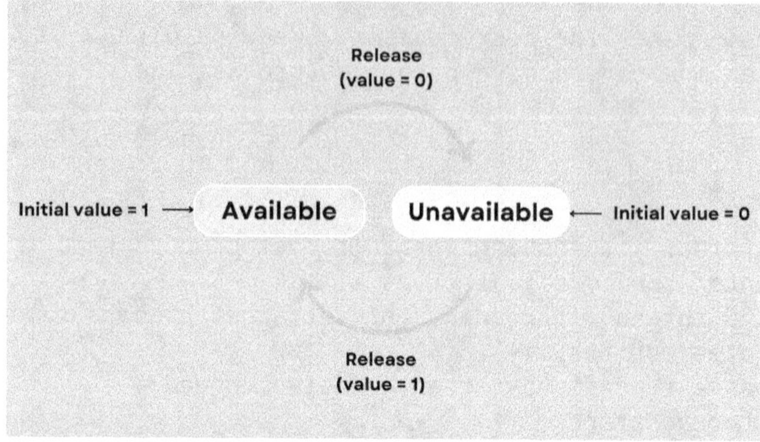

Figure 5.4: Semaphores: Counting locks for signaling and coordination between processes

Semaphores operate through two fundamental operations: **wait** and **signal**. The **wait** operation decreases the semaphore's value. If the value reaches zero, it suspends the process until the semaphore's value becomes non-zero. Conversely, the **signal** operation increments the semaphore's value.

Semaphores offer distinct advantages over other synchronization constructs, such as monitors and mutexes:

- **Simplicity:** Semaphores are straightforward to grasp and implement.
- **Portability:** They are versatile and adaptable to various operating systems and programming languages.
- **Efficiency:** Semaphores can be highly efficient, as they bypass the overhead associated with acquiring and releasing locks for every shared resource access.

However, semaphores do come with their limitations:

- **Expressiveness:** Semaphores may lack the expressiveness of monitors, rendering them less suitable for specific synchronization challenges.
- **Deadlock Risk:** Improper semaphore usage can lead to deadlocks, necessitating careful handling.

Let's illustrate the practical utility of semaphores with an example:

Imagine multiple processes contending for access to a shared database. A semaphore steps in to control concurrent access. When a process enters, it decrements the semaphore to signify database utilization. Upon exit, it increments the semaphore, granting access to others.

In this scenario, the database represents the shared resource, and processes act as users. The semaphore maintains a value of 1, symbolizing the available database connections. When a process intends to access the database, it invokes the wait operation on the semaphore. If the semaphore's value is 0, the process enters a blocked state. Upon completing database operations, the process executes the signal operation, enabling another process to access the database.

5.2.4.1 Semaphores in Python: Orchestrating Resource Access

Let's illustrate the practical utility of semaphores with a Python implementation:

```python
import threading

# Create a semaphore with an initial value of 1
semaphore = threading.Semaphore(1)

# Simulate a shared resource, initially available
shared_resource = "Initial data"

def access_shared_resource(thread_id):
    global shared_resource
    with semaphore:
        print(f"Thread {thread_id} is accessing the resource.")
        # Simulate resource access
        shared_resource += f" (modified by Thread {thread_id})"
        print(f"Resource data: {shared_resource}")
        print(f"Thread {thread_id} released the resource.")

# Create and start multiple threads
threads = []
for i in range(3):
    thread = threading.Thread(target=access_shared_resource,
args=(i,))
    threads.append(thread)
    thread.start()

# Wait for all threads to finish
for thread in threads:
    thread.join()
```

In this Python example, a semaphore ensures controlled access to a shared resource represented by `shared_resource`. Each thread attempts to access and modify the resource, but the semaphore manages concurrent access, preventing conflicts. The result demonstrates orderly resource utilization, with each thread safely modifying the data within the critical section.

These synchronization mechanisms equip programmers and system designers to impose order in the world of concurrent computing. Knowing when and how to employ them is pivotal for constructing resilient and dependable software in multi-process environments. Subsequent sections will delve deeper into these mechanisms and demonstrate their application to prevalent synchronization challenges.

5.3 SOLUTIONS TO SYNCHRONIZATION PROBLEMS

In the realm of concurrent computing, synchronization problems arise when multiple processes or threads must collaborate and coordinate their actions. These challenges often revolve around shared resources, demanding secure access to avoid conflicts and maintain program correctness. In this section, we'll explore classical synchronization problems, each presenting its unique set of hurdles.

5.3.1 The Producer-Consumer Problem: Balancing Data Flow

The producer-consumer problem, a classic challenge in operating systems, involves two roles: producers and consumers. Producers generate data items and deposit them into a shared buffer, while consumers retrieve and process these items. The goal is to maintain the buffer's integrity, preventing overflow and ensuring consumers don't access an empty buffer.

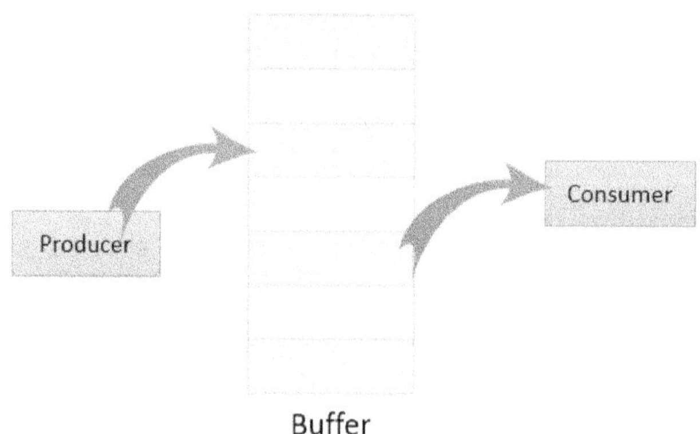

Figure 5.5: The Producer-Consumer Problem

One common solution employs semaphores as synchronization tools. Semaphores control access to shared resources, with the buffer acting as the shared entity in this context. The semaphore ensures that only one producer or consumer interacts with the buffer at any given moment.

Example: Taming the Producer-Consumer Challenge

Imagine a file download manager (producer) acquiring files from the web and storing them in a local directory (buffer). Concurrently, a video player (consumer) plays these downloaded videos. Effective synchronization mechanisms are paramount to avoid storage overflows and maintain seamless video playback.

Here's a Python implementation using a semaphore:

```python
from threading import Thread, Semaphore
import time
import random

# Size of the shared buffer
buffer_size = 10

# Create a buffer (list) to hold items
buffer = [0] * buffer_size

# Semaphore to control access to the buffer
semaphore = Semaphore(1)

# Producer thread
def producer():
    while True:
        # Acquire semaphore
        semaphore.acquire()

        # Produce random data and put in buffer
        data = random.randint(1, 100)
        print(f"Producer produced {data}")
        buffer.append(data)

        # Release semaphore
        semaphore.release()

        # Sleep to simulate production time
        time.sleep(0.5)

# Consumer thread
def consumer():
    while True:
        # Acquire semaphore
        semaphore.acquire()

        # Take data from buffer
```

```python
    data = buffer.pop(0)
    print(f"Consumer consumed {data}")

    # Release semaphore
    semaphore.release()

    # Sleep to simulate consumption time
    time.sleep(1)

# Start the producer and consumer threads
producer_thread = Thread(target=producer)
consumer_thread = Thread(target=consumer)

producer_thread.start()
consumer_thread.start()

# Wait for threads to complete
producer_thread.join()
consumer_thread.join()

print("Program completed.")
```

In this setup, the producer generates data and deposits it into the buffer, while the consumer retrieves and processes it. The semaphore ensures exclusive access to the buffer, avoiding conflicts and maintaining order.

5.3.2 The Dining Philosophers Problem

The Dining Philosophers problem epitomizes a classic deadlock scenario. In this setup, a group of philosophers gathers around a circular dining table, oscillating between contemplation and dining. To feast, philosophers require two forks, one on each side of their plate. The challenge is to devise synchronization mechanisms that circumvent the peril of deadlocks, where all philosophers endlessly yearn for forks.

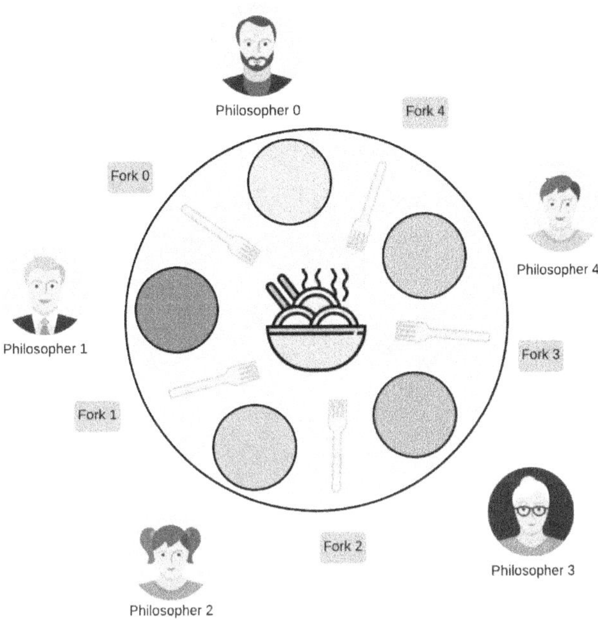

Figure 5.6: The Dining Philosophers Problem

A prevalent solution leverages dining philosophers with monitors. Monitors are synchronization constructs facilitating the secure access of shared resources by multiple processes. In this problem, the forks represent the shared resources, and a monitor ensures that only one philosopher accesses the forks at any given moment.

Example: Resolving the Dining Philosophers Problem

Envision five philosophers (processes) situated at a table with five forks. They can only indulge in their feast when they successfully secure both the left and right forks. Effective synchronization techniques are crucial to ensure philosophers dine without succumbing to deadlock predicaments.

Here's a Python implementation of the dining philosophers problem using monitors:

```python
from threading import Thread, Lock
import time


num_philosophers = 5
chopsticks = [Lock() for _ in range(num_philosophers)]

def philosopher(id):
```

```python
    while True:
        # Think
        time.sleep(0.5)

        # Pick up chopsticks
        print(f"Philosopher {id} grabbing chopsticks")
        chopsticks[id].acquire()
        chopsticks[(id + 1) % num_philosophers].acquire()

        # Eat
        print(f"Philosopher {id} eating")
        time.sleep(0.5)

        # Put down chopsticks
        print(f"Philosopher {id} putting down chopsticks")
        chopsticks[id].release()
        chopsticks[(id + 1) % num_philosophers].release()

threads = []
for i in range(num_philosophers):
    t = Thread(target=philosopher, args=(i,))
    threads.append(t)
    t.start()

for t in threads:
    t.join()

print("Done.")
```

In this implementation, the philosopher function takes the left fork, the right fork, and
the monitor as arguments. It begins by pondering for a while. Then, it secures both the
left and right forks, permitting it to dine. The monitor ensures that only one philosopher
interacts with the forks simultaneously, evading conflicts and deadlocks.

5.3.3 The Readers-Writers Problem

The Readers-Writers problem poses another classic synchronization puzzle, involving
multiple processes accessing a shared resource. Readers merely read the resource,
while writers both read and write to it. The challenge lies in crafting synchronization
that permits multiple readers simultaneous access while guaranteeing exclusive access
for writers to prevent data inconsistencies.

Example: Addressing the Readers-Writers Problem

Consider a database system with several clients. Many clients may read data from the database concurrently (readers), but only one client should modify the database (writer) at any given time. Effective synchronization mechanisms are essential to enable concurrent reading while upholding data integrity during writing.

5.3.4 Other Classical Synchronization Problems

Beyond the mentioned synchronization challenges, several other classical hurdles exist in concurrent computing. Each problem boasts unique attributes and solutions, serving as yardsticks to evaluate synchronization mechanisms and algorithms. Examples include the Sleeping Barber problem, the Cigarette Smokers problem, and the Bounded Buffer problem.

Solving these classical synchronization problems necessitates a profound comprehension of synchronization primitives such as semaphores, locks, and monitors, coupled with meticulous algorithmic design. This equips you with the knowledge to effectively address real-world concurrency dilemmas—a journey we'll embark upon in the forthcoming sections.

5.4 THE WORLD OF CPU SCHEDULING ALGORITHMS

Efficient CPU allocation stands as a pivotal pillar in the realm of operating systems, orchestrated by CPU scheduling algorithms that dictate multitasking environments. These algorithms wield substantial influence over system performance, equity, and the ability to cater to a spectrum of application requirements. In this section, we embark on a journey through diverse CPU scheduling algorithms, each meticulously crafted to tackle specific challenges and priorities.

5.4.1 Preemptive Scheduling: Empowering Fairness

Preemptive scheduling empowers the forceful interruption and preemption of a currently executing process, ushering in another contender. This approach not only ensures equitably distributed CPU allocation but also amplifies system responsiveness.

Example: Real-World Preemptive Scheduling

In the realm of multitasking operating systems, preemptive scheduling offers each application a just share of CPU time, preventing any single application from instigating system-wide sluggishness.

5.4.2 Non-Preemptive Scheduling: A Dance of Cooperation

Non-preemptive scheduling, often dubbed cooperative scheduling, grants the running process the liberty to voluntarily yield the CPU when it deems fit. Context switching relies on process cooperation, potentially optimizing efficiency while demanding responsible collaboration.

Example: The Harmony of Non-Preemptive Scheduling

In real-time systems and environments where processes closely coordinate their actions, non-preemptive scheduling shines. Processes release the CPU's grip only when pivotal tasks are accomplished.

5.4.3 SMT Multi-Core Scheduling: Leveraging Thread Power

SMT (Simultaneous Multithreading) technology introduces the capability for multiple threads to gracefully coexist on a single CPU core. SMT-aware scheduling algorithms harness this power to maximize CPU resource utilization, throughput, and energy efficiency.

Example: SMT's Impact in Modern CPUs

In the era of modern processors, equipped with SMT technology like Intel's Hyper-Threading or AMD's SMT, multitasking performance soars. SMT-aware scheduling ensures efficient thread resource sharing.

5.4.4 Real-Time Programming: Time as the Essence

Real-time programming necessitates scheduling algorithms that pledge predictability and punctuality in executing critical tasks. Failing to meet deadlines in real-time systems can bear grave consequences, making real-time scheduling the linchpin.

Example: Real-Time Scheduling in Autonomous Marvels

Autonomous vehicles, at the pinnacle of real-time systems, bank on real-time scheduling for swift sensor data processing, instantaneous decision-making, and precise vehicle control. Critical tasks like collision avoidance remain impervious to delays.

Comprehending these CPU scheduling algorithms lays the foundation for adeptly managing systems catering to a myriad of needs, spanning from general-purpose computing to the precise orchestration of real-time control systems. The choice of algorithm bears profound significance, shaping system performance, fairness, and the capacity to meet bespoke application demands.

5.5 SYNCHRONIZATION IN PYTHON: TAMING CONCURRENCY

In the realm of concurrent programming, synchronization is the linchpin, and Python arms developers with the tools to safeguard thread safety. In this section, we delve into Python's threading module, a robust toolkit for thread management, and explore synchronization mechanisms, including semaphores, monitors, and critical sections, all poised to tackle real-world conundrums.

5.5.1 Python's Threading Module: The Conductor of Threads

Python's threading module stands as the orchestral conductor of threads, offering a high-level interface that streamlines thread creation, management, and coordination. It gracefully abstracts away the complexities lurking beneath the surface.

Example: The Python Threading Module in Action

For a taste of its power, here's a fundamental example, showcasing the creation and simultaneous initiation of two threads:

```python
import threading

def task1():
    print("Task 1 is running")

def task2():
    print("Task 2 is running")

# Create threads
thread1 = threading.Thread(target=task1)
thread2 = threading.Thread(target=task2)

# Start threads
thread1.start()
thread2.start()
```

With Python's threading module, the intricacies of thread orchestration melt away, leaving developers to craft robust concurrent applications with ease.

5.5.2 Synchronization Tools in Python's Threading

In the world of Python threading, effective synchronization is paramount to manage shared resources and prevent conflicts when multiple threads run concurrently. Python's threading module offers a suite of synchronization tools to address these challenges. Here's an overview with examples:

Mutexes (Locks): Mutexes, or locks, are fundamental synchronization primitives that safeguard shared resources. Threads must acquire a mutex before accessing the resource, ensuring exclusive access. When the resource is no longer needed, the mutex is released.

```python
import threading

# Create a mutex
mutex = threading.Lock()

def protect_shared_resource():
    with mutex:
        # Access the shared resource safely
        pass
```

Semaphores: Semaphores control access to a limited number of resources. They are initialized with a count, and threads decrement this count when they acquire a resource. When a resource is released, the count increments.

```python
import threading

# Create a semaphore with 3 permits
semaphore = threading.Semaphore(3)

def access_shared_resource():
    semaphore.acquire()
    # Access the resource
    semaphore.release()
```

RLocks (Recursive Locks): RLocks allow a thread to acquire the same lock multiple times, useful for scenarios where a thread needs nested access to a resource without releasing the lock in between.

```python
import threading

# Create an RLock
rlock = threading.RLock()

def nested_access():
    with rlock:
        # First access
        with rlock:
```

```
        # Nested access
        pass
```

Condition Variables: Condition variables enable threads to wait for specific conditions to be met before proceeding. Threads acquire a lock and then wait on the condition variable. When the condition is met, another thread signals it to wake up.

```python
import threading

# Create a condition variable
condition = threading.Condition()

def wait_for_condition():
    with condition:
        while not some_condition:
            condition.wait()
        # Condition is met
```

Event Objects: Event objects are used to signal the occurrence of an event. Threads can wait for an event to be set and then proceed when it happens.

```python
import threading

# Create an event object
event = threading.Event()

def wait_for_event():
    event.wait()   # Wait for the event to be set
    # Event occurred
```

Choosing the right synchronization tool depends on your application's specific requirements. Mutexes for resource protection, semaphores for resource limiting, RLocks for nested access, condition variables for waiting on conditions, and event objects for signaling events provide a versatile toolbox for Python developers to manage threads effectively.

3.5.3 Example: Managing Print Jobs with Semaphores in a Print Shop

Scenario: Managing Access to a Limited Resource in a Print Shop

Imagine a busy print shop that offers printing services to customers. The print shop has a high-end color printer that can handle multiple print jobs simultaneously, but it has a limitation: it can only process three print jobs at a time due to its high cost and complexity.

In this scenario, semaphores can be used to manage access to the printer and ensure that only a limited number of print jobs are processed concurrently. Here's how it works:

1. **Semaphore Initialization**: Create a semaphore with an initial value of 3. This initial value represents the maximum number of print jobs the printer can handle simultaneously.

```python
import threading

# Create a semaphore with 3 permits
printer_semaphore = threading.Semaphore(3)
```

2. **Customer Threads**: Each customer who comes to the print shop is represented by a thread. When a customer wants to print a document, they must acquire a permit from the semaphore before using the printer. If all permits are currently in use (meaning three print jobs are already in progress), the customer thread will wait until a permit becomes available.

```python
def customer_thread(customer_id):
    print(f"Customer {customer_id} is waiting to print.")

    # Acquire a permit from the semaphore
    printer_semaphore.acquire()

    print(f"Customer {customer_id} is printing.")
    # Simulate the printing process
    print(f"Customer {customer_id} finished printing.")

    # Release the permit, allowing another customer to print
    printer_semaphore.release()
```

3. **Simulating Customer Arrivals**: Start multiple customer threads to simulate customers arriving at the print shop with print jobs.

```python
# Create and start customer threads
customer_threads = []
for i in range(10):  # Simulate 10 customers
    thread = threading.Thread(target=customer_thread,
args=(i,))
    customer_threads.append(thread)
```

```python
    thread.start()

# Wait for all customer threads to finish
for thread in customer_threads:
    thread.join()
```

In this real-world example, semaphores are used to control access to the limited resource (the printer). Only three print jobs can be processed concurrently, and additional customers have to wait until a permit becomes available. This ensures efficient resource utilization and prevents printer overload.

Semaphores play a crucial role in managing concurrency and resource allocation in various real-world scenarios, not just in print shops, but also in computer systems, manufacturing processes, and beyond.

6   DEADLOCK MANAGEMENT

Deadlock management stands as a pivotal pillar in operating system design and administration. Deadlocks, complex and potentially devastating scenarios in computing systems, demand our attention. This chapter delves deep into the realm of deadlocks, commencing with a comprehensive exploration of their nature and significance.

We embark on a journey to comprehend the components and dynamics underpinning deadlock situations, introducing the resource allocation graph as a foundational analytical tool.

Our odyssey continues with strategies for deadlock avoidance, prevention, and recovery, furnishing you with a toolbox for adeptly navigating these intricate scenarios. The chapter also unravels various deadlock detection algorithms and their practical applications.

Throughout this enlightening chapter, we harness the power of Python, a versatile programming language, to illuminate theoretical concepts through tangible examples. As we conclude, you will emerge as a proficient deadlock manager—an indispensable skill for systems engineers and developers alike.

6.1 UNDERSTANDING DEADLOCK: THE STANDSTILL SCENARIO

In the world of operating systems and concurrent programming, deadlocks resemble perplexing traffic jams. They occur when two or more processes find themselves in a state of inaction, each waiting for the other(s) to release a resource or trigger a specific action. This results in a standstill, akin to a gridlocked highway in the digital landscape.

6.1.1 Definition and Importance

A deadlock is precisely defined as a situation in which a set of processes becomes blocked, all eagerly anticipating a resource currently held by another process within the same group. To grasp the gravity of deadlocks, envision a real-world analogy: picture two cars, approaching a narrow bridge from opposing directions. Both drivers are courteous, refusing to yield, resulting in a traffic standstill with neither car able to cross. Similarly, in the computing domain, deadlock scenarios can bring an entire system to its knees, causing substantial disruptions, data loss, and even financial repercussions.

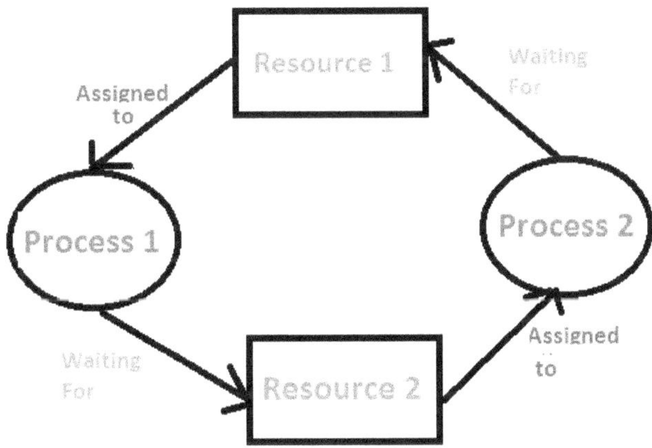

Figure 6.1: Deadlock: A state where two or more processes are waiting for each other to release resources

6.1.2 Characteristics of Deadlock

Deadlocks exhibit four distinct traits:

1. **Mutual Exclusion:** Processes in a deadlock vie for resources that cannot be concurrently shared. For instance, a printer can only serve one process at a time.

2. **Hold and Wait:** Processes involved in a deadlock clutch their allocated resources while yearning for additional ones. This perpetual waiting can trigger a domino effect, with processes patiently waiting for one another.

3. **No Preemption:** Resources are not forcibly taken from a process; they can only be voluntarily relinquished by the process currently holding them.

4. **Circular Wait:** A cyclic chain of processes exists, wherein each process awaits a resource held by the next in line. This cyclic interdependence is a hallmark of deadlock scenarios.

Understanding these characteristics provides a fundamental compass for recognizing and mitigating deadlock scenarios. In the following sections, we explore methods and techniques designed to effectively address deadlocks, preventing system-wide gridlock and ensuring the smooth operation of computing systems.

6.2 PARAMETERS FOR DEADLOCK HANDLING: UNRAVELING THE COMPONENTS

Effectively managing and addressing deadlocks in a computing environment requires a comprehensive understanding of the parameters that shape these intricate scenarios. These parameters encompass the critical elements contributing to both the emergence and resolution of deadlocks. In this section, we will dive into the vital parameters crucial for deadlock handling:

6.2.1 Resource Types

Resources serve as the foundational entities within deadlock situations. These resources span various types, encompassing printers, memory, CPU cycles, and more. Each resource type possesses distinct characteristics and requirements, necessitating differentiation when dealing with deadlocks. Resource types wield significant influence over resource allocation and contention, shaping the deadlock landscape.

6.2.2 Resource Instances

Resource instances denote the individual units or copies of a specific resource type. For instance, in the case of a printer resource type, resource instances correspond to the physical printers available within the system. Grasping the quantity and availability of resource instances proves pivotal for resource allocation and adept deadlock management. These instances are also interchangeably referred to as "resource units" or merely "instances."

6.2.3 Processes

Processes stand as the active entities within a computing system, actively soliciting and utilizing resources. In the context of deadlocks, processes represent the entities susceptible to entering a state of contention over resources. Each process articulates distinct resource prerequisites, which can evolve throughout its execution. Effectively orchestrating processes and their dynamic resource demands serves as a linchpin in proficient deadlock management.

These parameters constitute the foundational elements underpinning deadlock management. To navigate and mitigate deadlocks, meticulous scrutiny and control of resource allocation are essential, ensuring that processes maintain momentum without succumbing to deadlock paralysis. Subsequent sections will scrutinize methodologies and strategies for sidestepping, forestalling, detecting, and recuperating from deadlocks, all while considering the intricate interplay of these pivotal parameters.

6.3 INTRODUCING THE RESOURCE ALLOCATION GRAPH

In the realm of deadlock management, the resource allocation graph is a powerful tool used to **model** and **analyze** the allocation and utilization of resources in a computing system. It provides insights into the **current state** of resource allocation and helps identify potential deadlocks. This section introduces the resource allocation graph, its components, and its significance in understanding and mitigating deadlocks.

6.3.1 Nodes and Edges

The resource allocation graph consists of two primary components: **nodes** and **edges**. These elements represent the key entities involved in resource allocation.

- **Nodes:** Nodes in the resource allocation graph represent two types of entities: **processes** and **resource instances**. Each process and each resource instance is represented by a **unique node**. For processes, nodes are usually depicted as **rectangles**, while resource instances are shown as **circles or ellipses**.
- **Edges:** Edges in the graph represent the **allocation and request relationships** between processes and resource instances. There are two types of edges: **allocation edges** and **request edges**. An **allocation edge** from a process node to a resource instance node signifies that the process **currently holds** that resource. Conversely, a **request edge** from a process to a resource instance indicates that the process **is requesting** that resource.

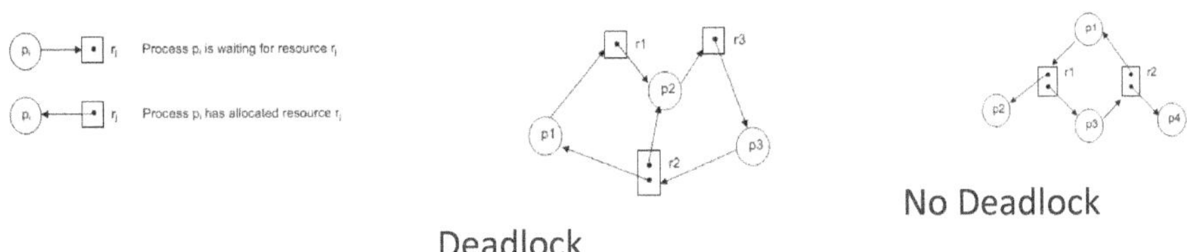

Figure 6.2: Resource allocation graph: Visualizing the allocation of resources to processes

6.3.2 Resource and Process States

Understanding the **states** of processes and resources is vital in the context of the resource allocation graph. The states can be categorized as follows:

- **Resource States:** Resource instances can be in one of two states: **allocated** or **available**. An allocated resource is **currently being used** by a process, while an available resource is **idle** and can be allocated to a requesting process.
- **Process States:** Processes can be in one of three states: **running, blocked**, or **requesting**. A running process is actively **executing**, a blocked process is **waiting** for a resource it has already requested, and a requesting process is actively **requesting** a resource it needs.

6.3.3 Graph Representation

The resource allocation graph provides a **graphical representation** of the resource allocation and request relationships in a system. It helps system administrators and developers **gain insights** into the current state of resource allocation and identify situations that could lead to deadlocks. The graph is **dynamic** and evolves as processes request and release resources.

In the subsequent sections, we will explore how the resource allocation graph is used in deadlock avoidance, prevention, detection, and recovery. It serves as a **fundamental tool** in managing and mitigating deadlocks in complex computing environments.

6.4 DEADLOCK HANDLING: AVOID, PREVENT, AND RECOVER

Deadlocks in computing systems pose challenges like resource contention and process stagnation. To combat this, three strategies are employed: deadlock avoidance, prevention, and recovery. Here's an overview of these techniques and their algorithms:

6.4.1 Deadlock Avoidance

Objective: Prevent deadlocks by analyzing resource allocation dynamically and ensuring it won't create circular waits.

Algorithm: **Banker's Algorithm** - It checks if granting a resource request would maintain a safe system state based on upfront declared maximum resource needs.

6.4.2 Deadlock Prevention

Objective: Proactively eliminate conditions conducive to deadlock (mutual exclusion, hold-and-wait, no preemption, circular wait).

Details:

- **Mutual Exclusion:** Allow multiple processes simultaneous resource access.
- **Hold-and-Wait:** Processes request and hold all needed resources before execution.
- **No Preemption:** Resources can be preempted from one process and allocated to another.
- **Circular Wait:** Processes can request resources with a lower priority, preventing circular waits.

6.4.3 Deadlock Recovery

Objective: Handle deadlocks after they've occurred.

Methods:

- **Process Termination:** Terminate one or more involved processes, freeing up resources.
- **Resource Preemption:** Preempt resources from processes to break the deadlock and allocate them to waiting processes.

Examples of operating systems that employ these methods include Windows, which uses a combination of deadlock avoidance and recovery techniques. Linux also utilizes similar strategies for deadlock management in its process scheduling and resource allocation algorithms.

The choice of technique depends on system requirements. Often, a combination of avoidance, prevention, and recovery methods is used for robust deadlock management. Understanding these techniques is essential for stable and efficient computing systems.

6.4.4 Safe State and Unsafe State in Deadlock Handling

In the realm of deadlock management, understanding the concepts of "Safe State" and "Unsafe State" is crucial. These terms are fundamental to deadlock avoidance and recovery strategies. Here's a concise explanation:

- **Safe State:** A system state where the processes can complete their execution without entering a deadlock. In a safe state, resources can be allocated to processes in such a way that they will eventually release them, ensuring progress. The Banker's Algorithm, mentioned earlier, is used to determine whether a system is in a safe state by analyzing resource allocation requests.

- **Unsafe State:** A system state where processes may enter a deadlock. In an unsafe state, resource allocation requests are such that, if all processes simultaneously request additional resources, it can lead to a deadlock.

Preventing the system from reaching an unsafe state is a key objective in deadlock avoidance.

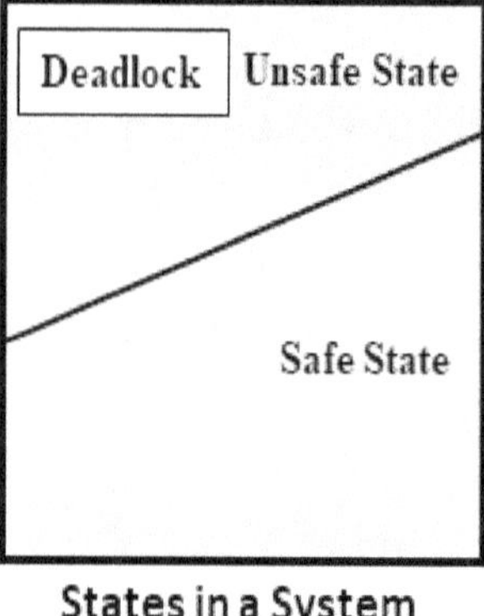

Figure 6.3: Deadlock handling: Safe states are free from deadlock, but unsafe states may lead to deadlock.

These concepts of safe and unsafe states are foundational for deadlock handling techniques. By carefully managing resource allocation and analyzing the system's state, operating systems can strive to keep the system in a safe state, minimizing the risk of deadlocks. When a system enters an unsafe state, recovery mechanisms, such as process termination or resource preemption, can be employed to bring it back to a safe state.

Examples of operating systems, such as Windows and Linux, utilize these concepts alongside deadlock avoidance, prevention, and recovery methods to ensure the stability and efficiency of computing systems. Understanding safe and unsafe states is essential for system administrators and developers when designing and maintaining deadlock-resistant systems.

6.5 DEADLOCK DETECTION ALGORITHMS: UNVEILING THE STRATEGIES

Deadlock detection is a pivotal aspect of deadlock management in computing systems. In this section, we explore various deadlock detection algorithms, tailored to diverse system configurations, providing crucial insights into their effective application.

6.5.1 Single Resource Instance: Deadlock Detection Simplified

Deadlock Detection Algorithm for Single Resource Instances

In systems where each resource type has only one instance, and tasks adhere to the single resource request model, the deadlock detection algorithm relies on graph theory.

The goal is to unearth cycles within the resource allocation graph, a telltale sign of the circular-wait condition and the presence of deadlocks.

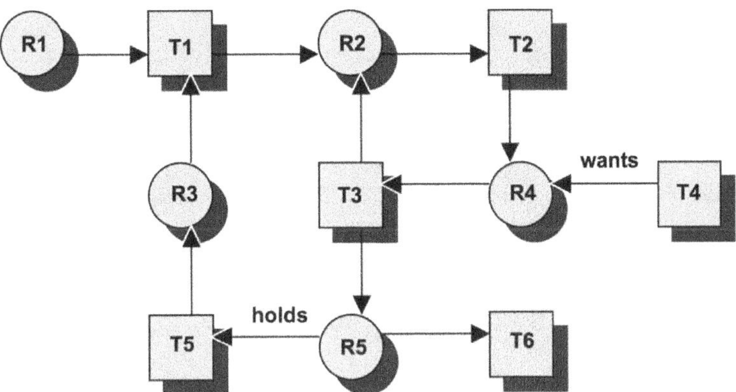

Figure 6.4 Resource allocation graph: Example

Figure 6.4 portrays the resource allocation graph, symbolized as follows:

- A circle represents a resource.
- A square represents a task or thread of execution.
- An arrow from a task to a resource signifies the task's desire for the resource.
- An arrow from a resource to a task signifies the resource's current allocation to the task.

Deadlock Detection Algorithm in Seven Steps:

1. Formulate a list of all nodes, denoted as N, from the graph.
2. Select a node from N. Create an initially empty list, L, to facilitate graph traversal.
3. Insert the node into L and check if it already exists there. If found, a cycle is present, signaling a deadlock. The algorithm concludes. If not, remove the node from N.
4. Verify if untraversed outgoing arcs exist from this node. If all arcs are traversed, proceed to step 6.
5. Choose an untraversed outgoing arc stemming from the node, mark it as traversed, and follow it to the new node. Return to step 3.
6. At this juncture, a path in the graph culminates, devoid of deadlocks. If multiple entries populate L, eliminate the last one. If more entries persist, designate the last entry as the current node and revisit step 4.
7. If list N isn't empty, revert to step 2. The algorithm ceases when N is exhausted,

affirming the absence of deadlocks in the system.

The algorithm's practical implementation, from step 3 to step 6, unfolds as a depth-first search of the directed graph.

When applied to the system depicted in *Figure 6.4*, the algorithm navigates as follows:

- Step 1: N = { R1, T1, R2, T2, R3, T3, R4, T4, T5, R5, T6 }
- Step 2: L = { <empty> }; node picked: R1
- Step 3: L = { R1 }; no cycles found; N = { T1, R2, T2, R3, T3, R4, T4, T5, R5, T6 }
- Step 4: R1 has one outgoing arc
- Step 5: Arc marked; reaches node T1; back to step 3
- Step 3: L = { R1, T1 }; N = { R2, T2, R3, T3, R4, T4, T5, R5, T6 }; no cycles found

The algorithm proceeds in this manner until it encounters a cycle at node T1, indicating a deadlock.

This meticulous approach captures the essence of deadlock detection in systems with single resource instances, ensuring efficient and reliable operation.

Here is a Python implementation of the deadlock detection algorithm for single resource instances:

```python
import networkx as nx

def deadlock_detection(resource_allocation_graph):
    """Detects deadlocks in a system with single resource instances.

    Args:
    resource_allocation_graph: A directed graph representing the
    resource allocation
    graph of the system.

    Returns:
    True if a deadlock is detected, False otherwise.
    """

    # Create a list to store the nodes in the resource allocation
    graph.
    nodes = list(resource_allocation_graph.nodes())
    # Initialize a list to store the nodes that have been visited
    during the
    # depth-first search.
    visited = []

    # Start the depth-first search from the first node in the list.
```

```python
stack = [nodes[0]]

while stack:
# Get the current node from the stack.
node = stack.pop()

# If the node has already been visited, then a cycle has been
found and a
# deadlock iş present.
if node in visited:
return True

# Mark the node as visited.
visited.append(node)

# Add all of the node's outgoing neighbors to the stack.
for neighbor in resource_allocation_graph.neighbors(node):
stack.append(neighbor)

# If the depth-first search completes without finding a cycle,
then there is
# no deadlock.
return False
```

This algorithm can be used to detect deadlocks in any system where each resource type has only one instance and tasks adhere to the single resource request model. To use the algorithm, simply pass in the resource allocation graph of the system to the `deadlock_detection()` function. The function will return `True` if a deadlock is detected and `False` otherwise.

Here is an example of how to use the deadlock detection algorithm:

```python
# Create a DiGraph object
resource_allocation_graph = nx.DiGraph()

# Add nodes
resource_allocation_graph.add_nodes_from(["R1", "R2", "R3", "R4",
"R5", "T1", "T2", "T3", "T4", "T5"])

# Add edges
resource_allocation_graph.add_edges_from([("R1", "T1"), ("T1",
"R2"), ("R2", "T3"), ("T3", "R4"), ("R4", "T4"), ("T4", "R3"),
("R3", "T5"), ("T5", "R5"), ("R5", "T2"), ("T2", "R1")])

# Now resource_allocation_graph is a proper networkx DiGraph
```

```
# Detect deadlocks
deadlock_detected = deadlock_detection(resource_allocation_graph)

# Print result
if deadlock_detected:
print("Deadlock detected!")
else:
print("No deadlock detected.")
```

Output:

```
Deadlock detected!
```

6.5.2 Multiple Resource Instances: A Graph-Based Approach

Deadlock Detection in Multi-Instance Resource Environments

In systems featuring multiple instances of each resource type, operating under the AND model of resource requests, a distinct deadlock detection algorithm comes into play. This algorithm operates within the framework of a resource allocation system, characterized by various resource types (R_1, R_2, R_3, ..., R_n), each with a fixed number of units. The core components of this system are the resource allocation table and the resource demand table.

Resource Allocation System Elements:

- **Total System Resources Table (N):** Captures the total number of units for each resource type (N_1, N_2, N_3, ..., N_k).

- **Available System Resources Table (A):** Reflects the remaining units for each resource type (A_1, A_2, A_3, ..., A_k) available for allocation.

- **Tasks Resources Assigned Table (C):** Records resource allocations to tasks, specifying units for each resource type.

- **Tasks Resources Demand Table (D):** Details additional resources needed by tasks to complete their execution.

In table C, for instance, C_{ij} signifies the units of resource R_j allocated to task T_i. Similarly, table D outlines the resource demands, with D_{ij} indicating the extra units of resource R_j required by task T_i for successful execution.

The Deadlock Detection Algorithm:

1. Identify a row (i) in table D where $D_{ij} < A_j$ holds for all $1 \leq j \leq k$. If no such row exists, a deadlock is confirmed, and the algorithm concludes.

2. Mark row i as complete and update $A_j = A_j + D_{ij}$ for all $1 \leq j \leq k$.

3. If an incomplete row remains, return to step 1. Otherwise, no deadlock exists, and the algorithm terminates.

Algorithm Insight:

Step 1 seeks a task whose resource demands can be satisfied. If such a task is found, it can proceed until completion. The resources freed from this task are returned to the pool (step 2), becoming available for other tasks, allowing them to continue and finish their execution.

The algorithm identifies a system deadlock when it ends, and table T contains incomplete rows, representing tasks in the deadlocked set.

Illustrative Example:

For clarity, consider an example with the following tables:

- N: [4, 6, 2]
- A: [1, 2, 0]
- C: [0, 2, 0]
    - Task 1: [1, 1, 0]
    - Task 2: [1, 1, 1]
    - Task 3: [1, 0, 1]
- D: [2, 2, 2]
    - Task 1: [1, 1, 0]
    - Task 2: [0, 1, 0]
    - Task 3: [1, 1, 1]

Following the algorithm's steps, it ultimately concludes that no deadlock exists in the system.

However, if task 3 required [0, 1, 1] instead of [0, 1, 0], a deadlock would emerge involving tasks 1, 3, and 4, underscoring the algorithm's ability to detect deadlocks.

Important Consideration: Executing a deadlock detection algorithm is not instantaneous and can have non-deterministic characteristics.

Here is a Python implementation of the deadlock detection algorithm for multiple resource instances:

```python
def deadlock_detection(total_system_resources,
available_system_resources, tasks_resources_assigned_table,
tasks_resources_demand_table):
    """Detects deadlocks in a system with multiple resource
```

```
instances.

  Args:
    total_system_resources: A list of the total number of units
for each resource
       type.
    available_system_resources: A list of the remaining units for
each resource
       type available for allocation.
    tasks_resources_assigned_table: A 2D list where each row
represents a task
       and each column represents a resource type. The value at
each row and column
       represents the number of units of the resource assigned to
the task.
    tasks_resources_demand_table: A 2D list where each row
represents a task
       and each column represents a resource type. The value at
each row and column
       represents the number of units of the resource demanded by
the task.

  Returns:
    True if a deadlock is detected, False otherwise.
  """

  # Create a list of the tasks that are still incomplete.
  incomplete_tasks = []
  for i in range(len(tasks_resources_demand_table)):
    if any(tasks_resources_demand_table[i][j] >
available_system_resources[j]
           for j in range(len(tasks_resources_demand_table[0]))):
      incomplete_tasks.append(i)

  # While there are still incomplete tasks, try to find a task
whose resource
  # demands can be satisfied.
  while incomplete_tasks:
    # Find a task whose resource demands can be satisfied.
    task_index = None
    for i in incomplete_tasks:
      if all(tasks_resources_demand_table[i][j] <=
available_system_resources[j]
             for j in
range(len(tasks_resources_demand_table[0]))):
        task_index = i
```

```python
      break

  # If no such task is found, then a deadlock exists.
  if task_index is None:
    return True

  # Mark the task as complete and update the available system
resources.
    incomplete_tasks.remove(task_index)
    for j in range(len(tasks_resources_demand_table[0])):
      available_system_resources[j] +=
tasks_resources_assigned_table[task_index][j]

  # If we reach this point, then there is no deadlock.
  return False
```

This algorithm can be used to detect deadlocks in any system where each resource type has multiple instances and tasks adhere to the AND model of resource requests. To use the algorithm, simply pass in the total system resources, available system resources, task resources assigned table, and task resources demand table to the `deadlock_detection()` function. The function will return `True` if a deadlock is detected and `False` otherwise.

Here is an example of how to use the deadlock detection algorithm:

```python
# Create the system resources tables.
total_system_resources = [4, 6, 2]
available_system_resources = [1, 2, 0]

# Create the task resources tables.
tasks_resources_assigned_table = [[0, 2, 0],
                                  [1, 1, 1],
                                  [1, 0, 1]]

tasks_resources_demand_table = [[2, 2, 2],
                                [0, 1, 0],
                                [1, 1, 1]]

# Detect deadlocks.
deadlock_detected = deadlock_detection(total_system_resources,
                                       available_system_resources,

tasks_resources_assigned_table,
                                       tasks_resources_demand_table)
```

```python
# Print the result.
if deadlock_detected:
  print("A deadlock has been detected.")
else:
  print("No deadlocks have been detected.")
```

Output:

```
A deadlock has been detected.
```

However, if we modify the task resources demand table such that task 3 requires [0, 1, 1] instead of [0, 1, 0], then the deadlock detection algorithm will return `True`.

6.5.3 BANKER'S ALGORITHM: A DEADLOCK AVOIDANCE STRATEGY

One of the most prominent deadlock avoidance algorithms in computing is the Banker's Algorithm. Named after its analogy to a bank managing customer resource requests, this algorithm operates on key principles:

- Advance declaration of maximum resource needs by each process.
- Incremental resource requests, with resources released before acquiring new ones.
- The operating system (OS) keeps track of available resources and process maximum demands.

By periodically examining a Resource Allocation Graph (RAG), this algorithm determines the presence of circular wait conditions. If a safe resource allocation sequence exists, processes proceed; otherwise, the system identifies deadlocked processes, necessitating corrective actions such as termination or resource preemption.

Understanding Banker's Algorithm

Banker's Algorithm operates under the assumption that there are n account holders (processes) in a bank (system) with a total sum of money (resources). The bank must ensure that it can grant loans (allocate resources) without risking bankruptcy (deadlock). The algorithm ensures that, even if all account holders attempt to withdraw their money (request resources) simultaneously, the bank can meet their needs without going bankrupt.

Characteristics of Banker's Algorithm

The key characteristics of Banker's Algorithm include:

- Processes requesting resources must wait if they cannot be immediately satisfied.
- The algorithm provides advanced features for maximizing resource allocation.
- Limited system resources are available.
- Processes that receive resources must return them within a defined period.
- Resources are managed to fulfill the needs of at least one client.

Data Structures in Banker's Algorithm

Banker's Algorithm employs several data structures for effective resource management:

1. **Available:** An array representing the number of available resources for each resource type. If `Available[j] = k`, it signifies that there are k available instances of resource type `Rj`.

2. **Max:** An `n x m` matrix indicating the maximum number of instances of each resource a process can request. If `Max[i][j] = k`, process `Pi` can request at most k instances of resource type `Rj`.

3. **Allocation:** An `n x m` matrix representing the number of resources of each type currently allocated to each process. If `Allocation[i][j] = k`, process `Pi` is currently allocated k instances of resource type `Rj`.

4. **Need:** A two-dimensional array (`n x m`) indicating the remaining resource needs of each process. If `Need[i][j] = k`, process `Pi` may need k more instances of resource type `Rj` to complete its task.

```
Need[i][j] = Max[i][j] - Allocation[i][j]
```

Banker's Algorithm Components

Banker's Algorithm comprises two essential components:

1. **Safety Algorithm:** Determines if the system is in a safe state. It iterates through processes to ensure their resource needs can be met.

2. **Resource Request Algorithm:** Determines whether a resource request can be safely granted to a process without causing a deadlock.

Disadvantages of Banker's Algorithm

Despite its effectiveness, Banker's Algorithm has some limitations:

- Processes cannot change their maximum resource needs during execution.
- All processes must declare their maximum resource requirements in advance.
- It only allows resource requests within a defined time frame (one year).

Understanding deadlock detection algorithms like Banker's Algorithm is crucial for system administrators and developers. These algorithms form the foundation of robust systems capable of effectively managing and troubleshooting deadlock scenarios in computing environments.

Example of Banker's Algorithm

An example demonstrates the functioning of Banker's Algorithm, showing how it allocates resources to processes and checks for a safe state. It ensures that the system can meet process resource demands without causing a deadlock.

Scenario:

Consider a computer system with three types of resources: A, B, and C. There are five processes (P0, P1, P2, P3, P4) in the system, each requesting resources at different times. The system needs to determine whether it can allocate resources to these processes without causing a deadlock.

Resource Information:

- Total available resources: A(10), B(5), C(7)
- Maximum resource need for each process:

```
       Max       Allocation      Need
P0    7 5 3      0 1 0          7 4 3
P1    3 2 2      2 0 0          1 2 2
P2    9 0 2      3 0 2          6 0 0
P3    2 2 2      2 1 1          0 1 1
P4    4 3 3      0 0 2          4 3 1
```

Step 1: Initial State

- Available resources: A(10), B(5), C(7)
- Work = Available
- Finish[i] = False for all processes

Step 2: Finding a Process to Execute

Start with process P0. Check if `Finish[P0] == False` and if `Need[P0] <= Work`:

- Finish[P0] == False (Process P0 is not finished).
- Need[P0] <= Work (7 4 3 <= 10 5 7)

Process P0 can proceed.

Step 3: Resource Allocation and Updating

Allocate resources to P0, and update Work and Finish:

- Work = Work + Allocation[P0] = (10 5 7) + (0 1 0) = (10 6 7)
- Finish[P0] = True

Step 4: Repeat Steps 2 and 3 for Other Processes

Continue the same process for the remaining processes:

- P1 can run as `Need[P1] <= Work`.
- Allocate resources to P1.
- P2 cannot run as `Need[P2] > Work`.

Step 5: Check for Safe State

Repeat the steps until all processes finish. If all processes finish, the system is in a safe state. In this case, the safe sequence is <P0, P1, P3, P4, P2>.

Here's a Python implementation of the Banker's Algorithm for deadlock avoidance:

```python
def bankers_algorithm(available, max_claim, allocation):
    num_processes = len(max_claim)
    num_resources = len(available)

    # Initialize data structures
    need = [[max_claim[i][j] - allocation[i][j] for j in
range(num_resources)] for i in range(num_processes)]
    finish = [False] * num_processes
    work = available.copy()

    safe_sequence = []

    # Main loop to find a safe sequence
    while True:
        # Find an unfinished process that can be satisfied with
the available resources
        found = False
        for i in range(num_processes):
            if not finish[i] and all(need[i][j] <= work[j] for j
in range(num_resources)):
                # Process can proceed
                work = [work[j] + allocation[i][j] for j in
range(num_resources)]
                finish[i] = True
                safe_sequence.append(i)
                found = True
```

```python
        # If no process can proceed, break the loop
        if not found:
            break

    # If all processes finish, a safe sequence exists
    if all(finish):
        return safe_sequence
    else:
        return None

# Example usage
if __name__ == "__main__":
    # Define available resources
    available_resources = [3, 3, 2]

    # Define maximum resource claims for each process
    max_claims = [
        [7, 5, 3],
        [3, 2, 2],
        [9, 0, 2],
        [2, 2, 2],
        [4, 3, 3]
    ]

    # Define allocated resources for each process
    allocated_resources = [
        [0, 1, 0],
        [2, 0, 0],
        [3, 0, 2],
        [2, 1, 1],
        [0, 0, 2]
    ]

    # Run the Banker's Algorithm
    safe_sequence = bankers_algorithm(available_resources,
max_claims, allocated_resources)

    if safe_sequence is not None:
        print("Safe Sequence:", safe_sequence)
    else:
        print("No safe sequence found. System is in an unsafe
state.")
```

In this implementation, you need to define the available resources, maximum resource claims for each process, and allocated resources for each process. The `bankers_algorithm` function will return a safe sequence if one exists or None if the system is in an unsafe state.

Please note that this is a simple demonstration of the Banker's Algorithm. In practice, you may need to adapt it to your specific use case and integrate it into your system's resource management.

6.6 HANDLING DEADLOCKS WITH PYTHON: LEVERAGING PYTHON'S VERSATILITY

This section explores Python's role in handling deadlocks, showcasing its libraries and tools for deadlock detection and resolution. We'll delve into Python's contribution to deadlock management, focusing on detection and resolution using Python.

6.6.1 Python's Role in Deadlock Management

Python, known for its versatility, extends its utility to deadlock management. While Python lacks built-in low-level operating system functions, it can interact with system-level libraries and tools to perform deadlock management tasks.

Python excels in high-level deadlock detection and resolution, thanks to its user-friendliness and extensive standard library. Let's examine Python's applications in deadlock management.

6.6.2 Detecting Deadlocks in Python

Detecting deadlocks in Python involves analyzing process and resource states to identify potential deadlocks. Python can gather relevant data, analyze it, and trigger alerts or corrective actions upon deadlock detection.

Here's a simplified Python example for deadlock detection:

```python
import threading

resource_locks = [threading.Lock() for _ in range(3)]

def process1():
    with resource_locks[0]:
        print("Process 1 acquired Resource 1")
        with resource_locks[1]:
            print("Process 1 acquired Resource 2")

def process2():
    with resource_locks[1]:
        print("Process 2 acquired Resource 2")
```

```
        with resource_locks[0]:
            print("Process 2 acquired Resource 1")

thread1 = threading.Thread(target=process1)
thread2 = threading.Thread(target=process2)

thread1.start()
thread2.start()

thread1.join()
thread2.join()

print("Both processes completed successfully")
```

In this example, we simulate a deadlock situation where two processes vie for
resources, resulting in a deadlock. Python's threading module represents processes as
threads and resources as locks. The code attempts to acquire two resources in reverse
order in two different threads, leading to a deadlock. Detection mechanisms can be
triggered if threads remain stuck.

6.6.3 Resolving Deadlocks in Python

Deadlock resolution in Python often involves techniques like process termination,
resource preemption, or waiting. Python enables the implementation of these strategies
based on system requirements.

Here's a simple deadlock resolution example using Python:

```
import threading

resource_locks = [threading.Lock() for _ in range(3)]

def process1():
    with resource_locks[0]:
        print("Process 1 acquired Resource 1")
        with resource_locks[1]:
            print("Process 1 acquired Resource 2")

def process2():
    while True:
        with resource_locks[1]:
            print("Process 2 acquired Resource 2")
            with resource_locks[0]:
                print("Process 2 acquired Resource 1")
```

```python
thread1 = threading.Thread(target=process1)
thread2 = threading.Thread(target=process2)

thread1.start()
thread2.start()

thread1.join()
thread2.join()

print("Both processes completed successfully")
```

This example introduces a basic deadlock resolution strategy. Process 2 continually attempts resource acquisition but releases them if a deadlock is detected, preventing prolonged deadlock persistence.

6.6.4 Deadlock Detection in Python: Unveiling Deadlock Detection

Detecting deadlocks entails scrutinizing the status of processes and resources to identify scenarios where processes wait indefinitely for resources that will never become available. Below is a Python example illustrating deadlock detection using a rudimentary resource allocation graph:

```python
import threading

# Simulated resource allocation graph
resource_locks = [threading.Lock() for _ in range(3)]

def process1():
    with resource_locks[0]:
        print("Process 1 acquired Resource 1")
        with resource_locks[1]:
            print("Process 1 acquired Resource 2")

def process2():
    while True:
        with resource_locks[1]:
            print("Process 2 acquired Resource 2")
            with resource_locks[0]:
                # Deadlock detected!
                break

# Create two threads representing two processes
thread1 = threading.Thread(target=process1)
thread2 = threading.Thread(target=process2)
```

```python
# Start the threads
thread1.start()
thread2.start()

# Wait for both threads to finish
thread1.join()
thread2.join()

print("Both processes completed successfully")
```

In this modified example, we introduce a deadlock detection mechanism. The `while True` loop in `process2()` ensures eventual deadlock detection. In a real-world scenario, continuous monitoring of thread and resource states is essential. If all threads are unresponsive, a deadlock detection mechanism can be triggered to rectify the situation.

6.6.5 Deadlock Recovery in Python: Navigating Deadlock Recovery

Deadlock recovery in Python typically involves designing your code to gracefully terminate threads when a deadlock is detected. This can be achieved by using shared variables or mechanisms to communicate between threads and request or signal them to exit in a controlled manner.

Here's an example of a straightforward deadlock resolution strategy employing resource preemption. In this example, we have two processes that acquire locks on resources, potentially leading to a deadlock:

```python
import threading
import time

# Simulated resource allocation graph
resource_locks = [threading.Lock() for _ in range(3)]

def process1():
    with resource_locks[0]:
        print("Process 1 acquired Resource 1")
        time.sleep(1)
        with resource_locks[1]:
            print("Process 1 acquired Resource 2")

def process2():
    with resource_locks[1]:
        print("Process 2 acquired Resource 2")
```

```python
        time.sleep(1)
        with resource_locks[0]:
            print("Process 2 acquired Resource 1")

# Create two threads representing two processes
thread1 = threading.Thread(target=process1)
thread2 = threading.Thread(target=process2)

# Start the threads
thread1.start()
thread2.start()

# Wait for both threads to finish
while True:
    if thread1.is_alive() and thread2.is_alive():
        # Deadlock detected!
        # Preempt one of the threads
        if thread1.is_alive():
            thread1.cancel()
        else:
            thread2.cancel()

        # Wait for the preempted thread to terminate
        thread1.join()
        thread2.join()
        break

print("Both processes completed successfully")
```

To implement the deadlock detection and resolution part, you will need to design a mechanism to detect the deadlock (e.g., by checking if both threads are alive) and preempt one of the threads gracefully, freeing the resources it holds. After preemption, the remaining thread can proceed without deadlock constraints.

The specific implementation of the deadlock detection and resolution mechanism would depend on your requirements and the details of your program. This code provides the foundation for handling deadlock situations, but you would need to customize it to your specific use case.

7   MEMORY MANAGEMENT

Efficient memory management is a cornerstone of robust operating systems. This chapter provides a comprehensive understanding of memory management, addressing key aspects:

1. **Significance:** Discover why memory management matters.

2. **Address Binding:** Explore the relationship between physical and logical addresses.

3. **Fragmentation Control:** Learn strategies to mitigate memory fragmentation.

4. **Paging:** Understand how paging enhances memory utilization.

5. **TLB:** Uncover the role of the Translation Lookaside Buffer in memory optimization.

6. **Advanced Techniques:** Delve into page sharing and its impact on memory efficiency.

7. **Python's Approach:** Examine how Python manages memory.

By chapter's end, you'll grasp the pivotal role of memory management in ensuring the seamless operation of operating systems and software.

7.1 INTRODUCTION TO MEMORY MANAGEMENT

Efficient memory utilization is a fundamental requirement in modern computing. Memory management encompasses the dynamic allocation and deallocation of memory to processes while addressing concerns like fragmentation. This chapter delves into the significance of memory management, elucidating its pivotal role in effective operating system memory allocation and management.

7.1.1 The Importance of Memory Management

Memory management is a critical component of efficient computing systems, serving several essential purposes:

- **Resource Utilization:** Memory management optimizes memory allocation, preventing wasteful use of resources and minimizing memory fragmentation.

- **Process Isolation:** It ensures that each process operates within its dedicated memory space, safeguarding data security by preventing unauthorized access or modification.

- **Concurrent Execution:** In a multitasking environment, memory management grants each process its own memory, preventing interference and conflicts among concurrent processes.

- **Fragmentation Mitigation:** Techniques like paging and segmentation effectively tackle fragmentation issues, enhancing memory organization and accessibility.

- **Optimized Performance:** Efficient memory management reduces memory access times, contributing significantly to system speed and overall performance.

- **Protection:** Memory management enforces memory protection mechanisms, shielding the operating system and processes from unauthorized manipulation.

- **Resource Allocation:** It establishes a structured approach to allocate resources like memory, based on the requirements, priorities, and constraints of processes.

In essence, memory management is the backbone of a smoothly functioning computer system. Without its proper implementation, systems face the risks of instability, crashes, and data corruption. Subsequent sections will delve into memory management intricacies, exploring concepts such as address binding, fragmentation, paging, and more, all integral to the robust operation of modern computing systems.

7.2 BINDING OF PHYSICAL AND LOGICAL ADDRESSES

In memory management, the binding of physical and logical addresses is a fundamental concept, pivotal to efficient memory handling. Here's why this binding is of utmost importance:

7.2.1 The Crucial Role of Address Binding

In the realm of computer architecture, the binding of logical addresses to physical addresses stands as a foundational concept. This process entails mapping the addresses generated by the CPU, known as logical addresses, to the precise physical locations in memory where the necessary data and instructions reside. The significance of this binding cannot be overstated, primarily because the CPU cannot directly access physical memory.

Figure 7.1: Physical vs. logical address: The MMU maps logical addresses to physical addresses.

Address binding takes on three primary forms:

1. **Compile-time binding:** This occurs during the compilation of a program and is the simplest form of binding. However, it offers limited flexibility.

2. **Load-time binding:** At this stage, the linker handles the binding during program loading. It provides greater flexibility compared to compile-time binding but is somewhat slower.

3. **Run-time binding:** Here, the operating system assumes responsibility for binding during program execution. This offers the highest degree of flexibility but comes at the cost of increased processing time.

The choice of address binding hinges on the specific requirements of the system. For instance, embedded systems often favor compile-time binding due to its speed and efficiency. General-purpose systems, on the other hand, typically opt for load-time or run-time binding to accommodate the need for flexibility.

Binding logical addresses to physical addresses bestows several invaluable benefits:

- **Versatile Memory Access:** It empowers the CPU to access data and instructions from any location within memory. Without this binding, the CPU would be limited to a small, contiguous memory region.

- **Shared Memory Resources:** Address binding allows multiple processes to coexist and share memory efficiently. In its absence, each process would necessitate its dedicated memory space, leading to resource inefficiency.

- **Efficient Memory Management:** The operating system harnesses the power of binding to allocate memory to processes, perform memory swaps between disk and RAM, and implement the concept of virtual memory.

These advantages underscore the critical role of binding logical addresses to physical addresses in computer systems. To shed further light, here are specific examples of how this binding is employed:

- **Process Loading:** When a process is loaded into memory, the operating system utilizes binding to map the logical address space of the process to a physical memory region. This enables the process to access its data and instructions from anywhere in memory, even if they are not contiguous.

- **Memory Swapping:** When a process needs data or instructions that are currently absent in memory, the operating system employs binding to swap these resources between disk and memory. This dynamic management enhances efficiency and facilitates memory sharing among multiple processes.

- **Virtual Memory:** This ingenious technique allows the operating system to provide more memory to processes than is physically available. It achieves this by dynamically binding logical addresses to physical addresses on demand, enabling seamless memory expansion and efficient resource allocation.

In essence, while the intricacies of binding logical addresses to physical addresses may be complex, its fundamental importance for the efficient operation of computer systems cannot be overstated.

7.2.2 How Logical Addresses Are Utilized

The Memory Management Unit (MMU), a core hardware component, plays a vital role in efficient memory management. Whether integrated into the CPU or as a standalone chip, the MMU is responsible for translating logical addresses into their corresponding physical counterparts.

At its heart, the MMU maintains a page table—a critical mapping tool that associates logical page numbers with their physical counterparts. Logical pages typically represent discrete memory blocks, usually 4KB in size, while physical pages mirror this size and reside in physical memory.

When the CPU needs to access memory, it sends a logical address to the MMU. The

MMU, with assistance from the relocation register, utilizes the page table to translate the logical address into the corresponding physical address. This resulting physical address is then sent to the memory controller, which handles the retrieval of data from memory.

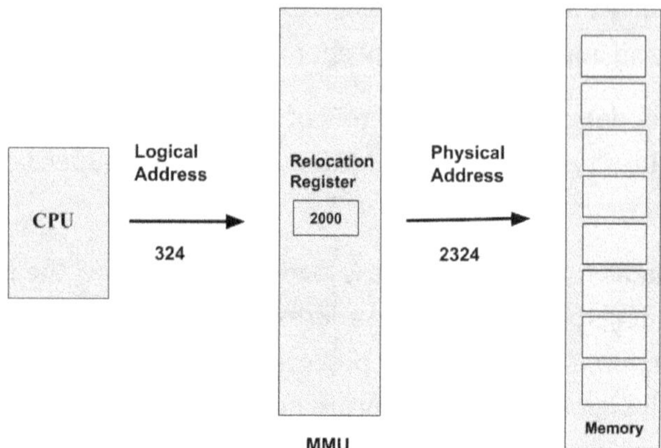

Figure 7.2: Relocation register: Logical address 324 mapped to physical address 2324

Beyond this essential translation function, the MMU, working alongside the relocation register, fulfills several other crucial roles:

- **Memory Protection:** The MMU enforces memory protection by imposing restrictions. It prevents processes from encroaching on each other's memory domains and maintains memory boundaries, ensuring that each process only accesses allocated memory segments.

- **Virtual Memory Implementation:** With the support of the relocation register, the MMU plays a central role in realizing virtual memory. This advanced technique empowers the operating system to offer processes more memory than is physically available. The MMU and the relocation register dynamically manage the binding of logical to physical addresses, enabling seamless memory expansion and efficient resource allocation.

- **Performance Enhancement:** The MMU, aided by the relocation register, boosts system performance by implementing caching mechanisms. Frequently accessed pages are intelligently cached in memory, reducing the need for repeated address translation operations and expediting data retrieval.

In summary, the MMU, often complemented by the relocation register, is an indispensable component within contemporary computer systems. It optimizes memory access, enforces security boundaries, facilitates virtual memory implementation, and efficiently manages memory resources, ensuring the seamless operation of modern computing environments.

7.3 FRAGMENTATION

Fragmentation is a major challenge in memory management, as it can degrade system performance and hinder the efficient use of memory resources. This section will explore the different types of fragmentation and the solutions used to mitigate their effects.

7.3.1 Types of Fragmentation

Fragmentation can manifest in two primary forms:

- **External Fragmentation**: This type of fragmentation occurs when free memory blocks are scattered throughout the memory space, making it challenging to allocate contiguous memory blocks to processes. Over time, as processes are loaded and removed, small gaps or fragments of unused memory accumulate, leading to external fragmentation.

- **Internal Fragmentation**: Internal fragmentation, on the other hand, occurs when allocated memory blocks are larger than what the process actually requires. In this case, a portion of the allocated memory remains unused, creating wasted space within the allocated block.

7.3.1.1 External Fragmentation

External fragmentation poses a significant challenge in memory allocation. As memory blocks are allocated and deallocated, free memory regions become scattered throughout the address space. When a process requires a contiguous block of memory, it may be challenging to find a single, contiguous block large enough to satisfy the request.

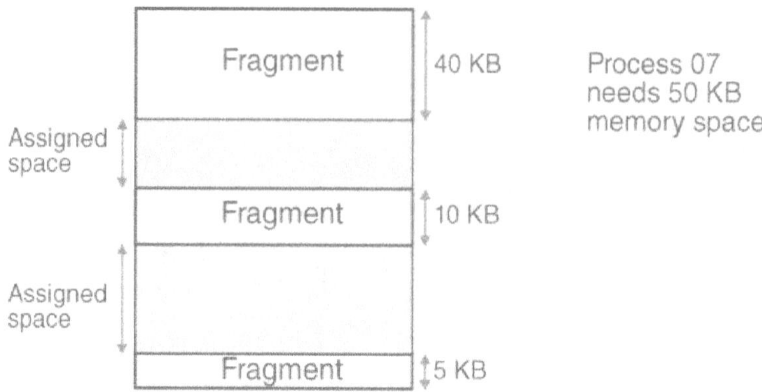

Figure 7.3

In the figure above, you can see how external fragmentation appears in the memory space. Various allocated and free memory blocks are interspersed, making it difficult to find a continuous region for a new process.

7.3.1.2 Internal Fragmentation

Internal fragmentation occurs when memory allocated to a process is larger than what the process needs. This results in inefficient use of memory since a portion of the allocated memory remains unused. Internal fragmentation is prevalent in memory allocation techniques like fixed partitioning, where processes are allocated fixed-size memory blocks.

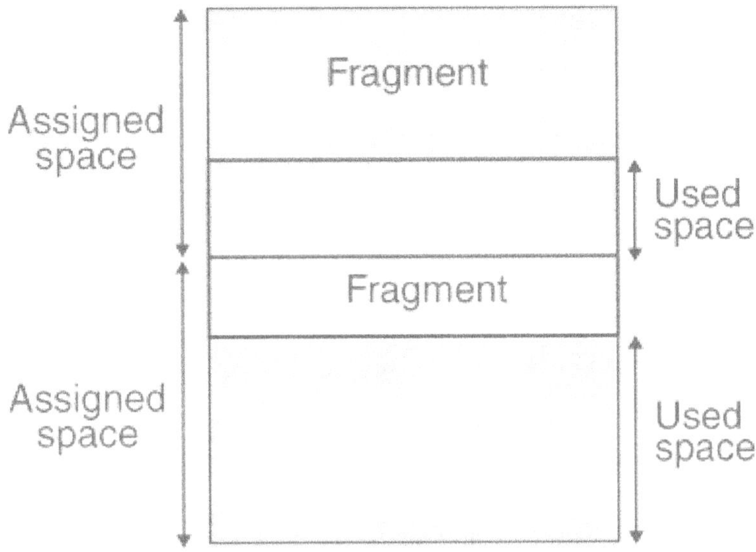

Figure 7.4: Internal fragmentation: Unused memory within an allocated block

In the figure above, internal fragmentation is demonstrated. The allocated memory block (in orange) is larger than what the process actually requires, leading to wasted memory space.

7.3.2 Fragmentation Solutions

Efficient memory management requires tackling fragmentation issues head-on. Several strategies are employed to mitigate fragmentation problems:

7.3.2.1 Compaction

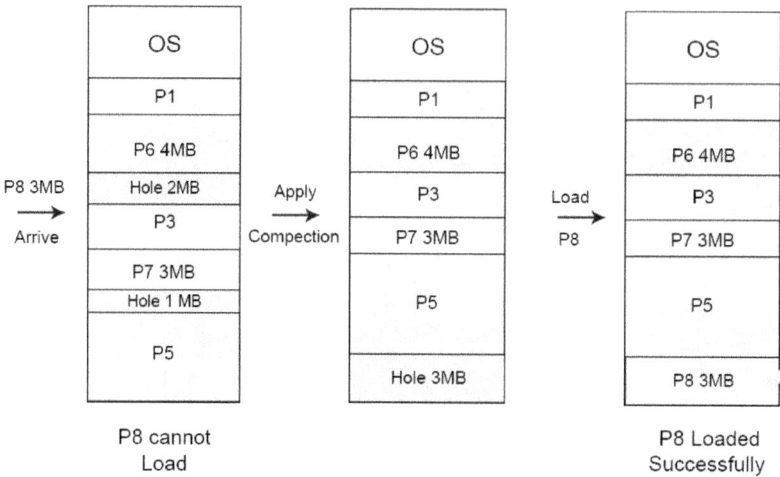

Figure 7.5: Compaction: Rearranging memory to eliminate fragmentation

Compaction, illustrated in Figure 7.3.4.1, involves rearranging memory contents to eliminate external fragmentation. It works by relocating allocated memory blocks to one end of the memory and consolidating free memory into a contiguous block at the other end. While effective, compaction can be resource-intensive and may require temporary process halting.

7.3.2.2 Segmentation

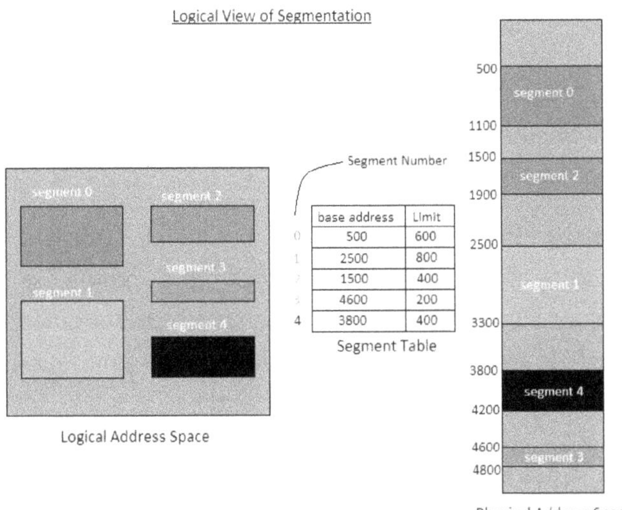

Figure 7.6: Segmentation: Dividing memory into logical segments

Figure 7.6 showcases segmentation, a technique that divides memory into logical segments of varying sizes. These segments can be allocated to processes as needed, reducing external fragmentation by allocating memory in variable-sized segments rather than fixed-sized blocks.

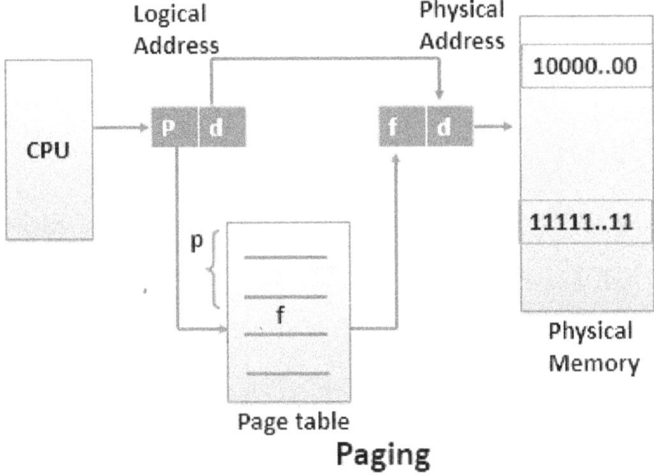

Figure 7.7: Paging: Memory management using fixed-size pages

7.3.2.3 Paging

Paging, as depicted in Figure 7.7, divides memory into fixed-size blocks called pages and allocates memory to processes in page-sized increments. This approach eliminates both external and internal fragmentation, simplifying memory management. Paging is widely adopted in modern operating systems.

Understanding and mitigating fragmentation are essential for efficient memory management. The choice of memory allocation technique and the use of compaction, segmentation, or paging strategies depend on the specific requirements and constraints of the system. In the following sections, we will delve deeper into the concepts of paging and its benefits in managing memory efficiently.

7.4 PAGING AND THE ROLE OF TLB

In this section, we'll delve into the concept of paging, a fundamental technique in memory management, and explore the vital role played by the Translation Lookaside Buffer (TLB) in optimizing memory access. Understanding paging and the TLB is essential for efficient memory allocation and retrieval within modern computer systems.

7.4.1 Paging Concept

Paging stands as a foundational memory management technique, strategically engineered to combat the persistent challenges of both external and internal fragmentation. It accomplishes this mission by partitioning both physical and logical memory into uniform-sized blocks known as "pages." However, to comprehend the complete picture of paging, it is essential to introduce the concept of "frames."

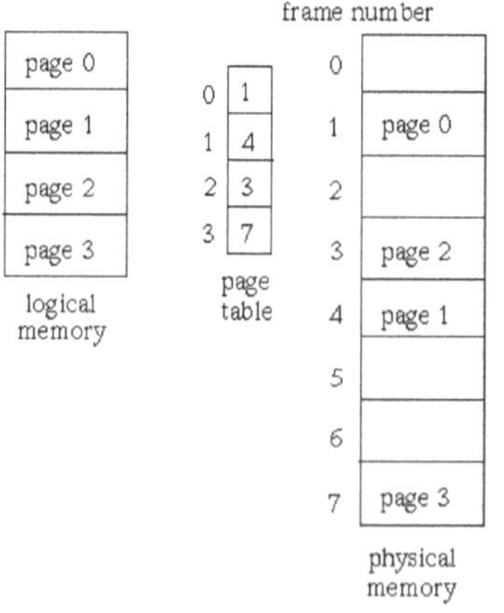

Figure 7.8: Paging Concept

As illustrated in Figure 7.8, both physical and logical memory undergo a transformation into discrete, uniform-sized pages. Each page is equipped with a unique identifier, simplifying the process of addressing. Yet, an integral aspect often mentioned in tandem with paging is the concept of "frames."

Frames: The Missing Piece

In the paging puzzle, frames serve as the counterpart to pages. While pages represent units of logical and physical memory, frames exclusively pertain to physical memory. The relationship between pages and frames is pivotal.

Advantages of Paging with Frames:

1. **Simplified Memory Management:** Paging, in conjunction with frames, streamlines memory allocation by dividing it into fixed-size units. This eliminates the need for intricate and resource-intensive variable-sized memory block management.

2. **Elimination of External Fragmentation:** By organizing memory into uniform-sized pages and frames, external fragmentation is effectively obliterated. This meticulous organization ensures there are no fragmented memory gaps between allocated blocks, resulting in efficient memory utilization.

3. **Reduction in Internal Fragmentation:** With the page and frame sizes aligned, internal fragmentation is significantly curtailed. Each process now receives entire pages, diminishing the presence of unused memory within a page to an inconsequential level when compared to the substantial reduction in overall fragmentation.

In essence, while pages serve as the units for logical and physical addressing, frames are the missing piece of the puzzle, exclusively dedicated to physical memory. Together, they form the foundation of efficient memory management in modern computer systems, assuring streamlined allocation and utilization of memory resources.

7.4.2 Translation Lookaside Buffer (TLB)

As modern computer systems grapple with the management of ever-expanding memory capacities, the efficiency of accessing data stored in pages has emerged as a paramount concern for achieving optimal performance. The Translation Lookaside Buffer (TLB), showcased in Figure 7.4.2, takes center stage as a mission-critical component, operating as a high-speed cache to significantly amplify memory access capabilities.

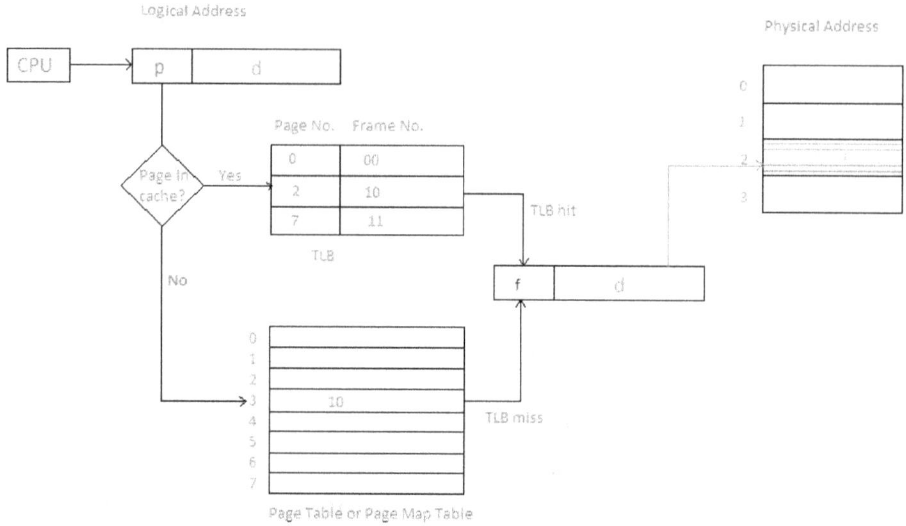

Figure 7.9: TLB: Cache of recently translated virtual addresses to physical addresses

The TLB assumes the role of a cache for page table entries, those invaluable records that establish the vital mappings between logical addresses and their real-world physical counterparts. When a process endeavors to access memory, the TLB springs into action, rapidly checking for the presence of the requisite page table entry. Once located, this entry acts as a shortcut to expedite memory access by promptly providing the essential address mapping.

TLB Hit and TLB Miss: Unveiling the Inner Workings

Let's delve into the inner workings of TLB operations to grasp the dynamics of effective memory access:

TLB Hit:

1. The CPU generates a virtual (logical) address.
2. The TLB is consulted to determine if the required page table entry is present (TLB hit).
3. Upon a successful hit, the corresponding frame number is retrieved, revealing the precise location of the main memory page.

TLB Miss:

1. The CPU generates a virtual (logical) address.
2. The TLB is examined, but the sought-after page table entry is not found (TLB

miss).

3. In this scenario, the page number becomes the key to accessing the page table residing in main memory (assuming that the page table encompasses all page table entries).
4. Once the page number is matched to the page table, the corresponding frame number is unveiled, divulging the main memory page's location.
5. Simultaneously, the TLB is updated with the new Page Table Entry (PTE). If there is no space available, one of the replacement techniques, such as FIFO, LRU, or MFU, comes into play to make room for the new entry.

Effective Memory Access Time (EMAT): Navigating Through Efficiency

The TLB plays a pivotal role in the quest to reduce memory access time. As a high-speed associative cache, it significantly contributes to enhancing system efficiency. The concept of Effective Memory Access Time (EMAT) encapsulates the benefits of TLB integration:

EMAT = h(c+m) + (1-h)(c+2m)

Where:

- **h** represents the hit ratio of the TLB.
- **m** signifies the memory access time.
- **c** denotes the TLB access time.

Let's illustrate the significance of EMAT with an example:

Example: Suppose we have a computer system where:

- **h (TLB hit ratio)** = 0.85, indicating that 85% of the time, the required page table entry is found in the TLB.
- **m (Memory access time)** = 10 nanoseconds, representing the time it takes to access data from main memory.
- **c (TLB access time)** = 1 nanosecond, showcasing the rapid TLB cache access time.

Now, let's calculate the Effective Memory Access Time (EMAT) using the formula:

EMAT = h(c+m) + (1-h)(c+2m)

EMAT = (0.85 * (1 + 10)) + (0.15 * (1 + 2 * 10))

EMAT = (0.85 * 11) + (0.15 * 21)

EMAT = 9.35 + 3.15

EMAT = 12.5 nanoseconds

In this example, the EMAT of 12.5 nanoseconds indicates that, on average, the system achieves a memory access time of 12.5 nanoseconds, considering both TLB hits and TLB misses. This calculation showcases how the TLB's high-speed cache can significantly optimize memory access, resulting in efficient and responsive system performance.

In essence, EMAT underscores the importance of TLB in memory management, portraying its role in minimizing memory access latency, reducing CPU overhead, and optimizing the utilization of virtual memory. The TLB, as a cornerstone of contemporary computer systems, ensures that data retrieval from memory unfolds swiftly, enhancing overall system performance.

7.5 PAGE SHARING TECHNIQUES

In modern computer systems, efficient memory management is not only about allocation and retrieval but also about resource optimization. Page sharing techniques play a pivotal role in achieving this optimization. These techniques enable multiple processes to share memory pages, reducing memory consumption and enhancing system efficiency. In this section, we delve into three essential page sharing techniques: Copy-on-Write (COW), Shared Memory, and Memory-Mapped Files.

7.5.1 Copy-on-Write (COW)

Copy-on-Write (COW) is a resource-efficient memory management technique that minimizes memory duplication when processes share data. It operates on the principle of deferred copying, meaning that data is duplicated only when a process attempts to modify it. Until that point, multiple processes can read the same memory page without incurring the overhead of duplicating the entire page.

Benefits of COW

COW offers several significant benefits, including:

- Reduced memory usage: COW can significantly reduce memory usage by eliminating the need to duplicate data that is shared by multiple processes. This is especially beneficial for systems that run multiple concurrent processes, such as web servers and database management systems.
- Improved performance: COW can improve performance by reducing the number of memory accesses required to read and write data. This is because COW only copies data when it is needed, and once it is copied, multiple processes can access it without incurring the overhead of additional memory accesses.

Challenges of Implementing COW

One of the challenges of implementing COW is page table overhead. The page table must be updated to track which pages are shared and which pages are private. This can require a significant amount of processing power, especially for systems with a large number of shared pages.

Another challenge is fragmentation. COW can lead to fragmentation if pages are frequently copied. This is because copied pages are typically allocated at the end of memory, which can lead to a situation where there are many small, scattered free pages throughout memory.

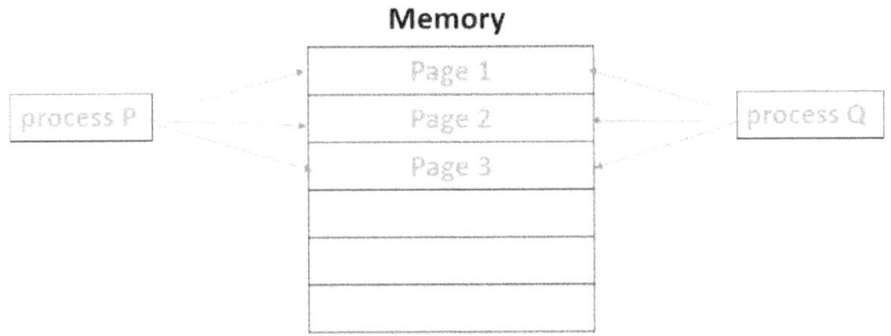

Before process P modifies Page 3

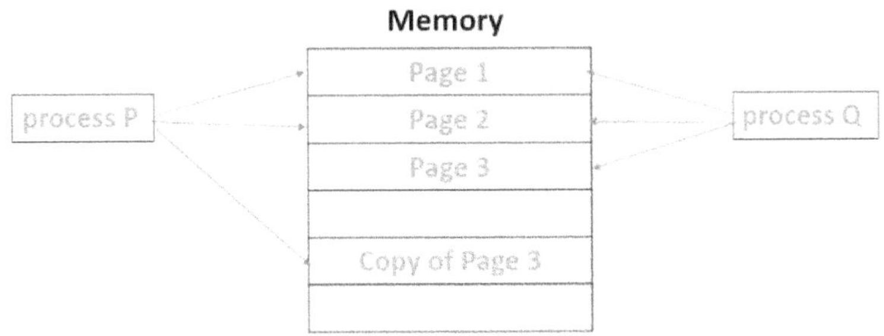

After process P modifies Page 3

Example

Consider the following example to illustrate the effectiveness of COW:

Suppose two processes, A and B, share access to a read-only file. In a conventional memory management system, both processes would receive separate copies of the file in their respective memory spaces, potentially consuming a significant amount of memory resources.

However, COW takes a smarter approach. Instead of duplicating the entire file, the memory manager assigns both processes pointers to the same memory page containing the file's data. As long as neither process intends to modify the file, they can efficiently share the same memory page without the need for additional memory allocation.

Now, let's say process A decides to modify the file. At this point, and only then, COW comes into play. When process A attempts to make changes, COW ensures that a duplicate page is created exclusively for process A. This new page contains the modified data, while process B continues to use the original shared page.

7.5.2 Shared Memory

Shared memory is a potent page sharing technique that enables multiple processes to access the same portion of memory concurrently, providing a fast and efficient means of inter-process communication. Unlike COW, where sharing occurs implicitly and is initiated by the memory manager, Shared Memory allows processes to explicitly request access to a common memory region.

Benefits of Shared Memory

Shared memory offers several significant benefits, including:

- **High performance**: Shared memory is a very efficient way to communicate between processes because it allows them to directly access the same data. This eliminates the overhead of copying data between process address spaces.
- **Scalability**: Shared memory can be used to scale applications to large numbers of processes because it does not require complex communication mechanisms.
- **Flexibility**: Shared memory can be used to implement a variety of inter-process communication patterns, such as producer-consumer, publisher-subscriber, and request-response.

Challenges of Implementing Shared Memory

One of the challenges of implementing shared memory is synchronization. When multiple processes access shared memory concurrently, it is important to ensure that they do not interfere with each other's data. This can be achieved using a variety of synchronization mechanisms, such as locks and semaphores.

Another challenge of shared memory is security. Shared memory can be vulnerable to attacks from malicious processes. It is important to implement appropriate security measures to protect shared memory from unauthorized access and modification.

Types of Shared Memory

There are two main types of shared memory:

- Global shared memory: Global shared memory is accessible to all processes on the system. It is typically used for system-wide data structures, such as the page table.
- Process-specific shared memory: Process-specific shared memory is only accessible to the processes that explicitly request access to it. It is typically used for data that is shared between a small number of related processes.

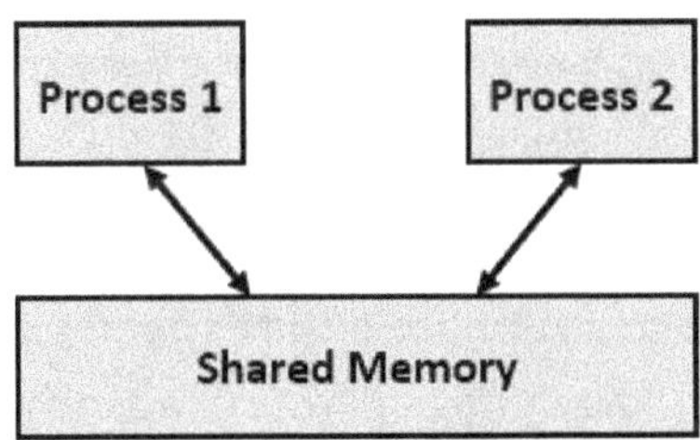

Figure 7.10: Shared Memory

Consider an example to illustrate Shared Memory:

Imagine two processes, P1 and P2, that need to collaborate on a data-intensive task. By creating a shared memory segment, both processes can access and manipulate the same data without the need for complex communication mechanisms. Changes made by one process are immediately visible to the other, making data synchronization seamless and efficient.

7.5.3 Memory-Mapped Files

Memory-Mapped Files (MMFs) provide a unique and flexible approach to page sharing by mapping a file directly into memory, blurring the distinction between file I/O and memory operations. This technique treats files as if they were portions of the process's address space, enabling straightforward and efficient file operations without the need for explicit read or write operations.

Benefits of Memory-Mapped Files

MMFs offer several significant benefits, including:

- Improved performance: MMFs can significantly improve performance by eliminating the overhead of copying data between file and memory.

- Efficient memory usage: MMFs can reduce memory usage by avoiding the need to create multiple copies of the same data.
- Simplified file I/O: MMFs simplify file I/O by allowing processes to access file data as if it were in memory.
- Concurrent access: MMFs can be used to share data between processes concurrently, allowing them to access and manipulate the same data without the need for complex synchronization mechanisms.

Challenges of Using Memory-Mapped Files

One of the challenges of using MMFs is synchronization. When multiple processes access the same MMF concurrently, it is important to ensure that they do not interfere with each other's data. This can be achieved using a variety of synchronization mechanisms, such as locks and semaphores.

Another challenge of using MMFs is data consistency. When MMFs are used to share data between processes, it is important to ensure that the data is consistent between all processes. This can be achieved by using appropriate synchronization mechanisms and by carefully managing the lifetime of MMFs.

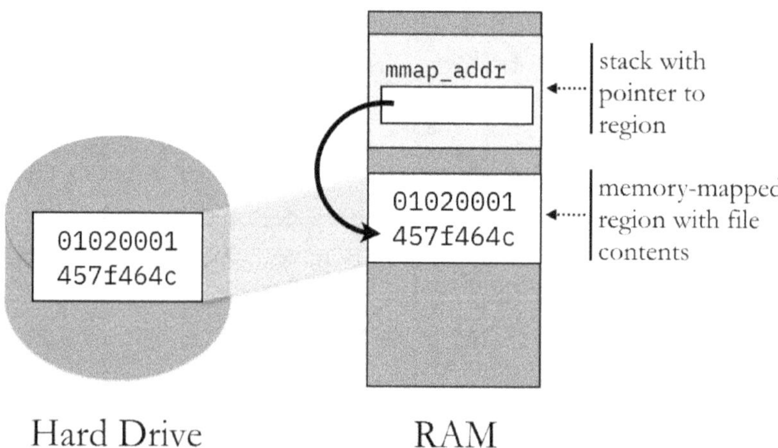

Figure 7.11: Memory-Mapped Files

Different Ways to Use Memory-Mapped Files

MMFs can be used in a variety of ways, including:

- File caching: MMFs can be used to cache frequently accessed files in memory, improving performance by reducing the number of disk accesses.
- Data sharing between processes: MMFs can be used to share data between processes concurrently, allowing them to access and manipulate the same data

without the need for complex communication mechanisms.
- Database mapping: MMFs can be used to map database files into memory, improving performance by allowing database systems to directly access the data in memory.

Consider an example to illustrate Memory-Mapped Files:

Suppose you have a large dataset stored in a file. Instead of reading the file in small chunks and processing it, you can map the entire file into memory. This allows you to access and manipulate the data as if it were in memory, which can significantly improve performance. Multiple processes can map the same file, and any changes made by one process are immediately reflected in the memory-mapped view accessible to other processes.

Memory-Mapped Files are advantageous for scenarios involving large files or when multiple processes require access to the same data concurrently. They offer a seamless and efficient means of sharing data among processes while also simplifying file I/O operations. However, developers must exercise caution when using Memory-Mapped Files to ensure data consistency and avoid potential conflicts between processes accessing the mapped file.

7.6 PYTHON FOR MEMORY MANAGEMENT

In this digital age, understanding memory management is crucial not just for system programmers but also for software developers who work with high-level languages like Python. While Python abstracts many low-level memory operations, having a grasp of memory management concepts can help developers write more efficient and optimized code. In this section, we will explore how Python, a versatile and widely-used programming language, handles memory management, and dive into implementing page sharing techniques using Python.

7.6.1 Implementing Page Sharing Techniques in Python

Python provides powerful tools and libraries for managing memory and implementing page sharing techniques. Let's explore how you can use Python to implement the three fundamental page sharing techniques we discussed earlier: Copy-on-Write (COW), Shared Memory, and Memory-Mapped Files.

1. Copy-on-Write (COW) in Python

Python's memory management simplifies the implementation of COW. You can create a shared read-only object and efficiently manage copy-on-write scenarios using Python's built-in data structures. Here's a Python example illustrating COW:

```python
# Create a shared read-only list
shared_data = [1, 2, 3, 4, 5]

# Create two processes
import multiprocessing

def process1(data):
    # Process 1 reads data
    print("Process 1 reads data:", data)

def process2(data):
    # Process 2 also reads data
    print("Process 2 reads data:", data)

if __name__ == "__main__":
    # Create a multiprocessing pool
    pool = multiprocessing.Pool(processes=2)

    # Both processes read the same data
    pool.apply(process1, (shared_data,))
    pool.apply(process2, (shared_data,))
```

2. Shared Memory in Python

Python provides robust mechanisms for inter-process communication and shared memory. You can use libraries like multiprocessing and ctypes to create shared memory regions. Here's a Python example illustrating Shared Memory:

```python
import multiprocessing

# Create a manager
manager = multiprocessing.Manager()

# Create a shared array in the manager
shared_array = manager.Array('i', [0, 0, 0, 0, 0])

def process1(data):
    # Modify shared memory
    data[0] = 1
    print("Process 1 writes to shared memory")

def process2(data):
    # Access shared memory
    print("Process 2 reads from shared memory:", data[0])
```

```python
if __name__ == "__main__":
    # Create a multiprocessing pool
    pool = multiprocessing.Pool(processes=2)

    # Execute both processes
    pool.apply(process1, (shared_array,))
    pool.apply(process2, (shared_array,))

    # Close the pool
    pool.close()
    pool.join()
```

3. Memory-Mapped Files in Python

Python offers the mmap module to work with memory-mapped files efficiently. You can map files into memory, enabling easy and efficient data manipulation. Here's a Python example illustrating Memory-Mapped Files:

```python
import mmap

# Create a memory-mapped file
with open("sample.txt", "r+b") as file:
    mmapped_data = mmap.mmap(file.fileno(), 0)

    # Access and manipulate the data in the memory-mapped file
    mmapped_data[0] = b'H'

    # Ensure changes are reflected in the file
    mmapped_data.flush()
    mmapped_data.close()
```

These Python examples provide a glimpse into how you can implement page sharing techniques in Python, making memory management accessible and efficient within a high-level language. Understanding these techniques can greatly benefit developers in optimizing their applications and achieving better memory efficiency.

8 VIRTUAL MEMORY MANAGEMENT

Virtual memory is a pivotal concept in modern computer systems that allows them to efficiently manage memory resources. It creates an abstraction layer between the physical memory hardware and the logical memory accessed by applications, enabling powerful capabilities:

Demand Paging - Only necessary pages of a program are loaded into physical RAM, the rest remain on disk until accessed. This optimizes memory usage and allows large programs to run.

Page Fault Handling - When a non-resident page is accessed, a page fault occurs. The OS fetches the required page from disk into memory. Effective page fault handling is critical for performance.

Copy-on-Write - Shared pages are not copied until modification is needed. This saves memory and simplifies forking new processes.

Belady's Anomaly - Contrary to intuition, increasing physical memory can sometimes increase page faults due to quirks in page replacement algorithms.

Frame Allocation - Strategies like equal allocation, priority-based, etc. allow the OS to efficiently distribute available memory frames among processes.

Memory Mapping - Files can be mapped into a process's address space for simplified access. Changes are reflected in both memory and the file system.

Overall, virtual memory is an elegant technique that transformed computing by bridging the gap between physical memory limitations and program memory requirements. Mastering virtual memory management enables optimizing modern systems for efficiency, responsiveness and multitasking capabilities.

Key aspects covered in this chapter:

- Introduced virtual memory and demand paging
- Discussed page fault handling and terminology
- Explained copy-on-write page replacement
- Explored Belady's anomaly
- Covered memory frame allocation strategies
- Discussed I/O optimization via memory mapping
- Provided Python examples to simulate virtual memory

In summary, this chapter provides a comprehensive overview of core virtual memory concepts using clear explanations, real-world examples, and actionable code samples. It develops strong foundational knowledge for operating system designers, developers, and professionals.

8.1 INTRODUCING VIRTUAL MEMORY

Virtual memory is a transformative concept that empowers computers to efficiently handle memory resources, effectively blurring the line between physical and logical memory. First proposed in the late 1950s and implemented in the early 1960s, virtual memory has evolved over time to become an essential part of all modern operating systems. Early virtual memory systems were simple and inefficient, but researchers and engineers have developed increasingly sophisticated and efficient virtual memory techniques, such as demand paging and page replacement algorithms.

Virtual memory allows computers to run programs that are much larger than the amount of physical memory available, enabling the development of more complex and powerful software applications.

8.1.1 Demand Paging and Its Advantages

Demand Paging Essentials:

Demand paging stands as a vital virtual memory technique, enabling computers to manage memory resources efficiently, transcending the limitations of physical memory. This technique revolves around loading only the necessary pages of a program into physical memory when required, meticulously tracked by a page table. When a process accesses a page not currently residing in memory, it triggers a page fault, subsequently resolved by the operating system by fetching the needed page from disk into memory.

The Benefits of Demand Paging:

Demand paging offers several advantages:

1. **Efficient Memory Utilization:** Demand paging optimizes memory usage by

loading only actively used program pages into memory. Inactive or seldom used pages remain on disk until called upon, preventing unnecessary memory consumption.

2. **Effective Multitasking:** Demand paging facilitates efficient multitasking, even in scenarios with limited physical memory. Each running process believes it possesses exclusive access to the entire memory space.

3. **Improved Responsiveness:** This technique enhances system responsiveness by minimizing program loading times. It retrieves only the essential components, reducing startup delays, and ensuring swift program launches.

4. **Resource Conservation:** By treating disk storage as an extension of physical memory, demand paging conserves valuable physical memory resources. This conservation allows the system to accommodate larger and more resource-intensive programs.

5. **Simplified Program Development:** Programmers can develop software without being hindered by physical memory constraints. The illusion of abundant memory streamlines the development process.

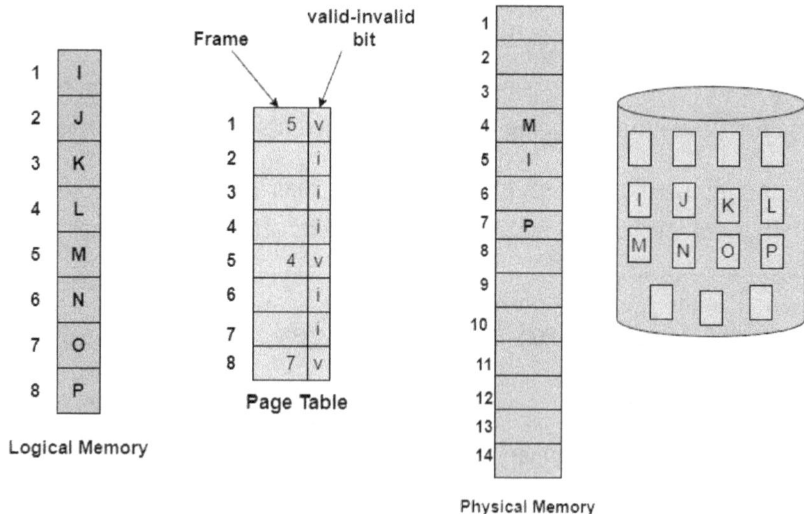

Figure 8.1: A visual representation of Demand Paging in action, optimizing memory usage.

Real-World Illustration:

Imagine a user running multiple applications simultaneously, including a web browser, word processor, and video player. Without demand paging, these applications would vie for limited physical memory, potentially leading to sluggish performance or system crashes. Demand paging empowers the operating system to allocate memory efficiently, ensuring each application receives the necessary resources precisely when needed, resulting in a smoother and more responsive computing experience.

8.1.1.1 Demand Paging and Its Implementation Details:

In addition to the high-level understanding of demand paging, it's crucial to delve into the intricacies of its implementation, which often involves specialized hardware and multi-level page tables. This subsection, "Demand Paging Implementation Details," will shed light on the inner workings of demand paging and the supporting components in modern computer systems.

Translation Lookaside Buffer (TLB) Cache:

As discussed in Chapter 7, modern processors are equipped with a Translation Lookaside Buffer (TLB) cache. This cache is designed to expedite the translation of virtual addresses to physical addresses by storing recent translations. The TLB is essentially a high-speed, associative memory that holds a subset of the page table entries, allowing for quick retrieval of virtual-to-physical mappings.

Multi-Level Page Tables:

Page tables in demand paging systems are typically organized in a multi-level hierarchy to efficiently manage the translation of virtual addresses to physical addresses. This hierarchical structure comprises different levels, each responsible for mapping specific address regions:

- **L1 Page Table:** This top-level page table handles entries for large virtual address regions. It provides a broad mapping of virtual addresses to intermediate-level page tables or directly to physical addresses.

- **L2 Page Tables:** Located below the L1 page table, these tables further refine the mapping by breaking down virtual address regions into smaller segments. Each entry in an L2 page table typically points to an L3 page table or directly to physical memory.

- **L3 Page Tables:** At the lowest level, L3 page tables focus on individual pages. They offer fine-grained control over page mappings. Each entry in an L3 page table corresponds to a specific page frame in physical memory.

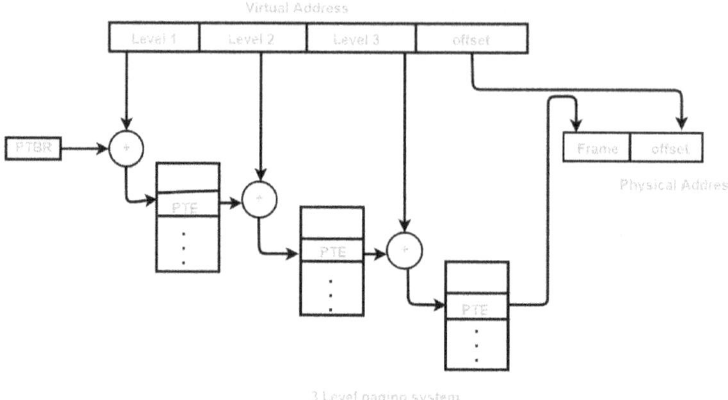

Figure 8.2: 3-Level Paging System

In the figure 8.2, PTBR stands for Page Table Base Register and PTE stands for Page Table Entry.

- **PTBR:** The PTBR is a register that stores the physical address of the L1 page table. The CPU uses the PTBR to start walking the page table when it needs to translate a virtual address to a physical address.
- **PTE:** A PTE is an entry in a page table. Each PTE contains information about a single virtual address region, such as the physical address of the page, the access permissions for the page, and whether the page is present in memory.

When the CPU needs to translate a virtual address to a physical address, it first checks the TLB. If the virtual address is not found in the TLB, the CPU walks the page table to find the PTE for the virtual address. The CPU uses the information in the PTE to access the memory location.

Here is an example of how the PTBR and PTE are used to translate a virtual address to a physical address:

1. The CPU starts by checking the TLB. If the virtual address is not found in the TLB, a TLB miss occurs and the CPU must walk the page table.
2. The CPU uses the PTBR to find the L1 page table.
3. The CPU walks the L1 page table to find the PTE for the virtual address.
4. The CPU uses the information in the PTE to access the memory location.

If the PTE for the virtual address is not found in the L1 page table, a page fault occurs and the operating system must load the PTE into memory. The operating system then updates the L1 page table with the new PTE and the CPU can retry the translation.

Multi-level page tables use the same basic principles, but the PTBR and PTEs are more complex. For example, the PTBR for a multi-level page table might point to an L2 page table instead of an L1 page table. The L2 page table would then contain pointers to L3 page tables, which in turn would contain the PTEs for individual pages.

The use of multi-level page tables allows the operating system to efficiently manage a large virtual address space while using only a small amount of physical memory.

Translation Process on TLB Miss:

When a TLB miss occurs, signifying that the desired virtual-to-physical translation is not present in the TLB cache, the processor initiates a translation process by walking through the multi-level page tables. Here's an overview of how this process unfolds:

1. **Starting at L1:** The processor begins the translation process by consulting the L1 page table, which provides a high-level mapping of virtual addresses.

2. **Progressing to Lower Levels:** If the L1 page table points to an intermediate page table (e.g., an L2 page table), the processor follows the pointer and proceeds to the next level. This process continues until it reaches the L3 page table or directly maps to a physical address.

3. **Caching Translations:** During this translation walk, the processor caches the encountered translations in the TLB. These cached translations expedite future lookups for the same virtual addresses.

Architecture-Dependent Variations:

It's important to note that the specific formats and structures of page tables can vary significantly across computer architectures. Different architectures may employ variations in the number of levels in their page tables, the sizes of page tables, and the format of page table entries. These details are highly architecture-dependent and are optimized for the particular characteristics and requirements of the hardware.

In summary, the demand paging mechanism leverages specialized hardware components like TLB caches and multi-level page tables to efficiently translate virtual addresses to physical addresses. These implementation details are critical for understanding how modern computer systems manage memory effectively and handle the demand for dynamic memory allocation.

8.1.1.2 Pure Demand Paging:

With pure demand paging, no pages are preemptively loaded into memory at program startup. Pages are only brought into physical memory on an on-demand basis when a page fault occurs. This approach maximizes memory utilization efficiency, since no unused pages occupy RAM. However, it can increase page fault frequency and the associated overhead, since every single page access initially triggers a page fault. This repeated paging activity can degrade program performance.

There is a tradeoff between minimal memory usage and performance - pure demand paging optimizes for the lowest memory footprint but suffers on throughput with the high page fault rate. In practice, a hybrid approach is commonly used, where a small subset of key pages are preloaded at process startup to amortize some of the page fault overhead. The rest are demand paged during execution. This balances memory efficiency with performance.

How Demand Paging Operates:

Demand Paging Mechanism:

1. The CPU generates a logical address to access memory.
2. The OS walks the multi-level page table to translate the logical address into a physical frame number and offset.
3. The page table entry contains a valid bit indicating if the page is resident in physical memory.
4. If valid bit is 1, the page is present in a memory frame. The CPU uses the frame number to directly access the contents.
5. If valid bit is 0, a page fault exception is triggered. This signals that the page needs to be demand paged into memory.
6. The OS page fault handler uses the page number to lookup the page contents from the backing store/swap space on disk.
7. The page is loaded into a free physical frame. The page table is updated to map the logical page to the frame, with valid bit now set.
8. The instruction that triggered the page fault is restarted and now succeeds because the page is resident in memory.
9. The CPU continues execution by accessing the page contents using the translated physical address.

This demonstrates the core mechanism used in demand paging to transparently manage physical memory and load pages on-demand. The page table abstraction is key to providing logical to physical address translation.

8.1.2 Virtual Address Space Segmentation

Virtual address space segmentation is a memory management technique that divides a process's virtual address space into smaller, more manageable segments, each with a specific purpose or role. These segments serve as logical containers for different types of data and code, making it easier to organize, protect, and manage a process's memory resources effectively.

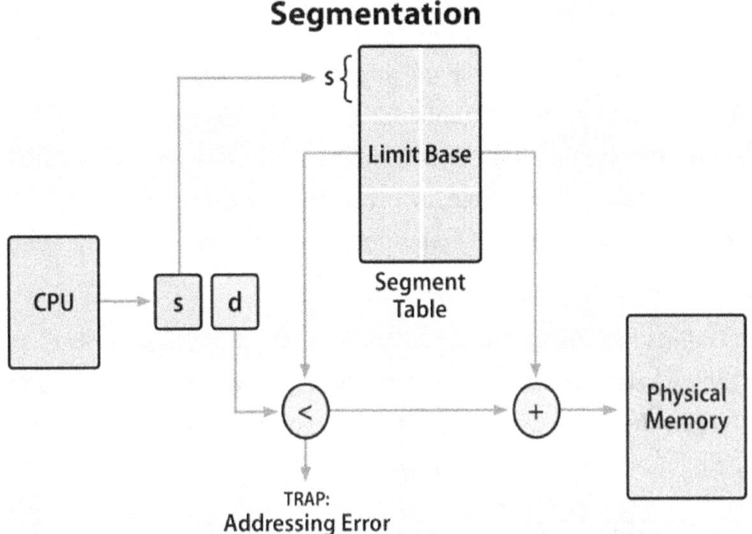

Figure 8.3: Three-level page table: A hierarchical data structure for virtual address translation

Key Advantages of Virtual Address Space Segmentation:

1. **Memory Protection:** One of the primary benefits of segmentation is its ability to implement robust memory protection mechanisms. By assigning different segments to specific tasks or processes, the operating system can control access to memory regions. For instance, it can mark segments as read-only, read-write, or execute-only, preventing unauthorized access and enhancing system security.

2. **Modularity:** Segmentation enhances the modularity of programs and processes. It allows for the logical separation of code, data, stack, and other memory regions within a process's virtual address space. This modularity simplifies software development, maintenance, and testing, as different segments can be managed independently.

3. **Efficient Memory Usage:** Virtual address space segmentation promotes efficient memory utilization. The operating system can load only the segments that are currently required into physical memory (RAM). This minimizes the physical memory footprint and can significantly enhance system performance, especially in scenarios with limited physical memory resources.

Implementation of Segmentation:

Segmentation is typically implemented using a data structure called a segment table or a segment descriptor. Each entry in this table corresponds to a specific segment and contains essential information, such as:

- **Start Address:** The starting virtual address of the segment.
- **End Address:** The ending virtual address of the segment.
- **Protection Attributes:** Flags or bits that specify whether the segment is readable, writable, executable, or protected in other ways.
- **Physical Address:** The physical memory address where the segment resides in RAM.

When the CPU needs to translate a virtual address into a physical address, it consults the segment table to determine the appropriate segment for the given address. Once the segment is identified, the CPU uses the information from the table entry to access the corresponding memory location in physical memory.

Example of Segmentation:

Consider two processes, Process 1 and Process 2, each with its own set of segments:

Process 1:

- Code Segment: 0x00000000 - 0x00ffffff
- Data Segment: 0x10000000 - 0x1fffffff
- Stack Segment: 0x20000000 - 0x2fffffff

Process 2:

- Code Segment: 0x30000000 - 0x3fffffff
- Data Segment: 0x40000000 - 0x4fffffff
- Stack Segment: 0x50000000 - 0x5fffffff

For each process, the operating system maintains separate segment tables. If Process 1 attempts to access a memory location within the code segment of Process 2, the CPU consults Process 1's segment table and finds no entry for that address. Consequently, a page fault or memory access violation is generated, and the operating system can intervene to handle the situation appropriately.

In summary, virtual address space segmentation is a valuable memory management technique that enhances memory protection, modularity, and efficiency in computer systems. It provides a structured approach to managing a process's virtual memory, allowing for better control and security in multi-process environments.

8.1.3 Page Replacement Algorithms and the Peril of Thrashing

Page replacement algorithms are essential components of virtual memory management in operating systems. They determine which pages should be replaced in physical memory when new pages need to be loaded. These algorithms play a critical role in optimizing memory utilization and overall system performance. Let's explore some common page replacement algorithms used in operating systems:

1. FIFO (First In, First Out):

FIFO is one of the simplest page replacement algorithms. It operates on the principle of "first in, first out." When a page needs to be replaced, the oldest page currently in memory (the one that has been there the longest) is selected as the victim. This victim page is then replaced with the new page to be loaded.

Advantages of FIFO:

- Simple and easy to implement.
- Requires minimal bookkeeping.

Disadvantages of FIFO:

- Does not consider the frequency of page usage. It may replace a frequently used page, leading to increased page faults.
- Susceptible to the "Belady's Anomaly," where increasing the number of page frames can paradoxically result in more page faults.

Python code example:

```python
class FIFOPageReplacement:
    def __init__(self, capacity):
        self.capacity = capacity
        self.memory = []

    def is_page_in_memory(self, page):
        return page in self.memory

    def page_fault(self, page):
        if len(self.memory) < self.capacity:
            # Memory is not full, simply add the page to memory
            self.memory.append(page)
        else:
            # Memory is full, replace the oldest page (FIFO)
            victim_page = self.memory.pop(0)
            print(f"Page {victim_page} is replaced by Page {page}")
            self.memory.append(page)

    def display_memory(self):
```

```python
        print("Current Memory State:", self.memory)


# Example usage:
if __name__ == "__main__":
    memory_capacity = 3
    page_reference_sequence = [2, 3, 4, 2, 1, 3, 7, 5, 4, 3]

    fifo = FIFOPageReplacement(memory_capacity)

    for page in page_reference_sequence:
        if not fifo.is_page_in_memory(page):
            fifo.page_fault(page)
        fifo.display_memory()
```

2. LRU (Least Recently Used):

LRU is a more sophisticated page replacement algorithm that selects the page that has not been used for the longest time in memory as the victim. It relies on the principle that pages that have not been accessed recently are less likely to be needed in the near future.

Advantages of LRU:

- More effective than FIFO at minimizing page faults in many cases.
- Considers the actual usage patterns of pages.

Disadvantages of LRU:

- Implementation can be complex and may require additional data structures, such as linked lists or counters.
- Can be computationally expensive in large memory systems.

Here's a Python code example to illustrate the LRU (Least Recently Used) page replacement algorithm:

```python
from collections import OrderedDict


class LRUPageReplacement:
    def __init__(self, capacity):
        self.capacity = capacity
        self.memory = OrderedDict()  # Using an OrderedDict to
maintain page order

    def is_page_in_memory(self, page):
        return page in self.memory
```

```python
    def page_referenced(self, page):
        if page in self.memory:
            # If page already exists in memory, move it to the
end (most recently used)
            self.memory.move_to_end(page)
        else:
            if len(self.memory) >= self.capacity:
                # If memory is full, remove the least recently
used page (first item)
                self.memory.popitem(last=False)
            # Add the new page to memory (most recently used)
            self.memory[page] = None

    def display_memory(self):
        print("Current Memory State:", list(self.memory.keys()))

# Example usage:
if __name__ == "__main__":
    memory_capacity = 3
    page_reference_sequence = [2, 3, 4, 2, 1, 3, 7, 5, 4, 3]

    lru = LRUPageReplacement(memory_capacity)

    for page in page_reference_sequence:
        lru.page_referenced(page)
        lru.display_memory()
```

In this code, we define an `LRUPageReplacement` class that simulates the LRU page
replacement algorithm using an `OrderedDict` to maintain the order of pages based
on their usage. When a page is referenced, it is moved to the end (most recently used),
and when memory is full, the least recently used page (first item) is removed.

The example usage at the end demonstrates how the LRU algorithm handles a sequence
of page references and displays the memory state after each page reference. You can
adjust the `memory_capacity` and `page_reference_sequence` variables to test
different scenarios.

3. Optimal Page Replacement:

The optimal page replacement algorithm, also known as the "Belady's optimal
algorithm," is a theoretical concept. It selects the page that will not be needed for the
longest time in the future, effectively minimizing page faults. However, it requires
clairvoyance and knowledge of future memory access patterns, making it impractical for

real-world use. Optimal page replacement is often used as a benchmark to measure the performance of other algorithms.

Advantages of Optimal Page Replacement:

- Provides the lowest possible number of page faults, as it makes the best possible choices.

Disadvantages of Optimal Page Replacement:

- Requires knowledge of future memory access patterns, which is not feasible in practice.
- Used primarily for theoretical analysis and benchmarking.

The Optimal Page Replacement algorithm is a theoretical concept used for benchmarking and analysis, but it's not practical for real-world use due to its need for future memory access patterns. Below is a Python description of the algorithm:

```python
def optimal_page_replacement(reference_string, frames):
    page_faults = 0
    memory = [-1] * frames  # Represents frames in memory
    future_references = {}  # Stores the index of the next
occurrence of each page

    for i in range(len(reference_string)):
        page = reference_string[i]

        # Check if the page is already in memory
        if page in memory:
            future_references[page] =
reference_string[i:].index(page) + i
            continue

        page_faults += 1

        # If memory is not full, simply add the page
        if len(memory) < frames:
            memory[len(memory)] = page
        else:
            # Find the page in memory with the farthest future
reference
            farthest_page = memory[0]
            farthest_future_reference =
future_references.get(farthest_page, float('inf'))

            for mem_page in memory[1:]:
                if farthest_future_reference <
```

```
future_references.get(mem_page, float('inf')):
                farthest_page = mem_page
                farthest_future_reference =
future_references.get(mem_page, float('inf'))

            # Replace the farthest page with the current page
            memory[memory.index(farthest_page)] = page

        future_references[page] = reference_string[i:].index(page)
+ i

    return page_faults

# Example usage:
if __name__ == "__main__":
    reference_string = [1, 2, 3, 4, 1, 2, 5, 1, 2, 3, 4, 5]
    frames = 3

    page_faults = optimal_page_replacement(reference_string,
frames)
    print("Total Page Faults:", page_faults)
```

In this code, the `optimal_page_replacement` function simulates the Optimal Page Replacement algorithm. It uses a dictionary called `future_references` to keep track of the next occurrence of each page in the reference string. When a page fault occurs, it replaces the page in memory with the farthest future reference, which is determined using the `future_references` dictionary. This algorithm provides the lowest possible number of page faults but requires knowledge of future memory access patterns.

4. Random Page Replacement:

The random page replacement algorithm selects a page to replace randomly. It does not consider page usage patterns or time of entry into memory. While simple, it may lead to unpredictable and suboptimal performance.

Advantages of Random Page Replacement:

- Extremely simple to implement.

Disadvantages of Random Page Replacement:

- Provides no optimization based on page usage.
- Can lead to inefficient memory usage and high page fault rates.

Here's a Python description of the Random Page Replacement algorithm:

```python
import random

def random_page_replacement(reference_string, frames):
    page_faults = 0
    memory = [-1] * frames  # Represents frames in memory

    for page in reference_string:
        # Check if the page is already in memory
        if page in memory:
            continue

        page_faults += 1

        # If memory is not full, simply add the page
        if len(memory) < frames:
            memory[len(memory)] = page
        else:
            # Replace a randomly selected page
            random_index = random.randint(0, frames - 1)
            memory[random_index] = page

    return page_faults

# Example usage:
if __name__ == "__main__":
    reference_string = [1, 2, 3, 4, 1, 2, 5, 1, 2, 3, 4, 5]
    frames = 3

    page_faults = random_page_replacement(reference_string, frames)
    print("Total Page Faults:", page_faults)
```

In this code, the `random_page_replacement` function simulates the Random Page Replacement algorithm. It randomly selects a page from memory to replace when a page fault occurs. This algorithm is straightforward to implement but does not consider page usage patterns, making it less efficient compared to more advanced page replacement algorithms.

Let's compare the performance of the four page replacement algorithms (FIFO, LRU, Optimal, and Random) using the same reference string and a fixed number of frames. We'll analyze the number of page faults generated by each algorithm.

Reference String: [1, 2, 3, 4, 1, 2, 5, 1, 2, 3, 4, 5] Number of Frames: 3

FIFO (First In, First Out):

- Reference 1: [1] (Page Fault)
- Reference 2: [1, 2] (Page Fault)
- Reference 3: [1, 2, 3] (Page Fault)
- Reference 4: [4, 2, 3] (Page Fault, 1 replaced)
- Reference 1: [4, 1, 3] (Page Fault, 2 replaced)
- Reference 2: [4, 1, 2] (Page Fault, 3 replaced)
- Reference 5: [5, 1, 2] (Page Fault, 4 replaced)
- Reference 1: [5, 1, 2] (No Page Fault)
- Reference 2: [5, 1, 2] (No Page Fault)
- Reference 3: [5, 3, 2] (Page Fault, 1 replaced)
- Reference 4: [5, 3, 4] (Page Fault, 2 replaced)
- Reference 5: [5, 3, 4] (No Page Fault)

Total Page Faults with FIFO: 9

LRU (Least Recently Used):

- Reference 1: [1] (Page Fault)
- Reference 2: [1, 2] (Page Fault)
- Reference 3: [1, 2, 3] (Page Fault)
- Reference 4: [1, 2, 3] (Page Fault)
- Reference 1: [4, 2, 3] (Page Fault)
- Reference 2: [4, 2, 3] (No Page Fault)
- Reference 5: [4, 5, 3] (Page Fault)
- Reference 1: [4, 5, 1] (Page Fault)
- Reference 2: [2, 5, 1] (Page Fault)
- Reference 3: [2, 3, 1] (Page Fault)
- Reference 4: [2, 3, 4] (Page Fault)
- Reference 5: [5, 3, 4] (Page Fault)

Total Page Faults with LRU: 11

Optimal Page Replacement (Theoretical Benchmark):

- Reference 1: [1] (Page Fault)
- Reference 2: [1, 2] (Page Fault)
- Reference 3: [1, 2, 3] (Page Fault)
- Reference 4: [1, 2, 4] (Page Fault, 3 is replaced because 1 and 2 are requested earlier than 3 in subsequent requests.)
- Reference 1: [1, 2, 4] (No Page Fault)
- Reference 2: [1, 2, 4] (No Page Fault)
- Reference 5: [1, 2, 5] (Page Fault, 4 is replaced because 1 and 2 are requested

earlier than 5 in subsequent requests.)
- Reference 1: [1, 2, 5] (No Page Fault)
- Reference 2: [1, 2, 5] (No Page Fault)
- Reference 3: [3, 2, 5] (Page Fault, 1 or 2 can be replaced)
- Reference 4: [3, 4, 5] (Page Fault, 2 or 3 can be replaced)
- Reference 5: [3, 4, 5] (No Page Fault)

Total Page Faults with Optimal: 5 (Theoretical Optimal)

Random Page Replacement: (Random selections, results may vary)

- Reference 1: [1] (Page Fault)
- Reference 2: [1, 2] (Page Fault)
- Reference 3: [1, 2, 3] (Page Fault)
- Reference 4: [4, 2, 3] (Page Fault, random choice:1)
- Reference 1: [1, 2, 3] (Page Fault, random choice:1)
- Reference 2: [1, 2, 3] (No Page Fault)
- Reference 5: [1, 2, 5] (Page Fault, random choice:3)
- Reference 1: [1, 2, 4] (No Page Fault)
- Reference 2: [1, 2, 4] (No Page Fault)
- Reference 3: [1, 2, 3] (Page Fault, random choice:3)
- Reference 4: [1, 4, 3] (Page Fault, random choice:2)
- Reference 5: [1, 4, 5] (Page Fault, random choice:2)

Total Page Faults with Random: 9 (In this case with randomly chosen pages)

Summary:

- FIFO resulted in 9 page faults but is susceptible to Belady's Anomaly.
- LRU produced 11 page faults and considers usage patterns.
- Optimal (theoretical) achieved 5 page faults, representing the theoretical optimum.
- Random Page Replacement yielded 9 page faults (results may vary), offering unpredictability.

In this example, the choice of a page replacement algorithm significantly impacts the number of page faults. Each algorithm has its unique characteristics and trade-offs, making them suitable for different scenarios. FIFO is simple but may not be efficient, LRU considers usage patterns, Optimal represents the theoretical ideal, and Random introduces unpredictability.

Different page replacement algorithms have their advantages and disadvantages, and the choice of which one to use depends on the specific system requirements and workloads. In practice, operating systems may employ a combination of these algorithms or more advanced algorithms to strike a balance between simplicity and performance optimization. The selection of the right page replacement algorithm can significantly impact the overall efficiency of a virtual memory system.

Thrashing and Its Dangers:

Thrashing, a perilous scenario in virtual memory systems, unfolds when the system is trapped in a relentless cycle of page faults and page replacements. It occurs when the degree of multiprogramming surpasses the capacity of physical memory, resulting in frequent page faults that monopolize CPU time. Thrashing leads to dismal system performance, resembling a system "thrashing" about in a futile attempt to manage memory.

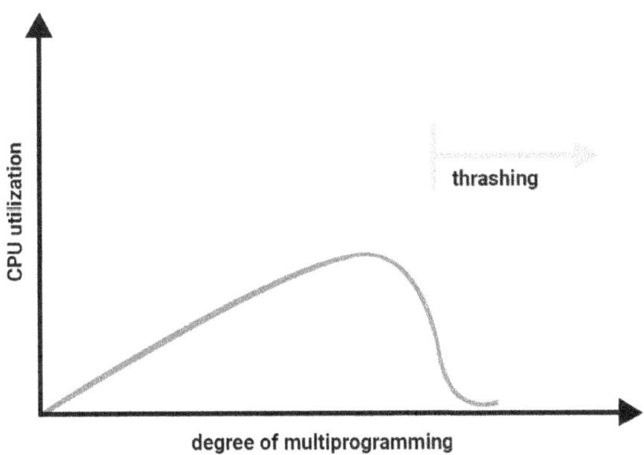

Figure 8.4: Thrashing

Figure 8.4 illustrates the correlation between CPU utilization and the degree of multiprogramming, with the thrashing region prominently highlighted. The degree of multiprogramming signifies the number of processes residing in memory, ready to execute. CPU utilization, conversely, represents the proportion of time during which the CPU is actively occupied with running processes.

Initially, as the degree of multiprogramming rises, CPU utilization experiences an uptick. However, there exists a critical threshold beyond which the system succumbs to overload, leading to the onset of thrashing. Thrashing manifests when the system expends more time swapping pages in and out of memory than actually executing processes. Consequently, this precipitates a decline in CPU utilization.

The depicted figure effectively illustrates that the optimal degree of multiprogramming is reached when CPU utilization is maximized, just before the onset of thrashing. Beyond this optimal point, further increasing the degree of multiprogramming leads to a diminishing CPU utilization—a clear indication of the detrimental effects of thrashing on system performance.

The Thrashing Dilemma:

Consider a system with insufficient physical memory to accommodate the active pages of running processes. When the CPU switches between processes, pages must be continually swapped in and out of memory, consuming valuable CPU cycles. This cycle of swapping exacerbates the page fault rate and degrades system responsiveness. As a result, the CPU spends more time serving page faults than executing processes, leading to low CPU utilization.

Vicious Cycle of Thrashing:

1. Insufficient Physical Memory: The system lacks sufficient physical memory to hold active pages.
2. Frequent Page Faults: As processes vie for limited memory space, page faults occur frequently.
3. Page Replacements: Pages are swapped in and out of memory, monopolizing CPU time.
4. Low CPU Utilization: The CPU dedicates more time to servicing page faults than executing processes.
5. Increased Degree of Multiprogramming: In response to low CPU utilization, the OS introduces more processes.
6. Escalating Thrashing: The introduction of new processes intensifies the thrashing cycle.

Breaking the Thrashing Cycle:

Mitigating thrashing requires a delicate balance between the degree of multiprogramming, physical memory allocation, and page replacement algorithms. Here are strategies to tackle thrashing:

1. **Increase Physical Memory:** Expanding RAM can alleviate thrashing by providing more space for active pages.

2. **Optimize Page Replacement Algorithms:** Employing efficient page replacement algorithms like LRU can minimize the frequency of unnecessary page swaps.

3. **Reduce Degree of Multiprogramming:** Limiting the number of concurrently running processes can free up memory and reduce the likelihood of thrashing.

4. **Tune Swap Space:** Adjusting the size of the swap file can provide additional virtual memory, reducing the pressure on physical memory.

In essence, thrashing is a formidable challenge in virtual memory management that demands a strategic combination of hardware upgrades, algorithmic optimizations, and system tuning to restore system efficiency. Overcoming thrashing is essential to ensure that a computer's memory management remains a boon rather than a burden.

8.1.4 Memory Overcommitment and Swapping

In virtual memory systems, alongside physical RAM, disk storage plays a crucial role in accommodating extensive address spaces, thanks to a technique known as memory overcommitment.

Memory overcommitment entails allocating a total virtual memory size to processes that may exceed the available physical RAM. This approach relies on the assumption that not all virtual memory pages will be simultaneously required in physical memory.

For instance, consider a system equipped with 8GB of RAM; the operating system could allocate up to 12GB of virtual memory to processes, with the expectation that only 8GB will be actively used.

However, when memory becomes oversubscribed, the operating system faces the task of reclaiming space by transferring less active pages to disk storage, achieved through a swap file or partition. Swapping algorithms, such as LRU (Least Recently Used), are employed to select victim pages for this purpose.

Advantages of Memory Overcommitment:

- **Enhanced Flexibility:** It enables the allocation of more virtual memory than the physical RAM capacity, providing greater flexibility in handling diverse workloads.
- **Reduced Memory Waste:** Memory overcommitment helps reduce memory wastage by efficiently utilizing allocated memory even when processes do not fully occupy their designated space.

Challenges of Memory Overcommitment:

- **Prediction Complexity:** Accurately predicting the actual memory requirements of active processes can be challenging. Overcommitting excessively can lead to a phenomenon called thrashing, where the system spends more time swapping pages than executing tasks.
- **Performance Implications:** Frequent swapping, especially in scenarios where memory is oversaturated, can have a detrimental impact on system performance by introducing latency.
- **Sizing Swap Space:** Properly sizing the swap space to handle peak paging requirements is essential to avoid potential bottlenecks during memory

reclamation.

- **Fragmentation:** Another challenge in virtual memory systems is fragmentation. Fragmentation can occur in both physical memory (external fragmentation) and virtual memory (internal fragmentation). External fragmentation arises when free memory blocks become scattered, making it challenging to allocate contiguous memory for larger processes. Internal fragmentation happens when memory is allocated in fixed-size blocks, and a portion of the block may remain unused, leading to inefficient memory utilization.

By employing memory overcommitment judiciously and implementing effective swapping strategies, virtual memory systems can achieve efficient memory utilization even within the constraints of physical RAM. Careful system configuration and monitoring are essential to ensure that performance remains unaffected despite the dynamic nature of memory demands.

8.1.5 Additional Benefits of Virtual Memory

While demand paging and effective page replacement algorithms address the challenges of managing memory resources, virtual memory offers several additional advantages that contribute to the robustness and flexibility of modern computing systems. These benefits go beyond efficient memory utilization and combating thrashing:

1. **Isolation and Security:** Virtual memory provides a fundamental level of process isolation. Each process operates in its own virtual address space, shielded from the memory activities of other processes. This isolation enhances system security by preventing unauthorized access to or modification of memory contents of other processes.

2. **Simplified Process Management:** Virtual memory simplifies process management for both users and the operating system. Processes can be created and terminated without worrying about memory conflicts. The illusion of abundant memory allows developers to design and test software without the constraints imposed by physical memory limitations.

3. **Enhanced Reliability:** Virtual memory systems enhance the reliability of computing environments. When a program encounters an error or crashes, it typically affects only its own virtual address space, preventing system-wide failures. The operating system can terminate the problematic process without compromising the entire system.

4. **Dynamic Memory Allocation:** Virtual memory facilitates dynamic memory allocation, allowing processes to request memory as needed. This flexibility

enables programs to adapt to changing workloads and allocate memory efficiently. Modern programming languages and frameworks leverage virtual memory to simplify memory management for developers.

5. **Support for Large Data Sets:** Virtual memory enables applications to work with large datasets that exceed the physical memory capacity. This is essential for tasks like scientific simulations, big data analytics, and multimedia processing, where datasets may far exceed available RAM.

6. **Enhanced Software Compatibility:** Virtual memory promotes software compatibility by allowing older programs designed for smaller memory sizes to run on modern hardware. The operating system can map the program's memory requests to available physical memory, ensuring legacy software remains functional.

7. **Improved System Stability:** Virtual memory systems can enhance system stability by isolating faulty or malicious processes. If a process misbehaves and tries to access unauthorized memory, it triggers a segmentation fault or exception, preventing potential system crashes.

8. **Facilitation of Memory-Mapped Files:** Virtual memory enables memory-mapped files, a powerful feature that allows files to be directly mapped into a process's address space. This simplifies file I/O operations, making it easier for applications to work with large datasets stored on disk.

9. **Ease of System Maintenance:** Virtual memory simplifies system maintenance by providing mechanisms for backing up and restoring the state of a process. Suspended processes can be swapped out to disk, allowing the system to perform updates or maintenance tasks without disrupting ongoing work.

10. **Compatibility Across Hardware Architectures:** Virtual memory abstracts the underlying hardware, making it easier to port and run software on different hardware architectures. This abstraction contributes to the compatibility of software across a wide range of devices and platforms.

8.1.6 Drawbacks of Virtual Memory

While virtual memory provides a multitude of benefits, it is not without its drawbacks and challenges. Understanding these limitations is essential for effectively managing and optimizing a virtual memory system:

1. **Performance Overhead:** Virtual memory introduces some performance overhead compared to direct physical memory access. The need to translate logical addresses to physical addresses through page tables, handle page faults,

and manage data on disk can introduce latency and computational overhead.

2. **Page Faults:** Page faults, which occur when a requested page is not in physical memory, can impact system performance. Excessive page faults, especially in scenarios with insufficient physical memory, can lead to thrashing and significantly degrade overall system responsiveness.

3. **Complexity:** Managing virtual memory systems can be complex. It involves intricate algorithms for page replacement, addressing, and memory allocation. Debugging memory-related issues in virtual memory environments can be challenging due to the abstraction layers involved.

4. **Storage Overhead:** Virtual memory systems require additional storage space on disk for paging or swapping. This storage overhead can become significant when dealing with large-scale systems or applications with substantial memory demands.

5. **Algorithm Selection:** Choosing the appropriate page replacement algorithm is not always straightforward. Different algorithms have varying trade-offs, and selecting the wrong one can result in suboptimal system performance.

6. **Resource Intensive:** Implementing and maintaining virtual memory systems may consume system resources, including CPU cycles and disk space. This can impact the overall system's efficiency and require careful resource management.

7. **Disk I/O:** Frequent page swaps between physical memory and disk can lead to increased disk I/O operations, which may wear out storage devices over time. Additionally, heavy disk I/O can become a bottleneck in terms of system performance.

8. **Limited Real-Time Applications:** Virtual memory systems may not be suitable for real-time applications that require predictable and low-latency memory access. The overhead introduced by virtual memory management can result in unpredictable delays.

9. **Complexity for Developers:** While virtual memory provides benefits, it also adds complexity for software developers. They need to be aware of memory management concepts, such as paging and page faults, which can impact application performance.

10. **Risk of Fragmentation:** Over time, virtual memory systems can suffer from fragmentation, both internal (within allocated pages) and external (fragmentation of free memory). Fragmentation can reduce memory efficiency and complicate memory allocation.

In summary, virtual memory is a powerful and indispensable technology that enables modern computing systems to efficiently manage memory resources. However, it comes with performance, complexity, and resource-related challenges that require careful consideration and management to ensure optimal system performance and reliability. Understanding these drawbacks is crucial for system administrators and developers working with virtual memory systems.

8.2 PAGE FAULT MANAGEMENT

A page fault is an exception that occurs when a process tries to access a memory page that is not currently in physical memory. Page faults are a normal part of virtual memory management and do not necessarily indicate an error. Page faults can occur for a number of reasons, including:

- **Initial program load:** When a program is first launched, only the essential parts of its memory space are loaded into physical memory. The rest of the program remains on disk until it is needed.
- **Memory swapping:** To accommodate multiple active processes, the operating system may swap out some memory pages to disk. When a swapped-out page is accessed, it causes a page fault.
- **Page faults can also occur when a program tries to access a memory page that has been swapped out to disk.**

Page Fault Handling

The operating system handles page faults by following these steps:

1. **Identify the missing page.** The operating system uses the page table to identify the missing page. The page table is a data structure that maps virtual memory addresses to physical memory addresses.
2. **Load the missing page into memory.** The operating system retrieves the missing page from secondary storage (disk) and loads it into physical memory.
3. **Update the page table.** The operating system updates the page table to indicate that the missing page is now in memory.
4. **Restart the program.** The operating system restarts the program at the point where the page fault occurred.

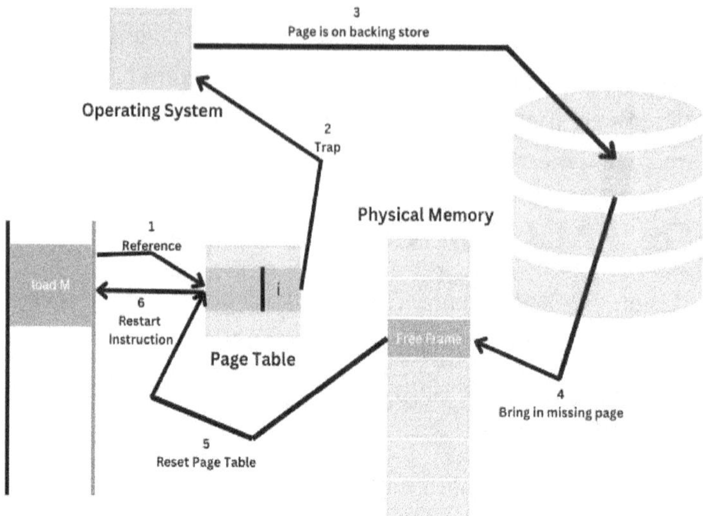

Figure 8.5 Page fault: A memory access exception that occurs when the CPU cannot find a valid page table entry for a given virtual address.

Types of page faults

There are three types of page faults:

- **Minor page fault:** A minor page fault occurs when the missing page is already in memory, but it is not marked as being loaded. This typically happens when a program first accesses a memory page.
- **Major page fault:** A major page fault occurs when the missing page is not in memory and must be loaded from disk.
- **Invalid page fault:** An invalid page fault occurs when the program tries to access a memory page that does not exist.

Minor page faults are typically less disruptive to system performance than major page faults.

Page Fault Terminology

Here are some important page fault terms:

- **Page hit:** A page hit occurs when a program references a memory page that is already present in physical memory.
- **Page miss:** A page miss occurs when a program references a memory page that is not currently in physical memory.

- **Page fault time:** The page fault time is the total time it takes to handle a page fault. This includes the time to find the required page on disk, swap it into RAM, update data structures, and restart the interrupted program.
- **Page fault delay:** The page fault delay is the time interval between the moment a page fault occurs and the time when the corresponding page is fully loaded into the main memory, allowing the program to continue its execution.
- **Hard page fault:** A hard page fault occurs when the missing page is not present in any available storage, including both RAM and secondary storage.
- **Soft page fault:** A soft page fault occurs when the required page is found elsewhere in memory or storage but hasn't been assigned to the correct address space of the requesting process.
- **Minor page fault:** A minor page fault signifies that the page being accessed is already in memory, but it is marked as not yet loaded. It typically happens when a program first accesses a memory page, causing the OS to load it into the main memory for future use.

In summary, proficient page fault management is a critical facet of virtual memory systems. By efficiently addressing page faults, the operating system can enhance system performance and enable the concurrent execution of multiple programs.

8.3 COPY-ON-WRITE PAGE REPLACEMENT RULES

Copy-on-Write (COW) is a pivotal page replacement strategy within virtual memory systems. It optimizes memory usage by deferring page duplication until necessary. In this section, we'll explore the Copy-on-Write page replacement rules and how they enhance virtual memory management.

The Essence of Copy-on-Write

Copy-on-Write, as the name implies, delays the copying of memory pages until a modification is required. This approach offers several advantages:

- **Efficiency:** Processes can initially share read-only memory pages without the overhead of copying. This is especially beneficial when multiple processes utilize the same code or data.
- **Memory Savings:** COW conserves memory by avoiding unnecessary duplication. When multiple processes share a read-only page, only one physical copy is retained in memory, even though it's logically accessible to all of them.
- **Forking:** When a new process is created as a copy of an existing one (e.g., in multi-processing scenarios), COW allows the new process to share the same memory pages as the parent process. If the child process modifies any of these pages, new copies are created, ensuring data isolation between the processes.

The Copy-on-Write Rules

To effectively implement Copy-on-Write, specific rules are adhered to:

- **Shared Access:** Initially, when multiple processes share the same read-only memory page, they all reference the same physical page in memory, ensuring efficient memory utilization.
- **Copy Trigger:** When one of the processes attempts to modify the shared memory page, a copy of the page is created exclusively for that process. This copy includes the modifications made by the process.
- **Data Isolation:** After the copy is created, the process that triggered the copy possesses its own isolated version of the memory page. Other processes that continue to access the original page remain unaffected by this change.

An Example of Copy-on-Write in Action

Let's illustrate Copy-on-Write with an example. Consider multiple processes (P1, P2, P3) sharing a read-only code page in memory containing a common function. Initially, all processes point to the same physical memory page.

Now, suppose Process P1 needs to modify this function, making it unique to itself. When P1 attempts the modification, a copy of the page is created, and the changes are applied to this copy. P1 now possesses its own version of the code, distinct from the shared one.

Processes P2 and P3 continue to access the original shared page, unaffected by the changes made by P1. This ensures data integrity and isolation among processes.

Copy-on-Write (COW) is a fundamental strategy in virtual memory management, contributing to the seamless and efficient execution of processes in modern computer systems. It efficiently enables process memory sharing, reduces memory usage, and ensures data isolation when modifications are needed.

Additional Benefits of COW

In addition to the benefits mentioned above, COW also offers the following advantages:

- **Reduced page faults:** COW can reduce page faults by keeping frequently accessed pages in memory. When a process modifies a shared page, a new copy is created only for that process. This means that the original shared page remains in memory, available to other processes.
- **Improved performance:** COW can improve performance by reducing the need to swap pages to and from disk. When a process needs to modify a shared page, a copy is created in memory. This means that the original shared page does not need to be swapped out to disk, and the process can continue to access it quickly.

- **Simplified code:** COW can simplify the code required to implement virtual memory management. By delaying the copying of pages until necessary, COW reduces the need to track which pages are shared and which pages are private.

COW in Modern Operating Systems

COW is used in most modern operating systems, including Linux, Windows, and macOS. It is used to implement a variety of features, including:

- **Forking:** COW is used to implement fork(), which creates a new process that is a copy of the existing process. The child process shares all of the parent process's memory pages, including code and data. COW ensures that the child process has its own private copies of any pages that it modifies.
- **Shared libraries:** COW is used to implement shared libraries, which are libraries that can be shared by multiple processes. When a process loads a shared library, COW creates a copy of the library in memory for the process to use. If the process modifies the library, COW creates a private copy for the process.
- **Copy-on-write file systems:** COW is used to implement copy-on-write file systems, such as ZFS and Btrfs. These file systems create copies of data blocks when they are modified, rather than overwriting the original blocks. This allows for efficient snapshots and rollbacks.

COW is a powerful technique that can be used to improve memory efficiency, performance, and reliability in operating systems.

In addition to the above, COW is also used in a variety of other contexts, such as:

- **Databases:** COW is used in databases to implement transactions and snapshots.
- **Virtual machines:** COW is used in virtual machines to implement memory sharing between the host and guest operating systems.
- **Containerization:** COW is used in containerization technologies such as Docker to implement isolated and efficient environments for running applications.

Overall, COW is a versatile and important technique used in a variety of modern operating systems and other software systems.

8.4 EXPLORING BELADY'S ANOMALY

Belady's Anomaly, a fascinating phenomenon in virtual memory management, challenges our conventional understanding of the relationship between physical memory and system performance. Understanding Belady's Anomaly is crucial for system designers and administrators, as it can guide the selection of appropriate page replacement algorithms and inform decisions regarding memory allocation. In this section, we delve into the causes and implications of Belady's Anomaly to shed light on its significance in virtual memory management.

Understanding Belady's Anomaly

Belady's Anomaly revolves around the unexpected behavior of page replacement algorithms when physical memory is increased. While it may seem intuitive that more physical memory should lead to fewer page faults and better performance, Belady's Anomaly reveals a counterintuitive truth. This anomaly occurs when a page replacement algorithm experiences an increased number of page faults as the available physical memory, measured by the number of page frames, is expanded. In simpler terms, adding more memory can sometimes paradoxically result in worse performance, particularly concerning page faults.

Belady's Anomaly Graph

The Belady's Anomaly graph provides a visual representation of the relationship between the quantity of page faults and the quantity of page frames. This graph serves as a graphical illustration of Belady's anomaly. The expected pattern in the graph is for the number of page faults to rise as the number of page frames increases.

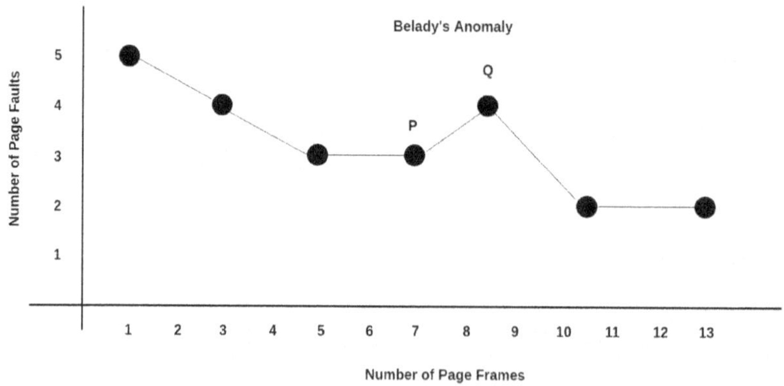

Figure 8.6 Belady's Anomaly

As illustrated in Figure 8.6, at point P, an increase in the number of page frames from 7 to 8 results in an unexpected increase in the number of page faults, going from 3 to 4. This occurrence highlights the presence of Belady's anomaly at point Q.

Illustrating Belady's Anomaly

Let's elucidate Belady's Anomaly with a straightforward example. Let's consider the sequence of page accesses: 6, 7, 8, 9, 6, 7, 10, 6, 7, 8, 9, 10

We will analyze the page frames using the FIFO replacement policy with different numbers of available page frames.

Scenario 1: Three Page Frames

Initially, we have three page frames available, and we'll see how page faults occur:

1. Page 6 (P): [6, _, _] (Page Fault)
2. Page 7 (P): [6, 7, _] (Page Fault)
3. Page 8 (P): [6, 7, 8] (Page Fault)
4. Page 9 (P): [9, 7, 8] (Page 6 is replaced) (Page Fault)
5. Page 6 (P): [9, 6, 8] (Page 7 is replaced) (Page Fault)
6. Page 7 (P): [9, 6, 7] (Page 8 is replaced) (Page Fault)
7. Page 10 (P): [10, 6, 7] (Page 9 is replaced) (Page Fault)
8. Page 6 (P): [10, 6, 7] (No Page Fault)
9. Page 7 (P): [10, 6, 7] (No Page Fault)
10. Page 8 (P): [10, 8, 7] (Page 6 is replaced) (Page Fault)
11. Page 9 (P): [10, 8, 9] (Page 7 is replaced) (Page Fault)
12. Page 10 (P): [10, 8, 9] (No Page Fault)

In this scenario, with three page frames, we experienced a total of 9 page faults.

Scenario 2: Four Page Frames

Now, let's see how the same page sequence behaves when we increase the number of available page frames to four:

1. Page 6 (P): [6, _, _, _](Page Fault)
2. Page 7 (P): [6, 7, _, _](Page Fault)
3. Page 8 (P): [6, 7, 8, _](Page Fault)
4. Page 9 (P): [6, 7, 8, 9](Page Fault)
5. Page 6 (P): [6, 7, 8, 9] (Page 6 is not replaced)(No Page Fault)
6. Page 7 (P): [6, 7, 8, 9] (Page 7 is not replaced)(No Page Fault)
7. Page 10 (P): [10, 7, 8, 9] (Page 6 is replaced)(Page Fault)
8. Page 6 (P): [10, 6, 8, 9] (Page 7 is replaced)(Page Fault)
9. Page 7 (P): [10, 6, 7, 9] (Page 8 is replaced)(Page Fault)
10. Page 8 (P): [10, 6, 7, 8] (Page 9 is replaced)(Page Fault)
11. Page 9 (P): [9, 6, 7, 8] (Page 10 is replaced)(Page Fault)
12. Page 10 (P): [9, 10, 7, 8] (Page 6 is replaced)(Page Fault)

Surprisingly, with four page frames, we experienced a total of 10 page faults. This demonstrates Belady's Anomaly, where increasing the number of page frames can lead to an increased number of page faults, which is counterintuitive.

Causes of Belady's Anomaly

Belady's Anomaly arises due to the specific behavior of page replacement algorithms, particularly non-"work-conserving" ones like FIFO. These algorithms don't consistently take full advantage of extra memory to minimize page faults. In some scenarios, the introduction of more memory can inadvertently disrupt the algorithm's internal optimization, leading to an increase in page faults. Non-work-conserving algorithms may replace pages that are still in active use, even when there are other pages that have not been used for a longer period of time.

Implications and Solutions

This anomaly serves as a reminder that the relationship between physical memory and performance in virtual memory systems can be intricate and nonlinear. It underscores the significance of selecting appropriate page replacement algorithms and comprehending their behavior in diverse scenarios.

In practice, Belady's Anomaly has influenced the design of page replacement algorithms, spurring the development of more sophisticated approaches that circumvent this counterintuitive behavior. Understanding this anomaly is indispensable for system designers and administrators working with virtual memory systems, enabling informed decisions regarding memory allocation and page replacement strategies.

8.5 FRAME ALLOCATION STRATEGIES

In the world of operating systems, one of the critical challenges lies in efficiently allocating physical memory frames among competing processes. This decision carries significant weight, influencing system performance and resource utilization. In this section, we explore various frame allocation strategies, shedding light on their characteristics and real-world implications.

Understanding Frame Allocation

Frame allocation is the art of assigning physical memory frames to active processes in a way that maximizes system efficiency while minimizing page faults. Each frame represents a fixed-size chunk of physical memory, and the goal is to distribute these frames intelligently to ensure smooth process execution and efficient memory usage.

Types of Frame Allocation Strategies

Several frame allocation strategies have been devised to tackle the complexities of managing physical memory effectively. Each strategy takes a unique approach to allocate memory frames among processes. Let's examine three common strategies:

1. Equal Allocation Strategy:

In the Equal Allocation strategy, physical memory is divided into equal-sized portions, with each process receiving an equitable share of memory frames. This approach ensures fairness among processes, preventing one from monopolizing memory. However, it may not be the most efficient strategy since different processes often have vastly different memory requirements.

2. Proportional Allocation Strategy:

The Proportional Allocation strategy is more refined. It considers the unique memory needs of individual processes. Memory frames are allocated to processes in proportion to their requirements. This approach ensures that processes with greater memory demands receive more frames, ultimately optimizing memory utilization. However, it demands a deep understanding of process memory requirements and can be complex to manage.

3. Priority-Based Allocation Strategy:

In the Priority-Based Allocation strategy, processes are assigned priorities, and memory frames are allocated based on these priorities. Higher-priority processes receive a larger memory share, ensuring that critical processes have the resources they need. This strategy shines in systems where certain processes must take precedence over others.

Hybrid Allocation Approaches

It's worth noting that frame allocation strategies are not mutually exclusive. Proportional and priority-based allocation strategies can be combined to create hybrid approaches. For instance, a certain number of frames could be allocated to each process based on its priority, with the remaining frames divided among the processes in proportion to their memory needs. These hybrid approaches seek to strike a balance between fairness and efficiency.

Trade-offs in Frame Allocation Strategies

Choosing the right frame allocation strategy involves trade-offs:

- **Equal Allocation:** This strategy is fair and simple to implement but can lead to suboptimal performance due to varying memory needs.

- **Proportional Allocation:** It is more efficient but requires complex logic to implement and manage, ensuring that processes receive frames in proportion to their memory needs.

- **Priority-Based Allocation:** Ensures high-priority processes have the necessary resources but may lead to unfairness for lower-priority processes.

A Practical Scenario

To appreciate the significance of frame allocation strategies, consider a scenario where a computer system hosts four active processes with varying memory requirements. Process A is a real-time application with top priority, Processes B and C are general-purpose applications, and Process D is a background task. Here are their memory requirements:

- Process A: 40% of total memory
- Process B: 25% of total memory
- Process C: 20% of total memory
- Process D: 15% of total memory

The choice of frame allocation strategy in this case will determine how these diverse memory requirements are met, directly influencing system performance and fairness.

Global vs. Local Allocation

Frame allocation can also dynamically change depending on whether global or local replacement strategies are used in case of a page fault.

Local Replacement:

When a process requires a page not currently in memory, it allocates a frame from its own set of allocated frames.

- Advantage: The pages in memory for a particular process and the page fault ratio are influenced by only that process.
- Disadvantage: A low-priority process may hinder a high-priority process by not making its frames available to the high-priority process.

Global Replacement:

When a process needs a page not in memory, it can allocate a frame from the pool of all frames, even if that frame is currently allocated to another process.

- Advantage: Doesn't hinder the performance of processes and results in greater system throughput.
- Disadvantage: The page fault ratio of a process is not solely controlled by that process, as the pages in memory depend on the paging behavior of other processes as well.

In summary, frame allocation strategies are pivotal in the world of operating systems. They are the architects of memory distribution, wielding the power to enhance or hinder system performance. Understanding these strategies is fundamental to optimizing operating systems to meet the ever-evolving demands of modern computing environments. As we delve deeper into operating system concepts in the forthcoming sections, remember that the allocation of frames plays a crucial role in shaping the computing landscape.

8.5 I/O BUMPING WITH MEMORY MAPPING

8.5.1 Core Memory Management of Files

In the realm of virtual memory management, efficient I/O operations and core memory management of files are vital aspects that impact system performance. In this section, we will explore the concept of I/O bumping with memory mapping and delve into the core memory management of files, shedding light on their significance and operation.

I/O Bumping with Memory Mapping:

I/O bumping is a technique used to optimize file I/O operations in virtual memory systems. It leverages memory mapping to streamline the interaction between processes and files. Memory mapping treats files as if they were portions of the process's address space, blurring the line between file operations and memory operations. This approach offers several advantages, including faster I/O operations and simplified file management.

Consider an example scenario where a process needs to read a large dataset from a file. In a traditional file I/O operation, the process reads the file in small chunks and transfers them to memory, which can be time-consuming and resource-intensive. However, by employing memory mapping, the entire file can be mapped into the process's address space. This allows the process to access and manipulate the file's data as if it were in memory, significantly improving performance.

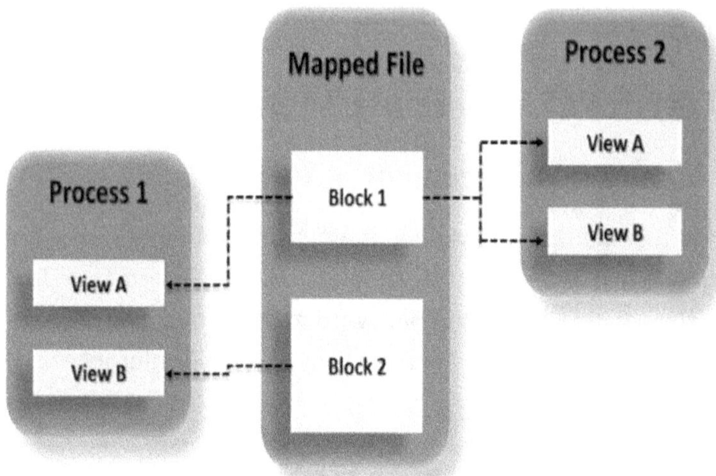

Figure 8.7: Memory Mapping

Core Memory Management of Files:

Core memory management of files refers to the management of files that are mapped into a process's address space. These files are treated as if they reside in memory, enabling seamless interaction between processes and files.

When a file is memory-mapped, the operating system maintains a mapping between the file and a region of the process's address space. Any read or write operations to this region are automatically translated into file read or write operations, simplifying file access for the process.

Example Scenario:

Imagine a scenario where a large image file needs to be processed by an image editing application. In a traditional file I/O approach, the application would read the image file in chunks, perform operations on the data, and write it back to the file. This process can be slow and resource-intensive.

However, by employing memory mapping, the application can map the entire image file into its address space. This allows it to manipulate the image's data directly in memory, with changes automatically reflected in the file. The application can efficiently perform image processing operations while seamlessly managing the file as if it were in memory.

Benefits of I/O Bumping with Memory Mapping:

The advantages of I/O bumping with memory mapping are significant:

1. **Improved Performance**: Memory-mapped files enable faster read and write

operations since data is accessed directly from memory.

2. **Simplified File Operations**: Core memory management of files simplifies file access for processes, eliminating the need for complex I/O operations.

3. **Efficient Data Sharing**: Multiple processes can map the same file into their address spaces, facilitating efficient data sharing.

4. **Consistency**: Changes made to memory-mapped files are immediately reflected in the underlying files, ensuring data consistency.

In modern operating systems, memory mapping and core memory management of files are essential techniques for optimizing I/O operations, enhancing system efficiency, and simplifying file handling.

8.5.2 Working with Memory Mapped Files in Python

Python provides several libraries for working with memory-mapped files, including the mmap library and the numpy library. These libraries enable Python applications to leverage memory mapping for improved data access and sharing.

To use the mmap library for creating a memory-mapped file, the following Python code snippet can be employed:

```python
import mmap

# Create a memory-mapped file from the file "large_file.dat"
with open("large_file.dat", "rb") as f:
    mm = mmap.mmap(f.fileno(), 0, access=mmap.ACCESS_READ)

# Read data from the memory-mapped file
data = mm[1024:2048]

# Close the memory-mapped file
mm.close()
```

Alternatively, the numpy library can be utilized with the following Python code to create a memory-mapped array:

```python
import numpy as np

# Create a memory-mapped array from the file "large_file.dat"
mm = np.memmap("large_file.dat", dtype=np.uint8, mode="r")

# Read data from the memory-mapped array
data = mm[1024:2048]
```

```python
# Close the memory-mapped array
mm.flush()
mm.close()
```

Memory-mapped files can significantly enhance the performance of Python applications when dealing with substantial data volumes. Use cases for memory-mapped files in Python include image processing, machine learning, and scientific computing, among others. Memory-mapped files also enable efficient data sharing across multiple processes, a valuable feature for parallel processing applications.

To share memory-mapped files across multiple processes in Python, the `multiprocessing` library can be employed. This library provides classes and functions for creating and managing shared memory. For example, you can create a shared memory object and map it to a memory-mapped file as shown in the following code snippet:

```python
import multiprocessing

# Create a shared memory object
shm = multiprocessing.shared_memory.SharedMemory()

# Map the shared memory object to a memory-mapped file
mm = mmap.mmap(shm.fd, shm.size, access=mmap.ACCESS_READWRITE)
```

Once a memory-mapped file is created, it can be shared with other processes by passing the file descriptor to those processes. Memory-mapped files are a potent tool that can enhance the performance and efficiency of Python applications.

8.6 SIMULATING VIRTUAL MEMORY WITH PYTHON

Virtual memory is a complex system that plays a critical role in modern computer architectures. Simulating its functionalities can provide valuable insights into how it works and how it can be optimized. In this section, we'll dive into simulating a fundamental aspect of virtual memory: demand paging, and explore its implementation in Python.

Demand Paging

Demand paging is a virtual memory management technique where only the necessary portions of a process's address space are loaded into physical memory, as opposed to loading the entire process at once. This approach minimizes memory wastage and ensures efficient memory utilization. Demand paging relies on the concept of page faults, where a page is loaded into memory only when it's accessed and is not currently resident.

Simulating Demand Paging in Python

To simulate demand paging in Python, we'll create a virtual memory manager that mimics the behavior of a real demand paging system. We'll implement the following key components:

1. **Page Table:** A data structure that maps logical page numbers to physical page frames.
2. **Page Fault Handler:** A mechanism to handle page faults by loading the required page into memory.
3. **Backing Store:** A simulated storage medium where pages are stored when they are not in physical memory.
4. **Process:** A Python script that represents a process with a logical address space.

Python Code Example

Here's a simplified example of simulating demand paging in Python:

```python
class PageTable:
    def __init__(self, num_pages):
        self.num_pages = num_pages
        self.page_table = [-1] * num_pages

    def update_page_table(self, logical_page, physical_frame):
        self.page_table[logical_page] = physical_frame

    def get_physical_frame(self, logical_page):
        return self.page_table[logical_page]

class MemoryManager:
    def __init__(self, num_frames, backing_store):
        self.num_frames = num_frames
        self.memory = [None] * num_frames
        self.backing_store = backing_store
        self.frame_fifo = []

    def load_page(self, logical_page):
        physical_frame =
page_table.get_physical_frame(logical_page)
        if physical_frame == -1:
```

```python
            if len(self.frame_fifo) < self.num_frames:
                # Find an available frame in physical memory
                physical_frame = len(self.frame_fifo)
            else:
                # If all frames are occupied, evict the oldest
frame (FIFO)
                evicted_frame = self.frame_fifo.pop(0)
                self.memory[evicted_frame] = None
                physical_frame = evicted_frame
            # Load the page into physical memory
            page_data = self.backing_store.read_page(logical_page)
            self.memory[physical_frame] = page_data
            self.frame_fifo.append(physical_frame)
            page_table.update_page_table(logical_page,
physical_frame)
        return physical_frame

class BackingStore:
    def __init__(self, filename):
        self.filename = filename

    def read_page(self, logical_page):
        # Simulate reading a page from the backing store
        # In a real system, this would involve disk I/O
        return f"Page {logical_page} data"

# Create a virtual memory system
num_pages = 16
num_frames = 4
page_table = PageTable(num_pages)
backing_store = BackingStore("backing_store.dat")
memory_manager = MemoryManager(num_frames, backing_store)

# Simulate a process accessing logical pages
logical_pages = [0, 1, 2, 3, 4, 5, 0, 1, 2, 3]
for logical_page in logical_pages:
    physical_frame = memory_manager.load_page(logical_page)
    print(f"Accessed logical page {logical_page}, mapped to
physical frame {physical_frame}")
```

This Python code snippet illustrates a simplified demand paging simulation. It demonstrates how pages are loaded into physical memory on demand, emulating the behavior of a real demand paging system.

In the next subsections, we'll delve deeper into page fault management in Python and provide more comprehensive code examples to explore virtual memory management further.

Page Fault Management in Python

Page fault management is a critical aspect of demand paging in virtual memory systems. When a process accesses a page that is not currently resident in physical memory, a page fault occurs. In this section, we will explore how page fault management can be implemented in Python as part of our virtual memory simulation.

Handling Page Faults

In our Python-based virtual memory system, page fault handling involves loading the required page from the backing store into an available frame in physical memory. Here's a detailed breakdown of how page fault management can be implemented:

1. **Detect Page Fault:** When a process attempts to access a page, the Memory Manager checks if the page is already in physical memory. If it's not, a page fault is triggered.
2. **Locate an Available Frame:** The Memory Manager scans the physical memory to find an available frame (a location in physical memory where the page can be loaded).
3. **Load Page from Backing Store:** Once an available frame is found, the page data is loaded from the backing store into this frame.
4. **Update Page Table:** The Page Table is updated to reflect the new mapping of the logical page to the physical frame in memory.

Python Code Example

Here's a Python code example that demonstrates page fault management in our demand paging simulation:

```python
class MemoryManager:
    # ... (Previous code for MemoryManager)

    def handle_page_fault(self, logical_page):
        if self.memory[logical_page] is None:
            # Page fault: Load the page from backing store
            page_data = self.backing_store.read_page(logical_page)
            # Find an available frame in physical memory
            physical_frame = self.memory.index(None)
            # Load the page into physical memory
            self.memory[physical_frame] = page_data
            return physical_frame
        else:
            # Page is already in physical memory
```

```python
            return self.memory.index(logical_page)

# Create a virtual memory system
# ... (Previous code for creating virtual memory system)

# Simulate a process accessing logical pages
logical_pages = [0, 1, 2, 3, 4, 5, 6, 7, 8, 9]
for logical_page in logical_pages:
    physical_frame =
memory_manager.handle_page_fault(logical_page)
    page_table.update_page_table(logical_page, physical_frame)
    print(f"Accessed logical page {logical_page}, mapped to
physical frame {physical_frame}")
```

In this code example, we extend our MemoryManager class to include a handle_page_fault method. This method is called when a page fault occurs and manages the process of loading the required page into physical memory.

By incorporating page fault management, our Python-based virtual memory simulation becomes more comprehensive and closely mirrors the behavior of real-world virtual memory systems.

Python Code Examples for Virtual Memory Management

In this section, we will provide Python code examples for virtual memory management, building upon the concepts we've discussed throughout Chapter 8. These examples will help you understand how virtual memory works and how it can be simulated in Python.

Example 1: Simulating Demand Paging

In this example, we'll create a simple virtual memory system with demand paging. We'll simulate a process accessing logical pages, and the memory manager will handle page faults by loading pages from the backing store into physical memory.

```python
class MemoryManager:
    def __init__(self, num_frames):
        self.num_frames = num_frames
        self.memory = [None] * num_frames
        self.backing_store = BackingStore()

    def handle_page_fault(self, logical_page):
        if logical_page < 0 or logical_page >= self.num_frames:
            # Invalid logical page number
            return None
```

```python
        if self.memory[logical_page] is None:
            # Page fault: Load the page from the backing store
            page_data = self.backing_store.read_page(logical_page)
            # Load the page into physical memory
            self.memory[logical_page] = page_data
            return logical_page  # Return the same logical page number
        else:
            # Page is already in physical memory
            return logical_page
class BackingStore:
    def read_page(self, logical_page):
        # Simulate reading a page from the backing store
        return f"Page {logical_page} data"
# Create a virtual memory system
memory_manager = MemoryManager(num_frames=4)

# Simulate a process accessing logical pages
logical_pages = [0, 1, 2, 3, 4, 5, 2, 1, 6, 0]
for logical_page in logical_pages:
    physical_frame = memory_manager.handle_page_fault(logical_page)
    if physical_frame is not None:
        print(f"Accessed logical page {logical_page}, mapped to physical frame {physical_frame}")
    else:
        print(f"Invalid logical page {logical_page}")
```

This Python code simulates demand paging, where pages are loaded into physical memory as needed. It uses a MemoryManager class to manage page faults and a BackingStore class to simulate the backing store.

Example 2: Page Replacement with FIFO

In this example, we'll extend the virtual memory system to include page replacement using the FIFO (First-In-First-Out) algorithm. When physical memory is full, the least recently used page is replaced with the incoming page.

```python
class MemoryManager:
    def __init__(self, num_frames):
        self.num_frames = num_frames
        self.memory = [None] * num_frames
        self.backing_store = BackingStore()

    def handle_page_fault(self, logical_page):
        if logical_page < 0 or logical_page >= self.num_frames:
```

```python
            # Invalid logical page number
            return None

        if self.memory[logical_page] is None:
            # Page fault: Load the page from the backing store
            page_data = self.backing_store.read_page(logical_page)
            # Load the page into physical memory
            self.memory[logical_page] = page_data
            return logical_page  # Return the same logical page
number
        else:
            # Page is already in physical memory
            return logical_page
class BackingStore:
    def read_page(self, logical_page):
        # Simulate reading a page from the backing store
        return f"Page {logical_page} data"
class MemoryManagerFIFO(MemoryManager):
    def __init__(self, num_frames):
        super().__init__(num_frames)
        self.page_queue = []

    def handle_page_fault(self, logical_page):
        if logical_page < 0 or logical_page >= self.num_frames:
            # Invalid logical page number
            return None

        if self.memory[logical_page] is None:
            if len(self.page_queue) < self.num_frames:
                # Frame is available, load the page
                physical_frame = len(self.page_queue)
            else:
                # Replace the oldest page using FIFO
                oldest_page = self.page_queue.pop(0)
                # No need to use self.memory to index logical
pages

                physical_frame = logical_page
                self.memory[physical_frame] = None

            # Load the page from the backing store
            page_data = self.backing_store.read_page(logical_page)
            self.memory[physical_frame] = page_data
            self.page_queue.append(logical_page)
            return physical_frame
        else:
            # Page is already in physical memory
```

```python
        return logical_page


# Create a virtual memory system with FIFO page replacement
memory_manager = MemoryManagerFIFO(num_frames=4)

# Simulate a process accessing logical pages
logical_pages = [0, 1, 2, 3, 4, 5, 2, 1, 6, 0]
for logical_page in logical_pages:
    physical_frame =
memory_manager.handle_page_fault(logical_page)
    if physical_frame is not None:
        print(f"Accessed logical page {logical_page}, mapped to
physical frame {physical_frame}")
    else:
        print(f"Invalid logical page {logical_page}")
```

This code demonstrates page replacement using FIFO. When physical memory is full, the oldest page is replaced with the incoming page.

These Python code examples provide hands-on experience with virtual memory management concepts, including demand paging, page fault handling, and page replacement strategies like FIFO. You can further explore and modify these examples to gain a deeper understanding of virtual memory in practice.

9 STORAGE MANAGEMENT

In the world of computing, storage management is pivotal. It shapes how we organize, access, and protect our data. This chapter delves into storage management, exploring file system architecture, storage allocation methods, and the crucial role of file system management in data integrity. We also reveal how Python, a versatile language, interacts seamlessly with the file system, enabling users to create, read, and manipulate files. A solid grasp of storage management optimizes data storage, retrieval, and system performance. Join us on this journey to uncover the techniques and principles of efficient data management.

9.1 STRUCTURE OF FILE SYSTEMS

File systems are the foundation of data organization and storage in computer science. Understanding file system structure is essential for anyone working with computers, from programmers to system administrators. In this section, we will explore the inner workings of file systems, shedding light on their components, hierarchies, and attributes.

9.1.1 File System Components

A foundational understanding of file systems begins with familiarity with their key components, each serving a vital role in data management. Let's shed light on these fundamental building blocks:

- **Files:** Files are the elemental vessels of data storage within a computer system. They can house diverse forms of information, ranging from text and programs to multimedia content.

- **Directories:** Think of directories as digital containers, often referred to as folders. They are designed to house not only files but also other directories. They create an organized, hierarchical structure for efficient data organization and navigation.

- **File Metadata:** Behind every file lies a treasure trove of metadata. This metadata encompasses essential information such as the file's name, size, type, creation date, and access permissions. It plays a pivotal role in file management and access control.

- **File Paths:** The concept of file paths is akin to a file's digital address. It represents the file's location within the directory hierarchy. Understanding file paths is essential for precisely locating and referencing files within the vast digital landscape.

These components form the bedrock of file systems, allowing users and computer systems to organize, access, and safeguard data with precision and efficiency.

9.1.2 File and Directory Hierarchy

File systems organize files and directories in a hierarchical manner, much like the branches of a tree. At the top is the root directory, which is represented as "/" in Unix-based systems. Below the root directory, there can be multiple subdirectories, each containing its own files and subdirectories. This hierarchy provides a structured and organized way to store and access data.

For example, the following file system hierarchy shows how files and directories might be organized on a personal computer:

```
/
├── Desktop
│   ├── Documents
│   │   ├── Projects
│   │   │   └── My Project
│   │   │       └── main.py
│   │   └── Other Documents
│   └── Other Files
├── Downloads
│   └── my_downloaded_file.pdf
├── Music
│   └── my_favorite_song.mp3
├── Pictures
│   └── my_favorite_picture.jpg
└── Videos
    └── my_favorite_video.mp4
```

In this example, the root directory contains the following directories:

- Desktop: This directory contains files and directories that the user accesses frequently.
- Downloads: This directory contains files that have been downloaded from the internet.
- Music: This directory contains music files.
- Pictures: This directory contains image files.
- Videos: This directory contains video files.

The Desktop directory also contains a subdirectory called Documents. This subdirectory contains two other subdirectories: Projects and Other Documents. The Projects subdirectory contains files related to the user's work on different projects. The Other Documents subdirectory contains other documents that the user has created or saved.

File paths are used to specify the location of a file within the file system hierarchy. For example, the file path `/Desktop/Documents/Projects/My Project/main.py` refers to the file `main.py` in the `My Project` subdirectory of the `Documents` directory on the desktop.

Understanding the file system hierarchy is essential for effective file navigation and management. By understanding how files and directories are organized, users can easily find and access the files they need.

9.1.3 File Attributes

Files in a file system possess various attributes that provide essential information about them. These attributes include:

- **File Name:** The name of the file, which serves as its identifier.

- **File Size:** The size of the file in bytes, indicating how much storage it occupies.

- **File Type:** The type or format of the file, such as text, image, or executable.

- **Creation Date:** The date and time when the file was created.

- **Permissions:** Access permissions that determine who can read, write, or execute the file.

- **Owner:** The user who owns the file and has control over its permissions.

Understanding these attributes is crucial for managing files, ensuring data integrity, and controlling access.

9.1.4 Storage Media Characteristics

The effectiveness of file system design is profoundly influenced by the underlying storage media where data resides. A well-optimized file system takes into account the specific characteristics of the storage media it operates on. Let's explore how different storage media impact file system design and functionality:

1. **Magnetic Hard Disk Drives (HDDs)**

- **Sequential Access Efficiency**: HDDs excel in sequential access scenarios, making them suitable for applications that require reading or writing data in a continuous manner.
- **Slow Random Access**: HDDs suffer from slower random access times due to seek time (the time it takes to position the read/write head) and rotational latency (the time it takes for the desired sector to rotate under the head). As a result, file systems designed for HDDs emphasize strategies that minimize head movement, such as optimizing for data locality and promoting contiguous storage.

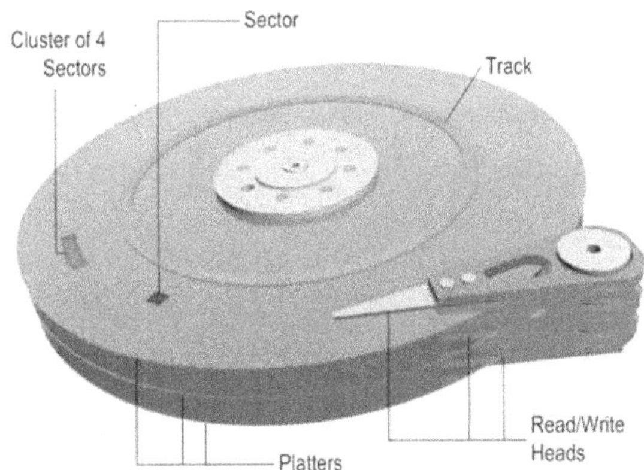

Figure 9.1Magnetic Hard Disk Drives

2. **Solid State Drives (SSDs)**

- **No Moving Parts**: SSDs have no mechanical components, making them exceptionally proficient in random access scenarios. This characteristic is leveraged in file systems to improve tasks like indexing and rapid data retrieval.
- **Erase-Before-Write**: SSDs require erasing data before new data can be written to a location. File systems designed for SSDs must manage this characteristic effectively to ensure longevity and performance.

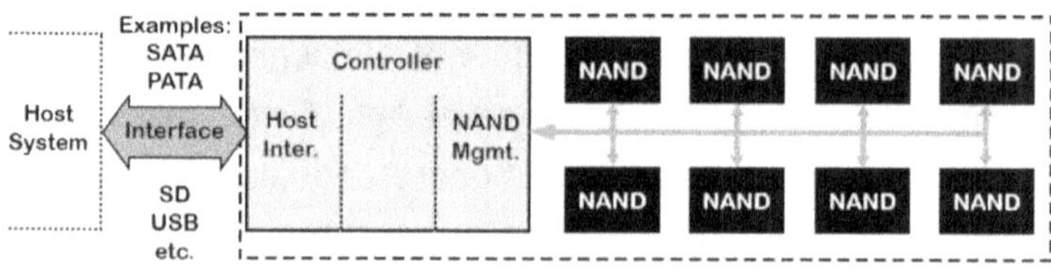

Figure 9.2: Solid State Drives

3. Tape Drives

- **Sequential Storage**: Tape drives are built for sequential access, excelling in scenarios where data is read or written in a linear fashion.
- **Buffering and Streaming**: File systems optimized for tape drives use buffering and streaming techniques to maintain a continuous flow of data. They also organize data in an append-only structure to simplify data storage.

Figure 9.3: Tape Drives

4. Optical Discs (CDs and DVDs)

- **Sequential Access**: Optical discs like CDs and DVDs primarily allow sequential access to data.
- **Cost-Effective Storage**: These storage media are relatively inexpensive, making them suitable for archival purposes.

- **Fragmentation Avoidance**: File systems for optical discs aim to minimize fragmentation to ensure efficient access. Directory information is strategically placed to enhance accessibility.

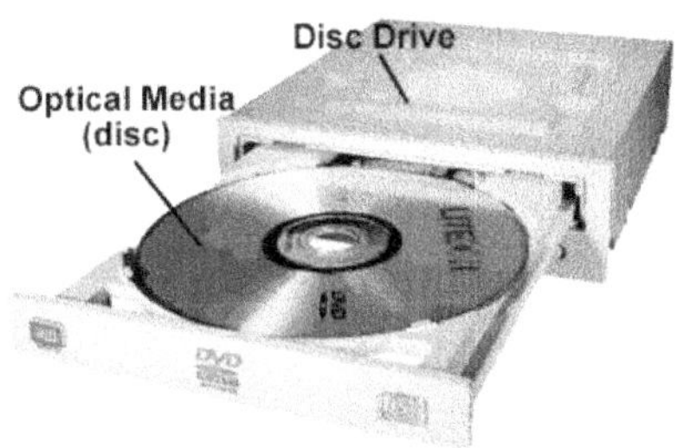

Figure 9.4: Optical Discs

5. Cloud and Object Storage

- **Remote Data Storage**: Cloud and object storage solutions store data remotely over the network, introducing unique challenges for file systems.
- **Latency Considerations**: File systems operating in the cloud environment must account for network latency, parallelism, and reliability requirements imposed by the distributed architecture.

By aligning file system implementations with the strengths and limitations of the underlying storage media, substantial improvements in performance, efficiency, and longevity can be achieved. A deep understanding of these characteristics is pivotal in designing file systems that meet specific data storage and access needs effectively.

Understanding these nuances allows system designers to make informed choices when selecting or designing a file system that optimally caters to their specific storage requirements.

9.2 STORAGE ALLOCATION METHODS

Efficient storage allocation methods lie at the core of judicious disk space utilization within a file system. These methods offer distinct strategies for orchestrating and overseeing files and their associated data on storage devices. In this section, we will embark on an exploration of three primary storage allocation methods: Contiguous Allocation, Linked Allocation, and Indexed Allocation, each endowed with its unique merits and limitations.

9.2.1 Contiguous Allocation

Contiguous Allocation bestows upon each file a continuous stretch of blocks on the storage medium, such as a hard disk. This entails storing all the file's data within an unbroken sequence of blocks, meticulously tracked by the file allocation table (FAT).

Advantages:

- Simplicity and efficiency shine when it comes to sequential access.
- Minimized disk arm movement translates to enhanced performance.

Limitations:

- The passage of time may breed fragmentation, leading to space wastage.
- Files are constrained by their initial allocated size and cannot expand beyond it.

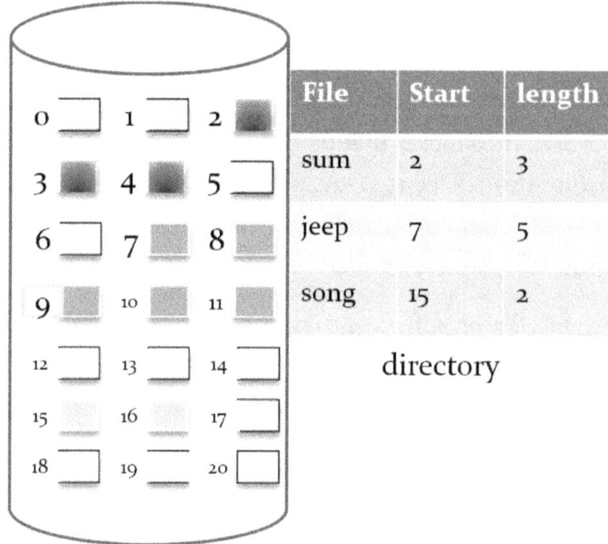

Figure 9.5: Contiguous Allocation

9.2.2 Linked Allocation

Linked Allocation dissects files into blocks or clusters of assorted sizes, with each block harboring a pointer to the subsequent block within the file. This intricate interplay generates a chain of blocks that collectively encapsulate the file's essence, with the ultimate block indicating the file's termination.

Advantages:

- Proficiently accommodates files of diverse sizes.
- Freedom from fragmentation concerns, as blocks are allocated dynamically.

Limitations:

- Random access is hampered due to the necessity of navigating the linked structure.
- The presence of pointers mandates additional storage space.

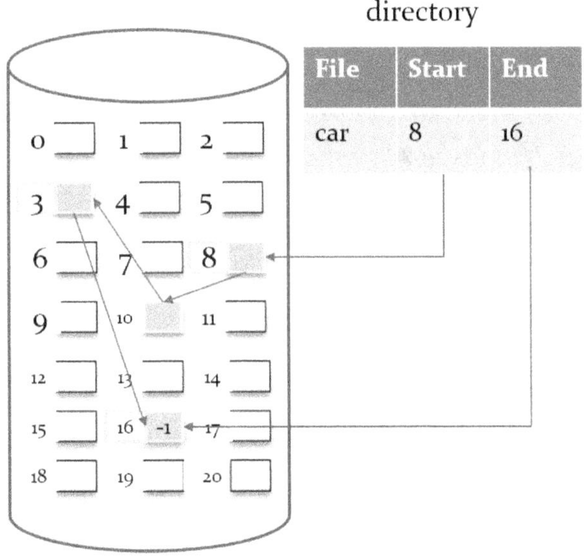

Figure 9.6: Linked Allocation

9.2.3 Indexed Allocation

Indexed Allocation embraces a master index block that houses pointers to individual blocks constituting a file. Each file possesses its dedicated index block, orchestrating references to all the data blocks assigned to it. This architectural elegance facilitates nimble random access, as the index seamlessly maps to the locations of the file's data blocks.

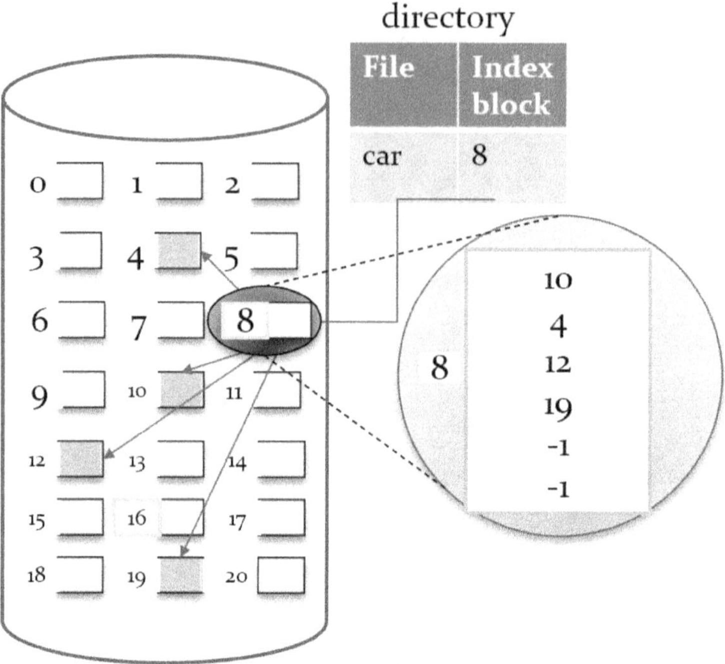

Figure 9.7: Indexed Allocation

Advantages:

- Empowers efficient direct access to any segment of a file.
- Keeps wastage and fragmentation at bay.

Limitations:

- Compulsory allocation of extra storage for the index blocks.
- The management of the index structure can introduce complexity.

The choice of storage allocation method depends on factors such as the type of data to be stored, access patterns, and storage device characteristics. Each method has its strengths and weaknesses, making it essential to select the most suitable approach based on specific requirements. Understanding these allocation methods is crucial for designing and managing file systems effectively.

Storage allocation methods play a vital role in optimizing disk space utilization and file access performance. By understanding the fundamental concepts of contiguous allocation, linked allocation, and indexed allocation, you can make informed decisions about choosing the right storage allocation method for your specific needs.

9.2.4 Selecting Block Size

An essential design decision in implementing storage allocation methods is the selection of the block or cluster size. This low-level parameter can significantly impact overall system performance and efficiency.

Advantages of Larger Block Sizes:

- **Reduced Disk Seeks**: Larger blocks reduce the number of disk seeks required for data retrieval, as more data can be read or written in a single operation.
- **Lower Block Metadata Overhead**: With larger blocks, the ratio of metadata (e.g., file allocation table entries) to data decreases, reducing storage overhead.
- **Improved Sequential I/O Throughput**: Large blocks are well-suited for sequential I/O operations, enhancing data transfer rates.
- **Simplified Free Space Tracking**: Managing free space with larger blocks often involves simpler techniques like bitmaps, reducing complexity.

Disadvantages of Larger Block Sizes:

- **Internal Fragmentation**: Large blocks can lead to internal fragmentation, where allocated space within a block is not fully utilized, especially when storing small files.
- **Limited Allocation Granularity**: The granularity of allocation is coarser with larger blocks, potentially leading to wasted space when allocating blocks for smaller files.
- **Waste for Small Files**: Small files may consume disproportionately large blocks, leading to space wastage.

Advantages of Smaller Block Sizes:

- **Reduced Internal Fragmentation**: Smaller blocks reduce internal fragmentation, as they provide finer granularity of allocation, allowing for a more efficient use of storage space.
- **Flexible Allocation**: Smaller blocks offer more flexibility in allocating space for files of varying sizes.
- **Suitable for Small Files**: Smaller block sizes are ideal for efficiently storing small files without significant wasted space.

Disadvantages of Smaller Block Sizes:

- **Increased Disk Seeks**: Smaller blocks require more disk seeks for I/O operations, potentially impacting I/O performance.
- **Higher Metadata Overhead**: With smaller blocks, the proportion of metadata relative to data increases, leading to higher metadata storage overhead.

Block sizes typically range from 512 bytes to 8192 bytes, depending on the specific usage and requirements of the file system. For example, database systems often favor smaller block sizes to optimize storage efficiency, while media streaming systems may use larger block sizes to maximize throughput.

In some cases, flexibility is provided through multi-block clustering, where logical blocks are grouped into larger physical clusters on disk while maintaining separate block allocation metadata. This approach balances the benefits of large and small block sizes.

Ultimately, selecting the appropriate block size requires a careful analysis of expected I/O patterns, typical file sizes in the workload, and the desired granularity of allocation. It is a crucial aspect of file system design that can significantly impact both storage efficiency and performance.

9.3 FILE SYSTEM MANAGEMENT AND DATA ORGANIZATION

In Chapter 9, we have embarked on a journey through the intricacies of storage management, and now it's time to explore how file systems manage data and maintain order within the digital world. Understanding how data is stored, retrieved, and organized is pivotal for efficient data management. In this section, we delve deeper into File System Management, examining its fundamental aspects.

9.3.1 Data Storage and Retrieval

At the core of file systems lies the primary task of storing and retrieving data. Files, whether they contain text documents, images, videos, or application code, are stored in a structured manner within the storage medium, be it a hard drive, solid-state drive, or cloud-based storage. The file system is responsible for managing the physical storage of these files, ensuring that data remains intact and accessible.

Data Organization: Files are organized into data blocks or clusters, depending on the file system's design. These data blocks are the smallest units of storage allocation. When a file is created or modified, it is divided into these blocks, and the file system maintains a table or index to keep track of which blocks belong to each file. This ensures that the file system can locate and retrieve the data efficiently when needed.

Data Retrieval: When a user or application requests a specific file or piece of data, the file system employs various techniques to locate and retrieve the data. These techniques include reading the file allocation table, traversing directory structures, and accessing the data blocks.

9.3.2 File Metadata

In addition to storing the actual data, file systems also maintain a wealth of information about each file, known as metadata. Metadata includes details such as the file's name, size, type, creation date, modification date, and permissions. This information is crucial for file management, as it allows the operating system and users to identify and work with files effectively.

File Attributes: File attributes are the specific properties associated with each file. They can include read, write, and execute permissions, owner information, group information, and access timestamps. The combination of these attributes determines how a file can be accessed and manipulated.

File Types: Files can have various types, such as regular files, directories, symbolic links, and device files. Understanding the file type is essential for determining how the file should be treated and processed.

9.3.2.1 Special File Types

In addition to regular files, directories, and symbolic links, some file systems support special file types and attributes, each serving distinct purposes:

Device Files: These files represent access points to I/O devices. Reads and writes to these files communicate directly with the associated hardware device.

Named Pipes/FIFOs: Named pipes act as conduits for inter-process communication. Processes can send and receive data through FIFOs, enabling efficient data exchange.

Sockets: Sockets serve as endpoints for networking and inter-process communication. They facilitate data exchange between processes running on the same machine or networked machines, playing a critical role in networked applications.

Hard/Soft Links: Hard links directly point to an inode, allowing multiple directory entries to reference the same file data. Soft links contain a path to the target file, offering flexibility but with the caveat that the target file can be relocated.

Sparse Files: Sparse files are files with empty or unset blocks, designed to save space on data that is inherently sparse. The file system optimizes storage allocation for such files, ensuring efficient disk usage.

Append-Only: Files marked as append-only can only have data appended to them and cannot be modified. This attribute is particularly useful for applications like logs and audit trails, where data integrity and preservation are critical.

Immutable: Immutable files cannot be altered after creation. This attribute ensures that once a file is set as immutable, its content remains unchanged, providing a safeguard against accidental modifications.

These special file types and attributes support a wide range of advanced functionalities, including hardware access, network communication, efficient data exchange between processes, and specialized data storage and preservation techniques. Understanding these features provides deeper insight into the advanced capabilities of file systems.

9.3.3 Directory Structures

A directory structure is a hierarchical organization of directories and files within a file system. Directories act as containers for files and subdirectories, allowing users to group related data together logically. Understanding the structure of directories is essential for navigating and managing files within a file system.

Root Directory: At the top of the hierarchy is the root directory, denoted by '/'. It serves as the starting point for the entire directory tree and contains all other directories and files.

Subdirectories: Directories within a file system can contain subdirectories, creating a nested structure. For example, a root directory may contain subdirectories for user profiles, documents, and system files.

File Paths: File paths are used to specify the location of a file within the directory structure. An absolute path starts from the root directory and provides a full path to the file, while a relative path starts from the current directory and specifies a path relative to the current location.

Understanding file paths and directory structures is vital for effective file navigation and management within an operating system.

In the upcoming sections, we will explore file system operations in Python, delving into practical examples of file creation, reading, writing, and manipulation. This hands-on approach will provide you with valuable insights into interacting with file systems programmatically, a fundamental skill for any software developer or system administrator.

9.3.4 Journaling and Crash Recovery

An important consideration for file system reliability is recovering from unexpected crashes or power failures. Journaling is a common technique used to ensure file system integrity after ungraceful shutdowns.

Journaling Concept: A journal keeps track of intended file system metadata operations before they are applied to the actual on-disk structures. It logs updates like inode changes and directory modifications.

Recovery Process: On reboot after a crash, the file system replays the journal to reconstruct unsaved updates and restore consistency. The specific journaling approach determines crash recovery performance.

Basic Journaling: Basic journaling only logs metadata, minimizing the amount of data to be replayed. More advanced techniques also journal actual file contents for faster recovery.

Crash Resilience Methods: Other crash resilience methods include consistency checking on reboot and incremental/immediate metadata updates. But basic metadata journaling provides good protection with reasonable overhead.

Overall, journaling is an essential capability for reliable file system implementations. By tracking critical file system changes, journaling enables rapid recovery from system crashes while preventing data corruption.

9.4 FILE SYSTEM OPERATIONS IN PYTHON

In this digital age, the ability to interact with the file system programmatically is a fundamental skill for developers, data scientists, and system administrators alike. Python, with its rich set of libraries and modules, provides robust support for file system operations, making it an ideal choice for working with files, directories, and data. In this section, we embark on a journey through the world of file system operations in Python, where we will learn how to interact with the file system, create and write files, read data from files, navigate directories, and even simulate the creation of a file system.

9.4.1 Interacting with the File System

Before diving into specific file operations, it's crucial to understand how Python interacts with the file system. Python provides a module called `os` (short for operating system) that offers a plethora of functions for performing file-related tasks. This module allows you to create, read, write, and manipulate files and directories. It also provides tools for checking file existence, permissions, and much more.

Example: Checking if a Directory Exists in Python

```python
import os

directory_path = "/path/to/directory"
if os.path.exists(directory_path) and
os.path.isdir(directory_path):
    print(f"The directory {directory_path} exists.")
else:
    print(f"The directory {directory_path} does not exist.")
```

9.4.2 Creating and Writing Files in Python

Creating and writing files is a fundamental file system operation. Python provides various methods for creating new files and writing data into them. Whether you need to create a new text file, open an existing one, or append data to an existing file, Python has you covered.

Example: Creating and Writing to a Text File in Python

```python
# Open a file in write mode
with open("sample.txt", "w") as file:
    file.write("Hello, World!\n")
    file.write("This is a sample text file.")
```

9.4.3 Reading Files in Python

Reading data from files is another crucial aspect of file system operations. Python allows you to read files line by line, read the entire file content, or iterate through specific sections of a file. Whether you're working with text files, CSV files, or binary files, Python provides versatile methods for reading data.

Example: Reading a Text File Line by Line in Python

```python
# Open a file in read mode
with open("sample.txt", "r") as file:
    for line in file:
        print(line.strip())  # Strip removes leading/trailing
whitespace and newline characters
```

9.4.4 File System Navigation

Navigating through directories and retrieving information about files and directories is essential for managing file systems efficiently. Python's os module offers functions to list files and directories, get file attributes, change the working directory, and more.

Example: Listing Files in a Directory in Python

```python
import os

directory_path = "/path/to/directory"
files = os.listdir(directory_path)

print(f"Files in {directory_path}:")
for file in files:
    print(file)
```

9.4.5 Creating a File System with Python

To build on the simple example, we can simulate additional file system capabilities like creating directories, setting file metadata, and defining a logical structure.

First, we'll create a root directory and some subdirectories:

```python
import os

os.mkdir('root')
os.mkdir('root/bin')
os.mkdir('root/usr')
os.mkdir('root/tmp')
```

Next, we can create files with various types, sizes and metadata:

```python
# Create text file
with open('root/file.txt', 'w') as f:
    f.write('This is a text file')

# Create large binary file
with open('root/bin/data.dat', 'wb') as f:
    f.write(os.urandom(1024*1024))

# Set access and modification times
os.utime('root/file.txt', (1000000, 2000000))
```

We can also simulate things like symbolic links:

```python
os.symlink('root/file.txt', 'root/link')
```

And listing directory contents:

```python
print(os.listdir('root'))
```

This allows us to model key aspects of a real file system like hierarchy, metadata and different file types. We could further extend the simulation by adding user permissions, directories as special files, free space management and other advanced features. Simulating file systems is a great way to understand how they work under the hood.

10 I/O MANAGEMENT

In the world of computing, Input/Output (I/O) operations are like the vital links that connect computers with the outside world. They're the bits and pieces that let your computer read data from storage, take input from your keyboard, and send info across the internet. Welcome to Chapter 10, where we're about to get our hands dirty and explore the intriguing realm of I/O Management, a fundamental building block of today's computer systems. Here, we're going to explore why efficient I/O management is a big deal, why interrupts are like the superheroes of I/O operations, the inner workings of the I/O subsystem, various ways to manage I/O, and how Python swoops in to save the day when it comes to handling I/O like a pro. Once you wrap up this chapter, you'll be packing some serious knowledge and tools in your tech arsenal to turbocharge your computer systems. They'll be running smoother, more reliable, and as responsive as a hot knife slicing through butter.

10.1 IMPORTANCE OF I/O MANAGEMENT

Getting to Grips with Effective I/O Management

In the realm of computer systems, Input/Output (I/O) operations are the unsung heroes bridging the digital universe of calculations with the tangible realm of hardware and external gizmos. These operations are like the Swiss Army knives of computing – they do it all, from reading and writing data on your hard drive to shooting information across the internet. But here's the kicker: efficient I/O management is the secret sauce that keeps your computer running smoothly.

Imagine you're typing away on your keyboard. You'd expect those letters to show up on the screen instantly, right? Well, that magic is all thanks to I/O management making sure things flow seamlessly behind the scenes.

Impact of I/O on System Performance

But why should you care about I/O management beyond speedy typing? Well, my friend, it's because I/O management doesn't just affect your user experience; it's the beating heart of your computer's performance and responsiveness.

Let's talk servers for a sec. When oodles of folks hop onto a website simultaneously, that server needs to juggle a ton of I/O operations to fetch web pages, images, and all sorts of goodies. If the I/O system isn't up to snuff, it can slow things down to a crawl or even bring the whole server crashing down.

That's where efficient I/O management swoops in as the hero of the day. It ensures those I/O operations happen lickety-split, cutting down on delays and turbocharging your system's responsiveness. Think of I/O management as that secret sauce that makes your computer go from good to great.It's the behind-the-scenes wizardry that keeps everything running smoothly, yet it doesn't always get the credit it deserves.But fear not, because in this chapter, we're pulling back the curtain to reveal all the tricks of the trade. You'll walk away with the skills to wield I/O management like a seasoned pro.

10.2 INTERRUPTS AND THEIR ROLE IN I/O OPERATIONS

Unpacking Interrupts

In the world of computing, especially when we're talking about I/O management, interrupts are like the secret sauce that makes everything work smoothly. Think of an interrupt as a digital "Hey, listen up!" signal sent to the CPU (Central Processing Unit). It's like your computer's way of saying, "I need your attention right now because something important just happened." These "important things" can range from hardware stuff like a keypress or mouse movement to software things like completing an I/O operation or spotting an error.

Interrupts are the CPU's way of staying on its toes. Instead of sitting around twiddling its digital thumbs, the CPU can keep doing its thing, and when an interrupt comes knocking, it knows it's time to switch gears and deal with whatever's happening.

Interrupt Handling in I/O Operations

Alright, time to get down to the real nitty-gritty. Let's talk about how interrupts totally change the game when it comes to I/O operations. Imagine your computer is busy reading data from a network card. Without interrupts, the CPU would be stuck in an endless loop, constantly checking the network card's status. It's like repeatedly asking,

"Are we there yet?" during a road trip—it gets old real fast, and it's not efficient.

Interrupts flip the script. Instead of bugging the network card every millisecond, the CPU can kick back and relax. When the network card has data ready to go, it sends an interrupt signal, like a digital smoke signal, and the CPU knows it's time to get to work. This game-changer makes the whole system run like a well-oiled machine, super-efficient and lightning-fast.

Types of Interrupts in I/O Management

Now, let's take a peek at the different flavors of interrupts in I/O management. Each one has its own special superpower:

1. **Hardware Interrupts**: These are like the bat signals of hardware, signaling events like data arriving, device glitches, or completing an operation.

2. **Software Interrupts**: Picture these as messages from software programs, often asking the operating system for help or flagging something out of the ordinary.

3. **Maskable Interrupts**: These are like the "Do Not Disturb" signs for interrupts. The CPU can snooze them temporarily to deal with more urgent stuff.

4. **Non-Maskable Interrupts**: These are the VIPs of interrupts, the ones that can't be ignored. They're reserved for super-critical events like hardware meltdowns.

Understanding interrupts and how they work in I/O operations is like having a backstage pass to the inner workings of a computer system. Think of it as the magic wand that keeps everything running smoothly.

Alright, buckle up because in the next sections, we're going to dig even deeper into I/O management and uncover some sweet tricks of the trade to make interrupts work their magic.

10.3 EXPLORING THE I/O SUBSYSTEM

Now, let's journey into the heart of the matter—the I/O subsystem. This baby is like the conductor of the computer orchestra, making sure every note plays just right. Here are the key players:

1. **I/O Devices**: These are the hardware whiz kids that let your computer talk to the outside world. Think keyboards, mice, monitors, hard drives, network cards, and printers.

2. **Device Controllers**: Picture these as the translators between the CPU and the I/O devices. They handle the nitty-gritty stuff like data transmission, error fixing, and speaking the device's language.

3. **I/O Channels**: These are the highways where data cruises between the CPU and I/O devices. Think of them as the express lanes for information flow.

4. **Interrupts**: As we've learned, interrupts are like the bouncers at the club, making sure the CPU knows when an I/O device needs some attention. They keep the party running smoothly.

I/O Devices and Their Interfaces

Now, let's zoom in on I/O devices and their various types:

1. **Block Devices**: These folks are all about dealing with data in fixed-size blocks or sectors. Hard drives and SSDs are the rock stars here. These devices do their thing using interfaces like SATA, NVMe, or SCSI.

2. **Character Devices**: These are the chatterboxes of the I/O world, sending data character by character. Think keyboards, mice, or serial ports.

3. **Network Devices**: These handle the data traffic on the information superhighway. Network interface cards (NICs) and modems are in the spotlight here, using protocols like Ethernet or Wi-Fi.

4. **Graphics Devices**: These are the artists, painting the pixels on your screen. GPUs (Graphics Processing Units) are the stars, and they speak languages like HDMI, DisplayPort, or VGA.

Smooth communication between the CPU and I/O devices is the secret sauce for peak system performance. It's like a well-choreographed dance:

a) **Initiation**: The CPU says, "Let's boogie!" and sends a command to the device controller, telling it what to do (read or write) and where to do it.

b) **Execution**: The device controller takes the lead, making sure the I/O device busts a move.

c) **Completion**: Once the dance is done, the device controller sends an interrupt to the CPU, letting it know how it went.

d) **Data Transfer**: Data glides between the device controller and the CPU through memory buffers or registers, depending on the device and system architecture.

Exploring the inner workings of the I/O subsystem, from its nuts and bolts to its communication wizardry, is like getting an exclusive backstage pass to the tech world's most exciting gig. We're here to help you build computer systems that are not just powerful but also nimble and responsive to your commands. As we move forward, we'll dive deeper into I/O management techniques and reveal how Python can be your trusty sidekick in conquering complex I/O tasks, making the developer's life a whole lot smoother.

10.3.1 The Role of Bus Architectures

Now, let's chat about the unsung heroes of the computer world—bus architectures. These are like the secret tunnels that let data flow smoothly between the CPU, memory, and all your gadgets. Choosing the right bus architecture is like picking the perfect road for a road trip. Here are some of the heavy hitters:

- **PCI Express (PCIe)**: This one's the speed demon, perfect for connecting powerhouses like GPUs and NVMe SSDs. It's got the bandwidth to make data zoom.

- **Universal Serial Bus (USB)**: USB is the friendly neighborhood connector, linking up everything from keyboards to printers and cameras. It's all about hassle-free connections.

- **Thunderbolt**: Thunderbolt is the lovechild of PCIe and DisplayPort, bringing not just speedy data transfer but also power delivery in a single cable.

- **Ethernet**: Ethernet is the network maestro, letting computers chat it up in LAN parties. Gigabit Ethernet is like the high-speed lane for network-attached storage.

- **Inter-Integrated Circuit (I2C)**: In the world of embedded systems, I2C is the go-to for short-distance chats between integrated circuits.

Picking the right bus architecture is like choosing the perfect car for a cross-country adventure. Absolutely, it's all about fine-tuning the data flow for your gadgets, ensuring they get the speed and attention they rightfully deserve. Understanding these bus technologies is like having a secret weapon for fine-tuning I/O performance, and we're about to unlock its potential.

10.4 I/O MANAGEMENT TECHNIQUES AND SYSTEM PERFORMANCE

Absolutely, let's get into the juicy details! This section is where the real I/O management magic happens, and you're about to discover some seriously cool techniques that can turbocharge your system's performance. So, grab your tech wizard hat, and let's jump in. Efficient I/O management is like the secret sauce for making your system lightning-fast and super responsive, and it's packed with some awesome concepts.

Buffering and Its Perks

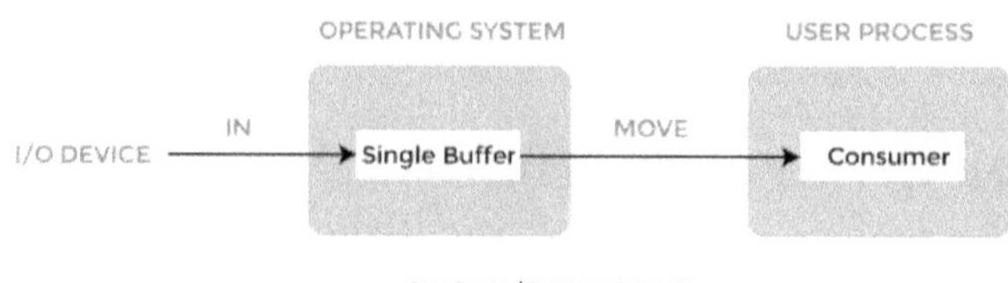

Figure 10.1: Buffering

Buffering is like having your own personal assistant in a bustling kitchen. Picture yourself as the head chef (that's your CPU), whipping up delicious dishes (which are your data) in the kitchen. Now, you don't want to serve each dish directly to hungry customers (those are your I/O devices) as soon as it's ready; that would be a recipe for chaos. Instead, you've got a savvy waiter (that's your buffer) who collects a bunch of dishes on a tray before gracefully delivering them to the customers' table. This way, you're not doing a mad dash to the dining room every time a dish is cooked. Buffers do the same thing but with data. They gather it up and serve it to the I/O devices in an orderly fashion. It's like a data traffic controller, making sure everything flows smoothly and efficiently.

Now, let's dig into why buffering is your system's best friend:

1. **Reduced Overhead:** Think of buffering as your CPU's personal time-saver. Imagine you're at a coffee shop (your CPU), and you're serving customers (I/O devices) cups of coffee (data). Without buffering, you'd have to brew and serve one cup at a time. It's like brewing a fresh cup, serving it, then going back to brew another one – a lot of back-and-forth. But with buffering, you brew a whole pot, and your friendly barista (the buffer) serves multiple cups from that pot. It's way more efficient and reduces all that back-and-forth running.

2. **Asynchronous Operations**: Now, this is where buffering gets really cool. It's like multitasking for your computer. Imagine you're cooking in the kitchen (your CPU), and you have to keep an eye on a simmering pot (I/O data transfer). Without buffering, you'd be stuck babysitting that pot, unable to do anything else. But with buffering, you have a sous-chef (the buffer) who takes care of the pot while you whip up other dishes (handle other tasks). You're not tied down to that one task, and your system becomes super responsive.

3. **Smoothing Data Flow**: This one's like traffic management for your data. Picture your CPU as a sports car and your output device as a slow-moving truck. Without buffering, you'd be racing ahead and constantly slamming on the brakes to match the truck's speed – not efficient at all. But with buffering, you have a traffic cop (the buffer) who lets the sports car (your CPU) cruise at full speed. The buffer collects data and makes sure it's handed over to the truck at a

pace it can handle, like a smooth relay race. No data gets lost, and everything flows like a well-choreographed dance. That's the magic of buffering!

Caching Strategies for Improved Performance

Caching is another key technique used to optimize I/O performance by storing frequently accessed data in a high-speed, easily accessible location. This location, known as a cache, can be located in various places within the I/O subsystem, such as the device controller, system memory, or even on dedicated cache hardware.

The advantages of caching include:

1. **Reduced Latency**: Cached data can be accessed much faster than fetching it directly from slower storage devices, reducing I/O latency and improving system responsiveness.

2. **Lower Bandwidth Usage**: Caching reduces the need for continuous data retrieval from slower storage, leading to lower bandwidth consumption and reduced wear and tear on storage media.

3. **Improved Data Availability**: Frequently accessed data is readily available in the cache, ensuring that applications can quickly retrieve it, further enhancing overall system performance.

Direct Memory Access (DMA) and Offloading CPU

Direct Memory Access (DMA) is a hardware feature that allows peripheral devices to transfer data directly to or from the system memory without CPU intervention. DMA controllers manage these data transfers, freeing the CPU from the time-consuming task of managing I/O.

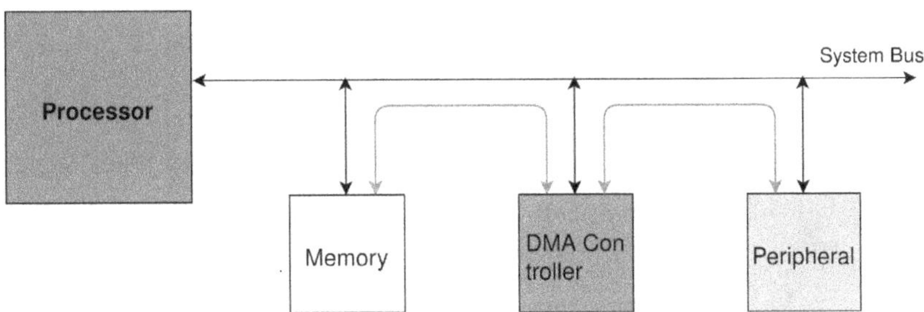

Figure 10.2: DMA

The advantages of DMA include:

1. **Reduced CPU Overhead**: By offloading data transfer tasks to DMA controllers, the CPU is free to execute other instructions, enhancing overall system efficiency.

2. **Faster Data Transfer**: DMA can transfer data at high speeds, outperforming CPU-managed data transfers and reducing I/O bottlenecks.

3. **Efficient Multi-Tasking**: DMA enables efficient multi-tasking, as the CPU can execute other tasks while I/O operations occur concurrently.

Incorporating these I/O management techniques into system design and software development is essential for achieving high-performance computing. These strategies not only enhance system responsiveness but also contribute to a smoother user experience and improved overall system reliability.

10.4.1 Orchestrating I/O with Scheduling Algorithms

In the realm of systems housing multiple I/O devices, the OS faces the intricate task of choreographing I/O requests to attain peak efficiency. Here, I/O scheduling algorithms emerge as the conductors of this intricate orchestra, harmonizing the symphony of data flow. Let's explore some of these algorithms, each fine-tuned to maximize throughput and minimize latencies:

Elevator Algorithm: Operating akin to an elevator, this algorithm services requests in either ascending or descending order. Its objective is to minimize disk head movement, mimicking the efficiency of a well-managed elevator.

Shortest Seek Time First: Armed with the knowledge of head movement, this algorithm chooses the request with the shortest distance to traverse from the current position. The goal is to optimize seek time, ensuring swifter data retrieval.

SCAN Algorithm: The SCAN algorithm meticulously services requests while moving the head in a single direction. Upon reaching the end, it reverses course. This strategy effectively reduces seek time.

C-SCAN: A variant of the SCAN algorithm, C-SCAN exclusively services requests in one direction, mitigating concerns of potential starvation by ensuring fair treatment.

Deadline Scheduling: With an eye on timeliness, this algorithm prioritizes requests with the earliest deadlines. It's a mechanism to ensure that time-sensitive tasks receive precedence.

Lottery Scheduling: Operating akin to a lottery, this algorithm allots each process a slice of time. Processes that exhaust their allotment receive more slices, preventing starvation and ensuring fairness in resource allocation.

Let's illustrate the operation of these algorithms with a numerical example:

Suppose there are five I/O requests pending:

- Request A at track 10
- Request B at track 22
- Request C at track 15
- Request D at track 40
- Request E at track 5

We'll compare how each algorithm schedules these requests starting from track 20.

- **Elevator Algorithm**: The elevator algorithm would go from track 20 to 40 (ascending order) and then reverse to 5, servicing requests in this order: C, A, B, D, E.

- **Shortest Seek Time First**: This algorithm selects the request with the shortest seek time from the current position. Starting at track 20, it would service E, A, C, B, and then D.

- **SCAN Algorithm**: The SCAN algorithm services requests while moving the head in one direction until it reaches the end. Starting at track 20, it would service C, A, B and then reverse to service D, E.

- **C-SCAN**: Similar to SCAN, but C-SCAN only services requests in one direction. Starting at track 20, it would service C, A, B and then move to the end and restart, servicing D and E.

- **Deadline Scheduling**: Deadline scheduling prioritizes requests based on their deadlines. Without specific deadlines, it may choose a default order, such as C, A, B, D, E.

- **Lottery Scheduling**: Lottery scheduling allocates time slices, so it might distribute time to processes based on random selection. The order of servicing requests can be random.

The choice of algorithm depends on the specific optimization metrics required, such as throughput, latency, or fairness. Sometimes, combining algorithms, like deadline scheduling with an elevator approach, can yield the desired results. It's worth noting that selecting the appropriate I/O scheduling algorithm is pivotal in optimizing system efficiency.

This comprehensive overview of I/O scheduling algorithms enriches our exploration of I/O management, providing valuable insights into enhancing I/O throughput and minimizing latency in environments bustling with multiple devices.

10.4.2 Memory-Mapped I/O

Okay, remember that cool trick we discussed in Chapter 9? Memory-Mapped I/O is like the sequel to that magic show. Memory-Mapped I/O is like inviting your devices to the memory party, where they get to hang out with the cool kids. No need for special secret handshakes (device instructions) – they can just blend in and chat like regular memory. It's like making your toaster feel at home in the world of 1s and 0s.

Advantages of Memory-Mapped I/O:

1. **Simplified Programming**: You know how you like things simple? Well, Memory-Mapped I/O makes programming a breeze. You can talk to your devices using the same language you use to talk to memory. It's like having a conversation with your toaster in plain English.

2. **No Special Device Instructions**: Forget about those fancy device instructions. Memory-Mapped I/O lets you use regular memory operations to chat with your devices. It's like having a universal remote control for all your gadgets.

3. **Bypassing DMA Operations**: Direct Memory Access (DMA) can be a headache sometimes. But with Memory-Mapped I/O, you skip the DMA line and go straight to the front. Devices and CPU caches talk directly, making data transfers a piece of cake.

4. **Memory-Mapped Files**: And guess what? Memory-Mapped I/O isn't just for devices; it can also work its magic on files. It's like having your favorite book always open on the table, ready for you to read. No need to keep flipping through pages – the story is right there at your fingertips.

But hold on, there's a catch. If you're not careful, this magic show can turn into a circus. Imagine your favorite book is open on the table, and it starts flipping pages all by itself. That would be chaos, right? Well, in the tech world, improperly accessed memory-mapped areas can lead to system crashes. It's like your book flying around the room – exciting at first, but then things get messy.

So, while memory-mapped I/O is a fantastic trick, it needs a responsible magician (or in this case, the operating system) to keep everything in check and prevent any bookish mayhem.

10.4.3 Emerging I/O Technologies - The Future Is Here!

Now, let's fast forward to the future. I/O tech is always evolving, and there are some new kids on the block shaking things up:

- **NVMe(Non-Volatile Memory Express)**: It's like a racecar for SSDs, speeding things up with PCIe. Say goodbye to slow storage!
- **Thunderbolt**: Think of it as a Swiss Army knife of connectors. It does it all – fast

data, video, and even powers your gadgets.

- **RDMA (Remote Direct Memory Access)**: Imagine devices talking directly to each other without bugging the CPU. That's RDMA for you, making networked storage a breeze.
- **USB 4**: It's like USB on steroids. More speed, more power, and it plays nice with Thunderbolt.
- **CXL (The Compute Express Link)**: Sharing is caring, and CXL lets devices share memory bandwidth. Data centers are getting a makeover!

These tech advancements are like turbochargers for your system. They boost speed, cut down delays, and bring new tricks to the table. Knowing about these shiny new toys helps you future-proof your system designs.

10.5 PYTHON FOR I/O OPERATIONS

Absolutely, let's keep the momentum going as we explore Python's prowess in the realm of I/O operations. Python, often hailed for its simplicity and adaptability, is your go-to tool for tackling I/O tasks like a seasoned pro. We're about to embark on a journey that will unveil Python's potential as your trusty sidekick in I/O management. But that's not all – we'll also roll up our sleeves and get hands-on with some practical code examples to make all of this come to life. So, are you ready to unlock the power of Python in the world of I/O operations? Let's dive right in!

Why Python Rocks for I/O Management

Python's appeal is like universal glue for I/O operations, and here's why:

1. **Cross-Platform Compatibility**: Python doesn't play favorites with operating systems. It's like the cool kid who gets along with everyone. Your Python-written I/O code will run smoothly on various platforms.

2. **Simplicity**: Python speaks plain English (well, almost). Its easy-to-read syntax and high-level abstractions make writing I/O operations feel like writing a grocery list. It's quick, straightforward, and minimizes those "I forgot to close the file" errors.

3. **Rich Ecosystem**: Python has a treasure chest of libraries and modules for all things I/O. Whether you're wrangling files, wrestling with sockets, or taming other I/O devices, Python's got your back.

Interrupts? Python's Got a Plan for That

Interrupts are like uninvited guests at your party, but Python knows how to handle them with grace. Here's how:

To dance with interrupts in Python, you can call on libraries and frameworks designed for event-driven programming, such as the crowd favorite `asyncio`. This library lets you create asynchronous, non-blocking I/O operations. It's like juggling flaming torches while keeping an eye on the door for new guests – all without missing a beat.

Python in Action: A Practical Example

Let's put Python's I/O prowess to the test with a real-world example. Imagine you're tasked with reading data from a sensor and jotting it down in a file. Python's got your back with a code snippet like this:

```python
import asyncio

async def read_sensor():
    while True:
        # Simulate reading data from a sensor
        sensor_data = await read_sensor_data()
        # Log the data to a file
        log_data(sensor_data)
        await asyncio.sleep(1)  # Sleep for 1 second

async def read_sensor_data():
    # Simulate reading data from a sensor
    return "Sensor data goes here"

def log_data(sensor_data):
    # Log the sensor data to a file
    with open("sensor_log.txt", "a") as file:
        file.write(sensor_data + "\n")

if __name__ == "__main__":
    asyncio.run(read_sensor())
```

In this script, Python's `asyncio` library takes the stage. It sets up an asynchronous loop that reads sensor data, logs it to a file, and takes a one-second nap between readings. No blocking, no fuss – just smooth, responsive I/O handling.

Python's adaptability makes it your go-to partner for I/O tasks, whether you're reading sensors or orchestrating intricate network communication. With Python's magic wand in hand, you can build efficient, reliable systems that play nice with various I/O devices and handle those surprise party crashers like a pro.

REFERENCES

- Silberschatz, Galvin, and Gagne. Operating System Concepts. 10th ed., Wiley, 2018. - This is a classic and comprehensive operating systems textbook that covers fundamental concepts and modern developments. It can be referenced for foundational OS topics.

- Tanenbaum, Andrew S., and Herbert Bos. Modern Operating Systems. 4th ed., Pearson, 2014. - Another seminal OS textbook with excellent coverage of theoretical concepts as well as practical implementations.

- Love, Robert. Linux System Programming. 2nd ed., O'Reilly Media, 2013. - Useful resource for Linux OS specifics, system calls, concurrency in Linux, and other topics.

- Nutt, Gary J. Operating Systems. 3rd ed., Addison-Wesley, 2004. - Provides good coverage of OS design and implementation considerations.

- Stallings, William. Operating Systems: Internals and Design Principles. 9th ed., Pearson, 2018. - Balanced analysis of key theoretical OS concepts along with practical examples and exercises.

- Arpaci-Dusseau, Remzi H., and Andrea C. Arpaci-Dusseau. Operating Systems: Three Easy Pieces. Arpaci-Dusseau Books, 2015. - Freely available e-book covering virtualization, concurrency, and crash consistency in addition to OS fundamentals.

- Xiao, Qing, et al. "The Linux Scheduler: a Decade of Wasted Cores." EuroSys '16, ACM, 2016. - Research paper providing useful insights into Linux scheduler implementations and their evolution.

- Gamsa, Benjamin, et al. "Tornado: Maximizing Locality and Concurrency in a Shared Memory Multiprocessor Operating System." OSDI '99, USENIX Association, 1999. - Seminal paper on Tornado operating system structure focused on efficient shared memory access.

ABOUT THE AUTHOR

Amir Keivan Shafiei is a lecturer of computer engineering at the University of Birjand, where he is also the head of the computer and civil engineering department. He has a master's degree in computer engineering from Ferdowsi University of Mashhad and a bachelor's degree in computer engineering from Najafabad University of Isfahan. He has taught various courses on software engineering, programming languages, and artificial intelligence. He has also served as the deputy of education at Hekmat Motahar Non-Profit University and the head of the computer department at Azad University of Sarakhs. He is interested in research topics such as data mining, machine learning, and natural language processing.